D0073422

GOLDEN LATIN
ARTISTRY

Gaius Lucilius...used to say that he wished to be read neither by the very unlearned nor by the very learned; for the former would understand nothing, the latter more perhaps than himself. CICERO, *De Oratore, II, 25.*

GOLDEN LATIN
ARTISTRY

BY

L. P. WILKINSON

University Orator and
Fellow of King's College in the
University of Cambridge

CAMBRIDGE
AT THE UNIVERSITY PRESS
1963

PUBLISHED BY
THE SYNDICS OF THE CAMBRIDGE UNIVERSITY PRESS

Bentley House, 200 Euston Road, London, N.W. 1
American Branch: 32 East 57th Street, New York 22, N.Y.
West African Office: P.O. Box 33, Ibadan, Nigeria

©

CAMBRIDGE UNIVERSITY PRESS

1963

Printed in Great Britain at the University Press, Cambridge
(Brooke Crutchley, University Printer)

To

Kenneth Fawdry

CONTENTS

CONTENTS

PART II: RHYTHMS

CONTENTS

CONTENTS

INTRODUCTION

Ever since I have been able to read Latin, it has been the sound and movement and architectonics of the language that have fascinated me, at least as much as the substance of anything most Romans had to say. Cicero made his Crassus complain of half-educated people who 'separate words from meaning as body from soul, which cannot be done without the perishing of both';[1] and of course form and content are really indissoluble. But there are literatures in which the formal element plays a far greater part than in others, and when we are not absorbed in reading them, we can sit back and obtain an intellectual pleasure, perhaps even increase our appreciation at the next reading, by examining how the writer, consciously or unconsciously, has obtained his effects. And one of the pioneers of this practice was, in fact, Cicero.

There must be—there are, I know—many whose experience has been the same as mine; who feel that much of the criticism of Latin literature they read is somehow irrelevant, springing from what critics expect to get out of modern literature, not from what Romans were intent on putting into theirs. In the notes of some commentators they will find observations which confirm or illuminate their experience; in the Latin compositions of sensitive scholars they will recognize the touch of a kindred spirit; but they will be at a loss for a book to which they may turn to find what most appeals to them in Latin literature given pride of place. There are, of course, such books, particularly as regards rhetoric, even a great book, Eduard Norden's *Die antike Kunstprosa*. The work that comes nearest to what I have in mind is J. Marouzeau's admirable *Traité de stylistique appliqué au latin* (1935), and I am greatly indebted to it.* There are also valuable compilations, such as R. Volkmann's *Die Rhetorik der Griechen und Römer*. But to many it is naturally poetry rather than prose which is of interest. Here again, there are useful compilations, particularly the Appendices to Norden's edition of *Aeneid* VI. There are full-scale works on *Lautmalerei* in Virgil and in Ovid.[2] But the phenomenon generally called by the misleading name

---

* 3rd edn. (1954). The refreshing Gallic humanity and good sense of Marouzeau's writings is found also in Laurand's studies of Cicero.

of 'onomatopoeia', which even those who value it highly must admit to be quite often a matter of subjective feeling, is quite unsuited to exhaustive treatment. And the plain fact is that detailed and exhaustive books, especially in a foreign tongue, cannot expect to be read by the ordinary devotee of Latin literature, even if they are available to him. It is to him that this book is addressed, to the undergraduate, the schoolmaster, the sixth-form boy, the civil servant on Sunday, the country parson on Monday—even perhaps to the don who has specialized in other departments of the classics, or to the critic of modern literature.

> Nec sum animi dubius verbis ea vincere magnum
> quam sit, et angustis hunc addere rebus honorem.

I have tried to be readable; and to be readable on any such subject one must select, letting a few illustrations suffice where a plethora would do more to repel than to reinforce; nor must one disdain to be discursive. If I have had any model in mind, it is such discourse as we find in Blair's thirteenth lecture, or in those numbers of the *Rambler*, 92 and 94, in which Dr Johnson, writing for a public educated in the classics (which still exists, and may indeed be no smaller numerically today), discussed with leisurely ease onomatopoeia, or as I would rather call it, 'expressiveness'. But on some important matters, such as the controversies over prose and verse rhythm, I have had to be more technical.

This book deliberately excludes all features of literature that concern imagery or meaning (except in so far as expressiveness, for instance, involves meaning). Let me say once for all that I do recognize the prime importance of these, not only in literature as a whole, but in much of Latin literature. But that is not what I have (unfashionably) chosen to write about on this occasion. I have also confined myself to Golden Latin, because in the preceding period artistry was less developed, and there is so much about its literature that is problematical, while in the Silver period verse at least lived on the artistic capital of the Golden.

ACKNOWLEDGEMENTS

Part I of this book was delivered as three open lectures in November 1958 at King's College, Newcastle-upon-Tyne. A better audience one could not wish to have.

INTRODUCTION

I am grateful to Mr F. H. Sandbach, Professor C. O. Brink and Mr A. G. Lee for reading my typescript and to Mr D. W. Lucas for reading the proofs. They have saved me from various pitfalls, and are in no way responsible for any that I have neglectfully or perversely fallen into. I am also grateful to my pupils Mr Hilary Newton and Mr Anthony Bulloch for help with the drudgery of checking references. The University Typewriting Office, Cambridge, must be complimented on its usual expert service. And finally I must thank the Cambridge University Press for its unfailing care and skill.

L. P. W.

CAMBRIDGE
November 1962

PART I

SOUNDS

Notes of substance are printed at the foot of the page, notes of reference at the end of the book. Superior figures in the text refer to the latter. Titles of modern works are there given in abbreviated form, to save space while avoiding the bugbear '*op. cit.*'; should any prove not self-evident, recourse may be had to the *Index of Modern Works Cited*. Finally there is an *Index of Passages Cited*, under authors' names. Thus the names of all authors, ancient and modern, are indexed. For subjects see the Table of Contents at the beginning.

1

PRONUNCIATION

About the year 1870 there came to a head in many quarters simultaneously a feeling that the chaos in the pronunciation of Latin could no longer be tolerated.[1] The stimulating causes can only be surmised. An important one must have been the development of scholarship in general, and of the science of comparative linguistics in particular. If any book should be singled out, it is probably that of W. Corssen on the pronunciation, vocalism and accentuation of the Latin language,[2] which appeared in 1858–9 and achieved a second edition in 1868–70. For the Vatican Council of 1870 reporters had to be trained to record speeches which would be made in the diverse national pronunciations of Latin, and one result of that Council was a movement in the Catholic Church towards standardization.[3]

In England there were subsidiary causes. The members of the Oxford Movement who seceded to Rome, eager to be more papal than the papists, had abandoned the traditional pronunciation of English Catholics for the Italianate, and this was officially adopted by the remaining Catholics in 1850, when territorial sees were established in this country.[4] Again, the increasing emphasis on verse composition incited some schoolmasters to revolt against the false quantities which were, for some reason, endemic in the old pronunciation (though in the 1880's, so Nathaniel Wedd used to recall, it was still a point of honour at City of London School to say, for instance, 'eego'). During the Christmas holidays of 1870 the Headmasters' Conference met at Sherborne to discuss the situation. H. A. J. Munro, then Professor at Cambridge, had already been approached by Cornish on behalf of some Eton Masters as well as by Lightfoot, Jebb and Mayor, and Edwin Palmer had written that Oxford was contemplating reform. At the request of the Headmasters Munro drafted a report which Palmer endorsed, advocating the adoption of the classical pronunciation as reconstructed by scholars.[5] But the Oxford Committee, led by Max Mueller, wanted a compromise in the interests of intelligibility to foreign scholars[1] (a short-sighted policy as it now seems, for the foreigners also were beginning to contemplate reform in the same direction). So the matter hung fire.

But in 1885 Cambridge returned to the charge, led by J. P. Postgate. At a meeting of the Philological Society held in St John's College on 29 October, with Skeat in the Chair, he was appointed, with J. S. Reid and J. Peile, to advise the Society; and this Committee reported that they had come to the conclusion 'that the Classical pronunciation of Latin has now been sufficiently ascertained for the purpose of drawing up a scheme which may reasonably be regarded as permanent'.* By the end of the ensuing twelve years all the responsible bodies in England representing schools, universities and learned societies had recommended its adoption to their members.†

It took at least a generation, however, for this to take effect completely,‡ owing partly to prejudice or inertia, partly to a natural but mistaken fear among masters that change would be a difficult process. Dr Johnson, in his *Life of Milton*, asserts that it is easy to adapt your pronunciation of Latin to that of the land in which you find yourself. That may be too sanguine; but it is certainly much easier to adopt a single new pronunciation permanently. There were, of course, the inevitable jokes about 'wayny, weedy, weeky', and *Punch* displayed a picture of a don surrounded by girls chanting 'We kiss 'im—by turns'. There were protests that Byron's 'tribe is' could not be made to rhyme with the new-fangled 'eebis', nor Browning's 'acacia' with 'grahtia'. When *The Times* in 1939 ran a correspondence on the subject (sup-

---

* *Proc. Camb. Phil. Soc.* For a convenient summary of the reformed pronunciation see J. P. Postgate, *How to Pronounce Latin* (1909). For fuller details, with evidence, W. M. Lindsay, *The Latin Language* (1894), ch. II; E. H. Sturtevant, *Pronunciation of Greek and Latin* (1920; 2nd ed. 1940); A. Traina, *L'alfabeto* (1957).

† The Modern Languages Association in December 1901; a joint Conference of the Oxford and Cambridge Philological Societies, by a three-quarters majority, in 1905; the Cambridge Philological Society, unanimously, on 1 February 1906; the Classical Association, almost unanimously, on 13 October 1906; the Headmasters' Conference, by a large majority, in December 1906; the Headmasters' Association and the Assistant Masters' Association in 1907. (J. P. Postgate, *How to Pronounce Latin*, pp. 13–29; Sir Frank Fletcher, *After Many Days* (1937), pp. 176–80.)

‡ By 1913 the reformed pronunciation had been officially adopted in 101 out of 110 of the Headmasters' Conference Schools. But a committee appointed by the Prime Minister in 1923 reported that, while reform was established in state schools and girls' schools, it was not consistently carried out in the boys' Public Schools, even where it was officially adopted. And in 1926 Alington recreated an area of chaos by telling the Preparatory Schools that Eton would continue to use the old pronunciation.

porting the old pronunciation, and suppressing a letter against it from the Kennedy Professor of Latin at Cambridge), the average age of the reactionaries whose letters were printed was sixty-six. But even in 1950 Sir Alan Herbert complained of the 'horrid "New" Pronunciation' of the Public Orator of Oxford University. Eight years later Mr Higham was able to make an effective reply: when presenting Sir Alan himself for an honorary degree he asked (drawing on Ovid, Virgil, Varro and Plautus),

> si 'sub aqua sub aqua' ranae 'cecinere querelam',
>   cur *sessineere* velis dicere, cur *sub akway*?
> balat ovis 'be be', vocem effert noctua 'tu tu'?
> haec *bee bee, tew tew* posse sonare putas?*

We are fortunate, indeed, to have (almost) completed our change in a generation, as the Germans have. In Italy the church pronunciation remains entrenched. In France the parallel attempts set off a characteristic chain-reaction, amusing enough as seen from this side of the Channel, but exasperating to good scholars over there. In 1892 the Congrès des Sociétés Savantes voted for reform, and by 1910 the movement, led by A. Macé, had captured several lycées. A ministerial inquiry was inaugurated, but halted in 1913 in the face of gathering resistance. For in 1912, following a letter to the Archbishop of Bourges from Pope Pius X, who was keen to encourage Gregorian chanting,[1] there was a crusade to spread the Italianate pronunciation through the Churches of France. This of course provoked not only an anti-clerical reaction, but a patriotic movement in favour of the old French pronunciation, perhaps the worst in Europe.† The First World War then intervened, and after it the fight has gone on, with scholars like Jules Marouzeau struggling against the 'Amis de la prononciation française du latin', founded in 1928 by M. Moissenet at the age of eighty.[2] In 1956 the Congrès international pour le latin vivant, held at Avignon, recommended all countries to adopt the reformed pronunciation.

---

* Or in his own translation (printed by kind permission):
> Frogs croaked *kwah kwah* and *keki* in old times as to-day:
> Why make their *keki* 'sessi'? why turn their *kwah* to 'kway'?
> Sheep cry *bey bey* as ever, and owls *tu-whit*: do you
> Think 'bee bee' sounds more sheeplike? Or that the owl cries 'tew'?

† Also the inevitable jokes about Kikero, and protests that Baudelaire's 'maudits' would not rhyme with the reformed sound of 'de profundis'.

But while it is agreed that we know in almost every case the value of the Latin vowels, diphthongs and consonants in the classical period, it is equally agreed that we can know nothing of Latin intonation, and the nature of Latin accent is still a subject of dispute.* In any case, readers may well have been asking, why this preamble? Does it matter how we pronounce this dead language, so long as we do it uniformly, at least within our island shores? It was in the time of Queen Elizabeth I that our pronunciation of Latin, which Italians of Erasmus' day approved as nearest to their own, began to diverge and became unintelligible to continental scholars such as J.-J. Scaliger.[1] This was a by-product, not of Reformation zeal, but of changes in the pronunciation of English itself; for our ancestors pronounced Latin as they did their own language.[2] And I must now ask in reply, why do we forthwith find James VI of Scotland deploring the Greek and Latin pronunciation of his English subjects as 'utterly failing the grace of those two learned languages'? Why did Milton recommend his Quaker friend Thomas Ellwood to learn the continental pronunciation, not only if he wanted to converse with foreigners, but also *if he wanted to read and understand Latin authors*?[3] And why did Gibbon refer to his countrymen's mode of uttering Latin as 'most corrupt and barbarous'?[4] It is these questions that Part I of this book sets out to answer.†

* The question of accent will be discussed later, pp. 90–2.

† Against my principles I have retained in this book Ramus's *v* for consonantal *u*, because I know how much the latter worries those unaccustomed to it, but I have not used his *j* for consonantal *i*, which seems to cause less trouble.

2

VERBAL MUSIC

I. THE CONTROVERSY

'Verbal music and melopoeia are, it seems to me, examples of metrical mythology with little or no basis in metrical fact. Onomatopoeia and hypnotic poetry, on the other hand, though they are not mere figments of the prosodist's imagination, are of doubtful poetic utility.'* F. W. Bateson thus puts in their place many reputable poets and critics of the past two thousand years. I will deal with the two subjects in separate chapters, but they are not wholly separable; for euphony or cacophony may be a form of expressiveness, and people who are sensitive to expressiveness seem also to be those who are sensitive to 'verbal music'. As Shelley divined, 'sounds as well as thoughts have a relation *between each other and towards what they represent*, and a perception of the order of their relations has always been found connected with a perception of the order of the relations of thought'.[1]

T. S. Eliot, in his lecture on 'The Music of Poetry', gives a warning: 'It would be a mistake, however, to assume that all poetry ought to be melodious, or that melody is more than one of the components of the music of words....Dissonance, even cacophony, has it place....And if the whole poem need not be, and often should not be, wholly melodious, it follows that a poem is not made only out of "beautiful words".'[2] It will be observed that he does not here deny that poetic melody, euphony and cacophony, and beautiful words, are realities; but when he proceeds to express his doubt 'whether, from the point of view of *sound* alone, any word is more or less beautiful than another', we must pause and take stock. It is true that Dr Johnson came to the conclusion

---

* *English Poetry* (1950), p. 30. '...the moribund belief that poetry depends for its effect in any large measure on the actual vowel and consonantal sounds that are used': Mr Philip Toynbee in *The Observer* for 14 August 1955, reviewing J. Press, *The Fire and the Fountain*, a book to which I am much indebted. Testimonies to the contrary by Lamartine, Sully Prudhomme, Valéry, Claudel, Verlaine and many ancient Greek and Roman authors are collected by N. I. Herescu, *La poésie latine* (1960), pp. 12–16. Friedrich Schlegel said that consonants are the body of speech, vowels the soul (*Alte und neue Literatur* (1812), I, p. 126).

that 'on many occasions we make the music which we imagine ourselves to hear',[1] but on *how* many? Those whose experience inclines
them to value their music are unlikely to bow to the authority of one
who found *Lycidas* unmusical.

Much of the argument on this subject is of the type 'I feel this'; 'No,
I don't'.* We must face the fact that respectable human beings approach
the arts with widely differing predispositions. The less pure an art is, the
less likely is it that those who have the misfortune not to be gifted with
the organ necessary for its specific appreciation will be aware of their
lack. The tone-deaf man realizes that instrumental music has nothing to
say to him, generally without accusing those who enjoy it of self-
deception. The man with no aesthetic sense is more likely to think he
appreciates painting, though his preferences and his reactions are likely
to reveal the extent to which his approach is literary. But with literature
the distinction is still more obscured, and disagreement therefore liable
to be more heated. A contrast partly relevant here was pointed in
a trenchant, if exaggerated, way by Rémy de Gourmont:

To the reader who draws his emotions from the very substance of what he
reads is opposed the reader who only feels what he reads to the extent that he
can apply it to his own life, to his griefs, to his hopes. He who enjoys the
literary beauty of a sermon by Bossuet cannot be touched by it religiously,
and he who weeps for the death of Ophelia has no aesthetic sense. These two
parallel categories of writers and readers constitute the two great types of
cultivated humanity. In spite of shades and overlappings, no understanding
is possible between them. They despise each other, for they do not understand each other. Their animosity extends in two wide, sometimes sub-
terranean, streams through literary history.[2]

* Mr Arnold Isenberg has discussed the implications of saying, 'I like Milton's line

But musical as is Apollo's lute

because of the pattern of *u*'s and *l*'s, which reinforces the meaning with its own musical quality':
although this statement is not related to any accepted psychological law, yet someone else, even
though not convinced in favour of the line by this argument, might still readily admit that the
quality alleged might have something to do with *my* pleasurable reaction, given *my* peculiar
mentality (*Aesthetics and Language*, ed. W. Elton, 1954, pp. 133–4).

II. ANCIENT IDEAS ABOUT EUPHONY AND CACOPHONY

(a) Letters, syllables, words

Let us begin by seeing what the ancients had to say, for they include intelligent and sensitive critics, and in any case they were in a better position than we are to know what their writers were trying to do. (It is remarkable how often their observations have been made and remade with pride in modern times.)* And let us first pose the question: Are particular letters, syllables or words euphonious or cacophonous regardless of their sense?

Homer was credited by ancient critics retrospectively with all sorts of verbal subtleties, and even the cautious Dr Johnson could not believe that he 'had no extraordinary attention to the melody of his verse when he described a nuptial festivity:

νύμφας δ' ἐκ θαλάμων, δαΐδων ὑπὸ λαμπομενάων,
ἠγίνεον ἀνὰ ἄστυ, πολὺς δ' ὑμέναιος ὀρώρει'.†

But the first tangible evidence we have of a Greek poet being self-conscious about sounds is a curious case of what looks like avoidance of cacophony. Lasus of Hermione, who was at the court of Hipparchus at Athens in the latter part of the sixth century B.C., composed at least one poem from which the letter sigma was excluded; and it was one of the most generally held opinions on these matters in antiquity that an excess of sibilants was cacophonous.‡

Sophists at the end of the fifth century, eager to examine phenomena of all kinds, including the artifices newly exploited by Gorgias and his

* How astonishing that a reputable French critic should have concluded that avoidance of hiatus is the only ancient principle of euphony to which we are now susceptible, as the late N. I. Herescu reports in his *La poésie latine: étude de structures phoniques*, a rich garner of examples relevant to the whole subject, which appeared (1960) after this Part of my book had been written. Herescu's insistence on the value and relevance of ancient criticism (pp. 36, 52, 205) is most timely. For a concise and useful account of Greek views on euphony see W. B. Stanford, *Hermathena* (1943), pp. 3–20.

† *Rambler*, no. 94; *Il.* 18, 492–3. I shall not append translations when the only point is the sound.

‡ ἄσιγμοι ᾠδαί, Athen. x, 455c (see p. 13). It seems likely that Lasus, Pindar's reputed master, was avoiding this letter for the sake of euphony. To a later and sillier age belonged those *tours de force*, 'Ιλιὰς and 'Οδύσσεια λιπογράμματος, in which the first book of each poem was written without an 'α', the second without a 'β', and so forth. John Thelwall wrote an 'English Song without a Sibilant' entitled *The Empire of the Mind* (W. Rhys Roberts, *Dion. Hal. On Lit. Comp.* (1910), p. 147 n.).

followers, whom Plato styles the λογοδαίδαλοι, set themselves to analyse sound-values. Licymnius, a pupil of Gorgias, distinguished verbal beauty (εὐέπεια) of sense and of sound.¹ The great Democritus (no mere word-taster, for he was also the propounder of the theory of poetic madness) wrote works 'On verbal beauty' and 'On euphonious and cacophonous letters'.² Isocrates maintained that even poetry mediocre in thought could beguile hearers by effects of harmony and symmetry in themselves.³ A century later Aristoxenus, a pupil of Aristotle and a great musicologist, wrote works on sounds and rhythms which seem to have had a wide effect on aesthetic and literary theory in general.⁴ But on the literary side the classic work was the treatise *On Diction* (περὶ λέξεως) of his rival, Theophrastus, whom Aristotle chose to succeed himself as head of the Peripatetic school. (There was a curious tradition that his name was originally Tyrtamus, but that Aristotle changed it to Theophrastus partly because that sounded better.)⁵ In discussing 'beautiful words' he developed Licymnius' idea, distinguishing between those that were pleasing in sound, those that appealed to the (inward) eye, and those that suggested noble thoughts.* Our best representative of this Peripatetic tradition is Dionysius of Halicarnassus' work *On Literary Composition*,† which is of particular interest for the purposes of this book because he was living and teaching in Rome from 30 B.C. at least until 8 B.C., that is, for precisely the period in which the *Aeneid*, the *Odes* and *Epistles* of Horace, the *Elegies* of Propertius and Tibullus and the *Amores* of Ovid were being composed. In his fourteenth chapter (which probably owes much to Aristoxenus) he discusses the qualities of the various letters. Thus λ is pleasant (γλυκύ), ρ noble (γενναῖον), σ unpleasant if used in excess. He arranges the long vowels in order of merit, α η ω υ ι (no short vowel is pleasant, though ο is better than ε), and deals likewise with the other letters according to the way in which the mouth produces them.‡ Another critic in the same tradition, Demetrius, author of the treatise *On Style* (περὶ ἑρμηνείας),

---

* That πρὸς τὴν ὄψιν refers to the *inward* eye is clear from the examples given by Demetrius, 'rose-coloured' and 'of flowery complexion' (ῥοδόχροον, ἀνθοφόρου χρόας) (*De Eloc.* 173–4).

† περὶ συνθέσεως ὀνομάτων, or *De Compositione Verborum*. (Useful notes in W. Rhys Roberts's edition.) Dionysius praised Isocrates as τὴν εὐφωνίαν ἐντείνων μουσικήν (*De Isoc.* 3, 540).

‡ The standard work on phonetics was Diogenes περὶ φωνῆς (late third century B.C.). I do not know whether T. H. Savory knew of this passage in Dionysius when he wrote of 'the brighter vowels, α, ε and ο, and the hard, anaemic ι and υ' (*The Art of Translation*, 1957, p. 61).

gave 'Kallistratos' and 'Annoön' as instances of euphonious names, the double *l* and *n* generating a sort of resonance (174). Both consonants were sounded in such cases, and indeed one may agree with Rhys Roberts that the full value given to double consonants in Italian, as in *la bella donna*, is delightful (though here we shall be told that we are confusing sound with associations).

Demetrius also mentioned that musicians called words consisting wholly or mainly of vowels 'smooth', and asserted that a concurrence of vowels within a word was euphonious—Αἰαίη, Εὔιος—and that ἠέλιος sounded better than ἥλιος, ὀρέων than ὀρῶν; the resolution had a sort of musical overtone (οἷον ᾠδὴν ἐπιγινομένην). And while concurrence of the same vowels and diphthongs imparted grandeur (μέγεθος), that of different ones imparted a pleasing variety also (ποικιλίαν ἐκ τῆς πολυηχίας.)[1] He had heard that in Egypt the priests, when singing hymns in praise of the gods, intoned the vowels in succession, and that people listened to this in preference to the flute or lyre, and he referred to the embellishment of songs by the trilling of a single long vowel.[2]

The Romans were no less interested in sounds. The early satirist Lucilius talked of euphony and cacophony,[3] and Messalla, the patron of Tibullus and Ovid, wrote treatises on *s* and other letters.[4] Quintilian liked the sound of open vowels.[5] He found Latin harsher (*durior*) than Greek: it lacked what he felt to be the two most euphonious of Greek letters, upsilon and zeta.* He observed that when a borrowed word like 'zephyri' occurred, a sentence seemed instantaneously to cheer up and smile—'velut hilarior protinus renidet oratio'.[6] He probably relished such a line as Propertius'

> grata domus nymphis umida Thyniasin
> *moist dwelling dear to the Bithynian nymphs*

---

* Dionysius considered ʒ the most pleasing of the double semivowels (*De Comp.* XIV). Appius Claudius Caecus, on the other hand, objected to *z* in early Latin because to pronounce it you had to set your teeth like a dead man's skull (Mart. Cap. III, 261, from Varro). It had not yet the prestige of association with Greek. Upsilon was *ü* (Latin *u* being an *oo*-sound transliterated as ου in Greek); zeta was a voiced *s*. From the first century B.C. these were represented in Latin by *y* and *z*. Quintilian also expresses dislike of *f*, consonantal *u* (including *qu*), words ending in *m*, none of which are features of Attic Greek; also of syllables ending in *b* and *d* before a consonant. And there was less variety in the incidence of the accent in Latin (XII, 10, 27–33).

and would understand why Virgil called the river of Rome 'Thybris' nineteen times, whereas he used 'Tiberis' only twice (in passages of highly Italian colouring).* Other poets also took pleasure in seasoning their Latin with words and forms borrowed from the Greek,† the practice of retaining Greek declensions to taste being introduced by the tragic poet Accius.[1] Lucilius went too far, peppering his satires with actual Greek words as freely as Cicero does his letters, and (so Horace indicates) being admired for doing so by certain literary circles who followed the Neoteroi:

> at sermo lingua concinnus utraque
> suavior, ut Chio nota si commixta Falerni

> *But diction harmonized from the two languages is more pleasing, as when Falernian wine is blended with Chian.*[2]

Horace himself was deprecating this excess, presumably including the writing of words in Greek characters; nevertheless some of his own lines seem to me to gain charm from a moderate admixture of words and forms taken from the Greek, whether exactly or 'parce detorta'— such as

> si neque tibias
> Euterpe cohibet nec Polyhymnia
> Lesboüm refugit tendere barbiton.[3]

Munro observed that Lucretius, when he wished to represent something beautiful, would tune his lines with Greek words, as in

> *musaea mele per chordas organici*, quae
> mobilibus digitis expergefacta figurant,

and

> et *cycnaea mele Phoebeaque daedala chordis*
> carmina.[4]

Ovid makes music of the Greek names of flowers:

> has, hyacinthe, tenes, illas, amaranthe, moraris;
> pars thyma, pars casiam, pars meliloton amant;

---

* *G.* I, 499; *Aen.* VII, 715. Ovid used only 'Thybris' in the *Met.*, 'Tiberis' often in the *Fasti* (Norden on *Aen.* VI, 87). It is noteworthy that Virgil adapted Ennius' line (*Ann.* 54)

> tuque, pater Tiberine, tuo cum flumine sancto

as (*Aen.* VIII, 72)

> tuque, O Thybri, tuo genitor cum flumine sancto.

(M. Leumann, 'Die lateinische Dichtersprache', *Mus. Helv.* 1947, p. 135 n. 12.)

† Quint. XII, 10, 33; N. I. Herescu, *Poésie* (1960), pp. 78–81.

and of places:

> Isi, Paraetonium genialiaque arva Canopi
> quae colis, et Memphin palmiferamque Pharon,

sounds which pleased him so much that he repeated them in varied form in the *Metamorphoses*.* Boileau recognized the enhancement that foreign names can give;[1] and is there not a charm in the mingling of Latin with English in some of our early poems, as in many carols?

Cicero remarks in passing that poets are more addicted to sound than sense—'vocibus magis quam rebus inserviunt'.[2] He gives as an example of a sonorous line 'lit up by splendid place-names' ('locorum splendidis nominibus illuminatus')

> qua pontus Helles supera Tmolum et Tauricos,

where his feeling may be partly due to the un-Latin *tm*-sound in *Tmolum*; and while deprecating excessive attention to such things in oratory, he does recommend that euphonious words be preferred as far as possible, even to the detriment of strict grammar† (and so does Quintilian).[3] 'Voluptati aurium debet morigerari oratio', he says, and again, 'The ears of the people are flutes to the orator'.[4]

As already indicated, there was one point on which all ancient critics were agreed—that an excess of sibilants was peculiarly cacophonous.‡ There was a strange tradition that Pericles substituted ττ for σσ in Attic Greek for the sake of euphony.[5] Cicero, who discusses sound at some length in the *Orator* (149–68), thought that for the same reason *x* had dropped out of certain words, and he called *f* a most unpleasing letter.[6] Quintilian, who agreed, tells us of one Servius who eliminated from his work every case in which a final preceded an initial *s*, as in 'ars studiorum.'[7]

---

* *F.* IV, 439 f.; *Am.* II, 13, 7–8, cf. *M.* IX, 773–4. Note that he is careful not to overdo it by writing 'Paraetoni*on*'; nor did Horace (above) write 'Lesboön'. For names of Aegean islands so used see *Ars*, II, 79–82.

† Fr. 43, p. 142 Baiter. It has been suggested that the ablative of quality was often used by good writers in preference to the orthodox genitive in order to avoid an excess of the termination -*is* (both letters of which, in Dionysius' account, were potentially unpleasing), for example 'vir singulari virtute' for 'vir singularis virtutis' (E. Vandvik, *Symb. Osl.* 1934, pp. 82–3). Similarly, Mr T. S. Eliot has maintained that Tennyson was justified in preferring appropriate sound to strict grammar when he wrote in *Mariana* 'The blue fly *sung* in the pane' (for *sang*: and had he the same object in putting 'in' for 'on'?). (See F. L. Lucas, *Style* (1955), p. 250 n.)

‡ 'σ is an unattractive, disagreeable letter, very offensive when used to excess. A hiss seems a sound more suited to a brute beast than to a rational being': Dion. Hal. *De Comp.* 14, tr. Rhys Roberts, who has an informative note *ad loc.* Cf. Aristoxenus, *ap.* Ath. XI, 467 A.

Tennyson did the same, and called the process 'kicking the geese out of the boat'.* Nor is it surprising that Milton, in revising his draft, substituted 'art sitting' in the song which had originally begun

> Sabrina fair
> Listen where thou sitst—

But it should be noticed that only an excess was, and is to be, condemned. Milton had clearly no intention of being cacophonous when he wrote

> In solemn troops and sweet societies,

nor Virgil when he wrote

> si canimus silvas, silvae sint consule dignae.†

Indeed Robert Graves has fancied that he might leave as his own literary testament, 'The art of poetry consists in knowing exactly how to manipulate the letter *s*'.[1]

It was long ago observed that Milton distinguished in practice what he felt to be harsh and harmonious sounds respectively. Blair drew attention to the contrast of sound between two passages in *Paradise Lost*:

> on a sudden, open fly
> With impetuous recoil and jarring sound
> Th'infernal doors: and on their hinges grate
> Harsh thunder,

whereas

> Heav'n open'd wide
> Her ever-during gates, harmonious sound,
> On golden hinges turning.[2]

And Johnson would not venture to declare that he 'did not intend to exemplify the harmony which he mentions' in

> Fountains! and ye that warble as ye flow,
> Melodious murmurs! warbling tune his praise.[3]

---

* Hallam Tennyson, *Memoir* (1897), II, 14; cf. 289. There is only one exception in the whole of *In Memoriam*,

> And dear to me *as* sacred wine.

Goodwin noted that in an admired passage, Demosthenes, *De Corona* 208, there are 50 sigmas in 67 words. In Latin *s* (15%) is second only to *t* (16%) in frequency among consonants (Förstemann, *K.Z.I.* 166; J. S. T. Hanssen, *Symb. Osl.* (1942), p. 90).

† N. I. Herescu, *Poésie* (1960), p. 38, suggests that he intended to evoke thus the rustling of leaves; but I doubt this, since the line is metaphorical rather than descriptive.

This, you may say, is an illusion generated by the meanings of the words. Then consider the following passages (for repetition of similar phenomena, especially by different poets, is a step towards an objective test). When Virgil's rustic taunts his fellow he says,

> non tu in triviis, indocte, solebas
> stridenti miserum stipula disperdere carmen?[1]

used you not, boor, at the crossroads, to spoil a wretched song on a strident pipe?

Here we have not only an excess of sibilants, but a significant prevalence of the less sonorous vowels, especially *i*, which came out bottom in Dionysius' list; and 'miserum' is an otiose epithet apparently selected as increasing both these sound-effects. Now who can deny that Milton, when he introduced into *Lycidas* the lines

> And when they list their lean and flashy songs
> Grate on their scrannel pipes of wretched straw,

was consciously emulating Virgil's sound-effect as well as his matter? 'Flashy' is hardly an obvious epithet, and he may even have invented *ad hoc* the word 'scrannel', which is found nowhere else. And why did he insert 'when they list', if not for the same reason that Virgil, as I suggest, inserted 'miserum'? These examples are the more striking as occurring in poems which for the most part may be felt to be even self-consciously melodious.

The ancient idea that certain letters or syllables were more beautiful than others was assumed by Dante in his discussion on vernacular words which were acceptable as 'dolata'—euphonious.[2] For him at least poetry was 'musice composita'. There seems to be a *prima facie* case for believing in some degree of musical value in words. And indeed the custom of saying that one word sounds beautiful and another ugly is so nearly universal that to deny any basis to it is a sophistication, though one which deserves to be taken seriously. We must grant that the ancients formulated things too crudely. Isolated letters, especially consonants, can only be said to have such qualities intrinsically to a limited extent. One is uncomfortably reminded of the man who declared that one note of Beethoven was worth the whole music of Bach. But can we detect any features that may tend to make an individual word euphonious or cacophonous?

It may be not too rash to say that some vowels are more sonorous than others; to agree with Dionysius that these contribute more obviously to beauty;[1] that the long surpass the short, and the open the closed, and that long *a* ('ah') has the pre-eminence assigned to it by singers. Certain consonants also spoil vowels. As Grierson has said:

Association doubtless makes even the sound of one's native language sweet to the ear. But no association will ever disguise the fact that Italian is a more euphonious language than guttural Dutch or German with its spluttering *sch—s—ts* (*z*) sounds.* What English has gained from the absorption of classical polysyllables rich in labials and open vowels the student of Shakespeare and Milton can judge:

> The multitudinous seas incarnadine.
> Then feed on thoughts that voluntary move
> Harmonious numbers.[2]

Coleridge, no Germanophobe, spoke of the 'woeful harshness' of the sounds of German.[3]

Marouzeau (independently of Demetrius, it seems, for he does not mention him) has suggested that there is beauty in the concurrence of vowels, especially within a word. He cites Virgil's lines

> Atque Ephyre atque Opis et Asia Deïopeia.
> Atque Getae atque Hebrus et Actias Orithyia.
> Glauco et Panopeae et Inoo Melicertae.

And he attributes to this feature the spell that has been exercised by Racine's simple and transparent verse,

> La fille de Minos et de Pasiphaë,

and by another that seems to haunt him, Musset's

> La blanche Oloössone à la blanche Camire.[4]

Such words often occupied an echoing place at the end of the line.[5] Many Greek proper names had this attraction to offer:

> Protesilaëam Laüdamia domum

---

* I find that I generally prefer, whether consciously or not, to use the relative 'that' rather than 'which', especially before an initial consonant.

was a line that Catullus probably enjoyed inventing, as Ovid probably relished his

> Amphiaraïades Naupactoö Acheloö.

Musing on his Lesbian models gave Horace opportunities to exploit the melodious word 'Aeolius'. There is no finer-sounding verse in Virgil than

> Laomedonteae luimus periuria Troiae,

and it is not surprising that its keyword reappears in another form in the *Aeneid*, 'Laomedontiadae'.[1] It is worth noting that, of the two words selected as examples of euphony by Demetrius on other grounds, one is 'Annoön', and that, of two words similarly chosen at random by Grierson, one is 'co-eternal'.* Have we here one explanation of the fact which puzzled Johnson, that Pope had declared the couplet of his by which his own ear was most gratified to be

> Lo, where *Maeotis* sleeps, and hardly flows
> The freezing *Tanaïs* through a waste of snows![2]

or of Julien Benda's singling out, as sounding poetic, Propertius' lines

> Mox *Amythaonia* nupta futura domo

and

> Dilapsus nusquam est *Amphiaraus* equis[3]?

Grierson mentions another probable factor. 'Some words are pleasant to utter, sweet on the tongue and gentle on the lips; others require an effort, a violent discharge of breath through the throat or lips.'[4] Even we, though we no longer read aloud when alone, as the ancients normally did, unconsciously frame with our throats and mouths, in sym-

---

* Dem. *De Eloc.* p. 174; Grierson, *Rhet. and Engl. Comp.* p. 30; cf. M. Grammont, *Les vers français* (1904), p. 275. Sanskrit, on the other hand, dislikes a concurrence of vowels even within a word (G. Gerber, *Die Sprache als Kunst*, 1871, I, 416–17). A clash of two *i*'s, combined with hissing, may have led the Romans, instinctively, to avoid forming a superlative such as 'piissimus', a solecism with which Cicero taunted Mark Antony (*Phil.* XIII, 43).

The grammarian Diomedes remarked that there are certain vowels which when fully sounded give splendour to the whole diction, and quoted in illustration some rather childish lines by Sextus Paconianus of the 'January brings the snow' type:

> Eoo Oceano Hyperion fulgurat Euro;
> Arctoo plaustro Boreas bacchatur †Rheno;
> Hesperio Zephyro Orion volvitur [austro];
> fulva Paraetonio vaga Cynthia proruit Austro.

'Alte producta elocutione sonantibus litteris universam dictionem illustrant' (I, 499 K.) (Morel, *Frag. Poet. Lat.* p. 123).

pathy, the words we do not articulate. How much more important must this factor have been to them. Writing, said Aristotle, should in general be 'easy to read, or easy to utter—which comes to the same thing'.[1] Latin tended to discard such tongue-twisting words as the early 'stlites' and 'stlocus',[2] and it broke up such awkward collocations of consonants as it found in Greek, saying 'Aesculapius' for 'Asklepios', 'Alcumena' for 'Alkmene'.* Cicero preferred the words 'formarum', 'formis' to their synonyms, 'specierum', 'speciebus' on grounds of comfort in utterance ('commoditatem in dicendo').[3] Further, it has been noted that when a Latin critic or grammarian says a word is, or is not, euphonious, he often seems to mean that is slips more, or less, easily from the mouth. Thus Priscian says that the *p* in 'demptum' was inserted 'euphoniae causa'.† Indeed someone criticized by Philodemus, the Greek scholar-epigrammatist and friend of the Augustan poets, held that the *only* form of cacophony was that caused by difficulty of enunciation.[4] Lucretius thought that 'mel' (honey) and 'lac' (milk) were so named because the words were pleasant to relish in the mouth:

> huc accedit uti mellis lactisque liquores
> iucundo sensu linguae tractentur in ore,

and Augustine said the same: '*Mel* quam suaviter res ipsa gustum tam suaviter nomen tangit auditum'; on the other hand *vepres* (brambles) were as rough as they sound. Lucretius exploits *r* in describing the wry effect of absinth and centaury:

> at contra taetra absinthi natura ferique
> centauri foedo pertorquent ora sapore.[5]

---

* Velius Longus found it hard to pronounce the *m* in 'etiamnunc' (78, 19 K.). Cf. Istambul for Istanbul (εἰς τὰν πόλιν), and the English vulgarisms, Westminister, Admiralty. Similarly, Italian, which has dropped the final consonants of Latin may prefix *i* to an initial impure *s*. It is not surprising that the full form of the word 'ispse' did not maintain itself in Latin.

† Cf. O. Jespersen, *Language* (1922), p. 278: 'Euphony depends not only on custom, but even more on ease of articulation and on ease of perception: what requires intricate or difficult movements of the organs of speech will always be felt to be cacophonous, and so with anything that is indistinct or blurred.' The Greek words were εὐπρόφορον and δυσέκφορον (Dion. Hal. *De Comp.* XII); the difference in the preposition in the middle seems onomatopoeic in intention. Εὐφωνία and εὐστομία were synonyms. (Blair gives the same explanation: *Rhetoric*, no. 13 (1783).)

(b) Collocation of words

It does seem plausible, then, to say, as Grierson does not hesitate to do, that there are euphonious and there are unpleasing words.* But this does not take one very far. We must now consider the effect of words in combination. Dionysius realized that euphonious composition might be not merely a matter of stringing euphonious words together, but of subtly blending with them neutral or even ugly words, like generals distributing indifferent troops among the good, and paying great attention to timely variety.[1]

If we have comparatively little explicit indication of what sounded beautiful to a Greek or Roman ear, still less of any explanation, we do at least gather that that ear was extraordinarily sensitive to 'iucunditas in situ'. A story in Aulus Gellius[2] about the eminent Neronian critic Probus is worth quoting at length:

Valerius Probus, as I heard from a friend of his, was once asked whether one should say 'has urbis' or 'has urbes', 'hanc turrem' or 'hanc turrim'. 'If you have to use those words', he replied, 'whether in writing verse or prose, pay no attention to the musty, school-room rules of the grammarians, but consult your own ear as to what is best in each place. What it advises will surely be most correct.' 'What do you mean by consulting my ear?' 'Doing what Virgil did, when in different passages he used "urbis" and "urbes" according to the taste and judgement of his ear. For in *Georgics* I, which I have read in a copy corrected by his own hand, he wrote "urbis" with an *i*. These are his words:

> urbisne invisere, Caesar,
> terrarumque velis curam.

Change it to 'urbes', and somehow you will make it blunter and heavier. On the other hand in *Aeneid* III he wrote 'urbes' with an *e* in

> centum urbes habitant magnas.

Change this to "urbis" and the word will be too thin and bloodless, such

---

* 'Beautiful name, that *Magdalen*!' exclaimed Keats (letter to Reynolds of 14 March 1818). K. M. Wilson selects from *Lycidas* as words beautiful in themselves 'Neaera', 'enamel', 'Lesbian' (!), 'Amaryllis', 'mellowing', 'violet', 'laborious' (*Sound and Meaning*, 1930, p. 52). (For what it is worth one may note that the first has a concurrence of vowels, and the rest have the letter *l* in common: in Dionysius' opinion, ἡδύνει τὴν ἀκοὴν τὸ λ, καί ἐστι τῶν ἡμιφώνων γλυκύτατον, *De Comp.* XIV.) But for some healthy though not extreme scepticism see F. L. Lucas, *Style* (1955), pp. 248-50.

a difference does combination make to the harmony of adjacent vowels. Moreover Virgil said "turr*i*m" not "turr*e*m", "secur*i*m" not "secur*e*m":

turrim in praecipiti stantem

and

incertam excussit cervice secur*i*m.

These forms have, I think, a more agreeable lightness than if you used those in *e* in both places.' His questioner, surely an uneducated fellow with no ear, insisted: 'I simply don't understand why one or the other is better or more correct in any of these passages.' 'Then,' said Probus with some heat, 'don't worry whether you ought to say "urb*e*s" or "urb*i*s". For being the sort of man I perceive you are, you won't suffer from any error; you'll lose nothing, whichever you say.'

In one respect some of the ancients (especially the Greeks) went much further than any of the moderns, presumably because their literature was designed to be spoken aloud—the pursuit of smoothness. The catch of the breath occasioned by the collision of an unelided final with an initial vowel, Stevenson's 'jaw-breaking hiatus', was generally avoided in Greek drama and in Latin poetry. Marked avoidance of such hiatus in prose was found already in Thrasymachus and Gorgias, but was first systematically cultivated by Isocrates. Though some disdained it as pernickety (no wonder, said Plutarch, that a man who shrank from the clash of two vowels shrank also from the Macedonian phalanx),[1] and though Demosthenes was not rigid, even Plato paid attention to it in his later works, and subsequent Greek prose writers also in varying degrees.*

We must however note the curious fact that hiatus in poetry could be felt to be positively pleasing. Demetrius speaks of its avoidance as making composition possibly smoother but as depriving it of the considerable euphony that results from the collision of vowels;[2] and Dionysius cites as a passage whose gentle and harmless flow matched the beauty of its subject

ἡ δ' ἴεν ἐκ θαλάμοιο περίφρων Πηνελόπεια
Ἀρτέμιδι ἰκέλη ἠὲ χρυσῇ Ἀφροδίτῃ.[3]

Whether by chance or intention the three lines of Virgil quoted above (p. 16) as selected by Marouzeau for euphony all exhibit hiatus between

* For example, *Hellenica Oxyrhynchia*, sometimes at the expense of natural order (Grenfell and Hunt, *Ox. Pap.* v, 124). The 'ephelcystic' *v* was a mitigant of hiatus in general use.

words. Cicero, after quoting some instances from older Latin poets (and one, a Grecism, from himself

> Etesiǎe in vada ponti,

which involves *correptio*, that is, shortening of the final vowel or diphthong), adds 'the Greeks tend even to praise this'.[1] Stranger still, Aulus Gellius particularly liked hiatus of the *same* vowel, remarking that he found so many examples of this 'suavitas' in famous poets. He quotes Homer, Virgil and finally Catullus, 'most elegant of poets':[2]

> minister vetuli puer Falerni
> inger mi calices amariores,
> ut lex Postumiae iubet magistrae,
> ebria acina ebriosioris,

(where however 'ebria' for the more normal masculine might seem intended rather to induce an effect of hiccup). On the other hand Quintilian particularly deprecates synaloepha of the *same* vowels, though many cases occur in reputable authors.[3]

The orthodox view was that hiatus, as the word implies, created a gasping and laboured effect—in Pope's expressive phrase,

> Tho' oft the ear the open vowels tire.*

The treatise to Herennius repeats the precept 'avoid frequent clashes of vowels', instancing 'bacae aeneae amoenissime impendebant'.[4] But when Cicero follows suit (presumably likewise echoing some Grae-culus), the contrast with Latin realities (he has just written 'ut in legendo oculus') pulls him up for once; for Latin differed from Greek because in it a final long vowel as well as a short was elided, or rather slurred, before an initial vowel, even by the illiterate.[5] So he shakes himself free with 'But the Greeks must see to that: we cannot keep our vowels apart even if we wish'.[6] And indeed the slurring (*synaloepha*), such as occurs in Italian, seemed not unpleasing to him:† it was a lubricant—'habet

---

* *Essay on Criticism*, I, 345. French only became sensitive to hiatus after Malherbe (Boileau, *A.P.* I, 107). English and German are said to mind only concurrence of the same vowel: G. Gerber, *Die Sprache als Kunst* (1871), I, 416–17. M. Grammont (*Les vers français*, 1904, pp. 273–85) dislikes it only in cases where no modulation of the voice results. 'Dryden got a bee in his bonnet about hiatus; but who minds it?' (F. L. Lucas, *Style*, p. 252).

† It did not always take place, in prose or poetry. For a full discussion (in Latin) of hiatus and synaloepha see C. Zander, *Eurhythmia*, II (1913), 555–660.

molle quiddam' (and incidentally those who meticulously avoided it might give the impression of being more interested in style than in clients).[1] Analysis of Cicero's practice has shown that his ear was not in fact offended by collision of vowels.[2]

There was also a tendency among some authors, both Greek and Roman, particularly exponents of the 'periodic' style of oratory, to avoid excessive or ugly clash of consonants at the junctures of words, and in general to cultivate a smooth, flowing movement. Again the *locus classicus* is a chapter in Dionysius' *De Compositione Verborum* and again I will quote to show how sensitive an ancient ear could be, or could profess to be.[3] 'This style (the smooth, or γλαφυρά) resembles finely woven stuffs, or pictures in which the lights melt insensibly into the shadows. It requires that all its words shall be melodious, smooth, soft as a maiden's cheek; and it shrinks from harsh, clashing syllables, and carefully avoids everything rash and hazardous.' He distinguishes certain poets for this quality as well as prose-writers, fortunately including Sappho, whose *Hymn to Aphrodite* (fr. 1) was preserved by his quoting it here in full. His comments on this poem show that it even mattered whether or not the successive sounds were such as easily followed one another in the mouth:*

Here the euphonious effect and the grace of the language arise from the coherence and smoothness of the junctures. The words nestle close to one another and are woven together according to certain affinities and natural attractions of the letters. Almost throughout the entire ode vowels are joined to mutes and semivowels,† all those in fact which are naturally prefixed or affixed to one another when pronounced together in one syllable. There are very few clashings of semivowels with semivowels or mutes, and of mutes and vowels with one another, such as cause the sound to oscillate. When I review the entire ode I find, in all those nouns and verbs and other kinds of words, only five or perhaps six unions of semivowels with mutes which do not naturally blend with one another, and even they do not disturb the smoothness of the language to any great extent. As for juxtaposition of vowels, I find that those which occur in the clauses themselves are still fewer, while those

---

* Cf. Robert Graves, *Asphodel* (1949), p. 15: '[The skilled craftsman] takes care not to interrupt the smooth flow of the line, if this can possibly be avoided, by close correspondence between terminal consonants and the initial consonants that follow them—e.g. *break ground, maid's sorrow, great toe.*'

† The semivowels are given as λ, μ, ν, ρ, σ, 3, ξ, ψ, in ch. XIV. For the smooth harmony of Greek in general see T. H. Savory, *Translation* (1957), p. 61.

which join the clauses to one another are only a little more numerous. As a natural consequence the language has a certain easy flow and softness; the arrangement of the words in no way ruffles the smooth waves of sound.[1]

Cicero likewise had said: 'Such a collocation of words should be preserved as to make your style continuous, coherent, smooth, evenly flowing. This is achieved if you so manage the junctures of words that they do not clash harshly nor gape too wide.' But he is conscious that it is a matter of ear rather than rule, that such effects 'fiunt magnificentius quam docentur', and he apologizes for his discussion of such minutiae, as being perhaps beneath the dignity of a Senator.[2] Indeed he twice quotes a passage from Lucilius in which Scaevola pokes fun at one Albucius: 'Oh how daintily his compositions are created, the wording (λέξεις) all skilfully inlaid and intertwined like the little cubes in a mosaic pavement!'[3]

It is difficult to determine how far individual writers were consciously aiming at such an effect. In Horace's *Odes*, at any rate, there is a marked tendency to 'synaphea' or 'fitting together' through the avoidance of hiatus even between the end of one line and the beginning of the next.[4] The *Odes* are indeed remarkably smooth-flowing: collocations like 'fuga*x tr*epidare' are quite exceptional.* Again, whereas Ennius had twice described the sky as 'stellis fulgentibus aptum' and once as 'stellis ardentibus aptum', it is no surprise that Virgil appropriates the latter form, in which the inelegant thickness of *s* followed by *f* is avoided.[5] Quintilian thought that the termination -*erunt* had been smoothed out into -*ere* to avoid harshness.[6]

Variation of sounds is another of the prime alleged causes of euphony.† Wordsworth and Keats, for instance, are known to have set great store by it.[7] 'The vowel demands to be repeated', said Stevenson; 'the consonant demands to be repeated; and both cry aloud to be perpetually varied.'[8] Robert Graves speaks just as Dionysius might have spoken: 'The skilled craftsman varies the vowel sounds as if they were musical notes so as to give an effect of melodic richness; uses liquid consonants,

---

* II, 3, 12. Marouzeau finds this case 'expressive', but here seems fanciful. (*Traité*, p. 37.)

† N. I. Herescu, on 'la chaîne vocalique', gives some remarkable examples of vowel-patterning thrown into relief by the pulse of the metre (*Poésie* (1960), pp. 81–95); but perhaps he does not emphasize sufficiently the extent to which such patterns may be fortuitous, despite his interesting discussion of Virgil's choice between 'tres' and 'tris', 'illi' and 'olli', etc. (pp. 97–104).

labials and open vowels for smoothness, aspirates and dentals for force; gutturals for strength; sibilants for flavour, as a cook uses salt.'[1] When a line lingers in my memory, I often feel on introspection that this is the cause. A gradation can be particularly pleasing, as in

> Weed wide enough to wrap a fairy in

or

> To pluck bright honour from the pale-faced moon

(but then I must remind myself that Shakespeare probably said 'ploock'). Is it only the prettiness of the associations that creates the ineffable loveliness of Milton's climax?—

> Bid Amarantus all his beauty shed,
> And Daffadillies fill their cups with tears
> To strew the laureate hearse where Lycid lies.

In the last line I feel it is the gradation of vowel-sounds that makes the music, but in the two preceding ones there is the additional contrast imparted by an assonance—*Amarantus*, D*affadillies fill*, as, in the Shakespeare line, *honour from* and *pale-faced*.

It is on such interplay of variety and repetition that the harmonious patterns of all good writing depend.*

In antiquity a fastidious ear might be offended by too close recurrence of the same vowel. Dionysius criticized the Isocrateans for monotonous vowel-texture,[2] and we have seen that Demetrius considered variety (ποικιλία) of vowel-sounds euphonious. Aulus Gellius thought that Virgil used the uncommon feminine gender of 'finis' in the phrase 'haec finis Priami' because if he had written 'hic finis Priami' the ear would have spurned it as inharmonious.[3] It has been suggested that in *Eclogue* I, 18 he wrote

> qui sit, da, Tityre, nobis

to avoid the cacophonous series of 'i's (and thickening of consonants) that would disfigure the more normal

> quis sit, dic, Tityre, nobis.[4]

---

* See R. L. Stevenson's remarks and analyses in his well-known essay 'On Some Technical Elements of Style in Literature', Pentland edn. xv, 282. 'One sound suggests, echoes, demands, and harmonises with another; and the art of rightly using these concordances is the final art in literature.' Dame Edith Sitwell has much to say about this in the notes prefixed to her *Collected Poems* (1957).

(c) Alliteration

I have said little so far of the verbal music of alliteration and assonance, which is more palpable, and was in fact a recognized form of literary adornment (*ornatio*) in antiquity.

The word alliteration dates only from Pontanus (fifteenth century).* Strictly speaking it applies only to initial letters of words, but in literature initials of syllables also have their effect. (Herescu supposes that both alliteration and assonance were enhanced by coincidence with metrical 'ictus'.†) Though it was marked enough in some of the Presocratics (as contrasted with later Greek writers) to be more than fortuitous, and had its place in Greek rhetorical handbooks, it had independent roots in Italy and flourished much more in Latin.[1] It was partly used to make phrases memorable, distinctive, solemn or even magic: in proverbs—*mense Maio male nubent*; in legal formulae—*donum datum donatumque dedicatumque*; in prayers—*quod felix faustum fortunatumque siet*.[2] Here is a prophetic warning from a play of Ennius:

> puerum primus Priamo qui foret
> postilla natus, temperaret tollere.
> eum esse exitium Troiae, pestem Pergamo.[3]

It played a part in Saturnian verse, though not as regular a part as in Langland; for instance:

> immortales mortales flere si foret fas,
> flerent divae Camenae Naevium poetam;
> itaque postquam est Orci traditus thensauro
> obliti sunt Romai loquier lingua Latina.

In the fragments of Accius' tragedies we come across lines such as

> maior mihi moles, maius miscendum est malum.

Ennius retained alliteration in his hexameters, and the notorious line

> O Tite, tute, Tati, tibi tanta, tyranne, tulisti,

* The Greeks used παρήχησις, παρόμοιον or ὁμοιοκάταρκτον. For a general account see A. Cordier, *L'allitération dans l'Enéide* (1939).

† *Poésie* (1960), pp. 23–6; but he does not consider the effect of word-accent as well in this connection, assuming that it was effaced by ictus in reading verse (pp. 27–8). With this I cannot agree, believing that ictus was felt but not heard (see pp. 92–6).

even if, as some think, it is a parody, is at least evidence that there was a
recognizable feature to be parodied. There are plenty of lines in him
such as

> Marsa manus, Paeligna cohors, Vestina virum vis

whose genuineness are unquestioned; and he bequeathed this trait to
his admirer Lucretius:

> parare
> non potuit, pedibus qui pontum per vada possent
> transire et magnos manibus divellere montis
> multaque vivendo vitalia vincere saecla.[1]

Indeed Lucretius also ran to excess, and it was left to *his* admirer Virgil
to use alliteration with artistic restraint.[2]

It is in any case hard to distinguish intention from hazard, and in a
matter that does not admit of statistical analysis one must keep constantly in mind the overwhelming preponderance of non-occurrence.
But in certain poems one may plausibly detect a particular care, as when
Catullus (45) makes Septimius stammer out*

> mea...Acme
> ni te perdite amo atque amare porro
> omnes sum assidue paratus annos
> quantum qui pote plurimum perire...

and Acme answer,

> sic...mea vita Septimille
> huic uni domino usque serviamus
> ut multo mihi maius acriorque
> ignis mollibus ardet in medullis.

Did Horace have this music in his mind when he composed *his* lovers'
dialogue, *Donec gratus eram tibi* (III, 9), with its 'candidae cervici', 'alia...
arsisti', 'dulces docta', 'metuam mori', 'parcent puero', 'reiectae...
ianua', 'improbo iracundior', and its anaphora of *donec...donec, Lydia
...Lydia, pro qua...mori, si parcent...pro quo...mori, si parcent, tecum...*

---

* For stammering 'p-sounds' cf. Horace, *S.* 1, 6, 57 (Kiessling's note):
> infans namque pudor prohibebat plura profari;
also Plautus, *Men.* 252:
> non potuit paucis plura plane proloqui.
(For lisping, Lucretius has 'balba loqui non quit': IV, 1141.)

tecum, all in twenty-four lines that are like an antiphony on the virginals?
And did he remember this poem when he conceived another in the same
metre, *Festo quid potius die* (III, 28), with its *festo . . . faciam*, re*conditum**
. . . *Caecubum*, *sentis* ac *veluti stet volucris*,† *cessantem . . . consulis*,
*Neptunum . . . Nereidum, celeris . . . Cynthiae . . . carmine . . . Cnidon . . .
Cycladas, Nox . . . nenia*—all in sixteen exquisite lines?

I fancy also that poets sometimes had a natural care for their sounds
in the all-important opening line.‡ Catullus begins the poem already
quoted with

> *Acmen Septimius suos amores. . . .*

He begins his epyllion,

> *Peliaco quondam prognatus vertice pinus. . . .*

Other examples in hexameters strike the ear:

> *E tenebris tantis tam clarum extollere** lumen . . . ;*
> *Tityre, tu patulae recubans sub tegmine fagi . . . ,*

and in Horace's *Odes* we have

> *Motum ex Metello consule civicum*
> *bellique causas et vitia et modos . . .*

and

> *Angustam amice pauperiem pati*
> *robustus acri militia puer. . . .*[1]

But again we must bear in mind that the great majority of openings are
not alliterative. Nor must we impute intention too readily, remembering Tennyson's experience:[2] 'Why, when I spout my lines first, they
come out so alliteratively that I have sometimes no end of trouble to get
rid of the alliteration.'

W. M. Lindsay remarked of Plautus, 'not infrequently he revels in
an almost Celtic assonance, as at *Amphitryo* 1042, "Iam ad regem recta
me ducam resque ut facta eloquar" '.[3] An attempt was made by W. J.

---

* I have included such words because sometimes an *accented* syllable in the middle of a word can
have more alliterative effect than an unaccented initial, especially if it begins the verbal part of a
compound.

† Coleridge remarked that an alternate alliteration was 'perhaps, when well used, a great
secret in melody', citing Spenser's
> And on the grasse her *daintie limbs did lay.*
From Lecture III, 1818, pp. 512–13, Ashe.

‡ E.g. Erinna, fr. 2: πομπίλε, ναύταισιν πέμπων πλόον εὔπλοον ἰχθύ. . . . Pontanus noted that
alliteration pleased most at the beginning and end.

Evans in his *Allitteratio Latina* (1921) to discover fixed rules for alliteration in Roman poetry, such as exist in Welsh and, though now known
only to a few bards, exercise their effect on the audience. But he was
forced to admit so many licences that his rules became indistinguishable
from what hazard and a poet's natural ear would yield, though his collection of material has some value. In any case there is no mention in
ancient criticism of any such regularity. As for oratory, the treatise *Ad
Herennium* condemns 'excessive repetition of the same letter'.[1]

(d) Assonance

Alliteration is often bound up with assonance. This too was indigenous
to Latin before the influence of Greek oratory was felt. It characterizes
languages with an initial stress-accent (such as early Latin is believed to
have been), Germanic and Celtic verse, as against Greek and the earliest
Indian.[2] Again there are striking examples in early Roman drama, such
as

> mater optumarum multo mulier melior mulierum,
> missa sum,

or

> lassitudinemque minuam manuum mollitudine.[3]

In Lucretius assonance is as common as alliteration. It has been suggested
that in his case an additional factor was at work. He compares his atoms
several times to letters of the alphabet, and uses as a simile the way in
which different arrangement of almost the same elements will produce
lignis and *ignis*. His so-called puns are sometimes serious, being based
on his conception of the origins of language and the logical connections
of words—*amor* and *umor*, for instance, *terra* and *maternus*, *culmen* and
fulmen.*

But here again the rhetoricians warn against excess.[4] It appears that,
while a series of words with the same ending was classed as an adornment, too long a series was a blemish. It was also felt by ancient critics—
or hypercritics—to be a blemish if the same syllable ended one word and
began the next.[5] Needless to say, the poets provide numerous examples.

---

* IV, 1049 ff.; V, 795–6, 821–2, cf. II, 993, 998; VI, 296–8. See the suggestive article of P. Friedländer, 'Pattern of Sound and the Atomistic Theory of Lucretius', *A.J.P.* (1941), pp. 16–34. The
atoms of Democritus and Epicurus are like letters, the 'homoeomeria' of Anaxagoras fail by this
test.

But Herescu has observed that the commonest offender is Ovid, in the admittedly unfastidious poems from exile; Virgil has proportionally more in the unrevised *Aeneid* than in the *Eclogues* and *Georgics*, and Horace hardly any in the fastidious *Odes* (I, 12, 36, nobi*le le*tum; II, 17, 4, gran*de de*cus). He suggests that Horace was smiling up his sleeve when he wrote, of faults in style that are venial,

> sunt deli*cta ta*men quibus ignovisse velimus.
> *yet there are faults which we may be willing to pardon.*[1]

Not impossible: for we have an analogy in the caesura-less line about faults of rhythm that sometimes escape notice,

> non quivis videt immodulata poëmata iudex.[2]
> *not every critic can detect unharmonious verses.*

Victor Hugo, perhaps for the same reason, expelled Attila in favour of Genséric from his line which originally read,

> Avec les Atti*la la* nuit coïncidait.[3]

I confess that I do not care for the line in the hymn that goes

> Praise him with g*lad ad*oration.

It is a curious fact that Cicero was less fastidious in these matters than one would expect. Quintilian took him to task for his 'res mihi invisae visae sunt'. He let 'pleniore ore' stand, and 'eo equo quo', and 'civem bonarum artium, bonarum partium, bonorum virorum'.[4] Had he perhaps a shameless old-fashioned Roman delight in assonance? One thinks of those much-criticized verses of his,

> O fortu*natam natam* me consule Romam[5]

and

> cedant arma togae, concedat laurea linguae.*

In his youthful translation from the *Iliad* we read

> namque omnes memori por*tentum mente retentant*
> qui non *funestis* liquerunt lumina *fatis.*[6]

---

* *Linguae* must surely be the correct reading. The almost meaningless variant reading *laudi* may have been introduced by someone who recognized that jingle was in point, and saw a chance of intensifying it. Herescu emphasizes the amount of assonance that occurs in Cicero, Catullus and other Roman poets between the last vowels upon which ictus falls in the lines: *Poésie,* ch. v.

And he certainly made no attempt to avoid jingle, assonance or even rhyme in the endings of consecutive hexameters: here (reading downwards) are fifteen from the poem on his consulship:[1]

monebant	decore	morate
ferebant	ortus	locata
iubebant	senatus	hora
vereri	ortum	columna
teneri	videret	parata.

He remarked, of various forms of adornment in oratory involving repetition, that they sometimes lent energy (*vis*), sometimes grace (*lepos*),[2] and this seems to be true of verse also. Take *anaphora*. In the following line of Ovid it surely imparts energy:

ipse tuus custos, *ipse* vir, *ipse* comes;

in these of Tibullus it seems purely ornamental:

longa dies homini docuit parere leones,
longa dies molli saxa peredit aqua;
annus in apricis maturat collibus uvas,
annus agit certa lucida signa vice.[3]

In default of ancient testimony we cannot trust our own ear always to detect what would have been felt as euphonious or cacophonous by a Greek or a Roman. If the line

ἀτιμίας μὲν οὔ, προμηθίας δὲ σοῦ

had turned up unheralded in an undergraduate's iambics, would it have escaped censure? Yet Sophocles wrote it.[4] We can just swallow Demetrius' recommendation of Αἰαίη as a specially harmonious word, but that Virgil should have used it in the genitive *Aeaeae* is surely astonishing to us.[5] And was Ovid playing still, or sobbing, when he wrote in exile

si quis qui quid agam forte requirat erit?*

An almost xylophonic assonance chimes in with the neat elegance of the elegiac couplet: as in

ne tibi neglecti mittant mala somnia manes,
maestaque sopitae stet soror ante torum.[6]

* *Tr.* I, I, 18. For sobbing cf. Catullus (see p. 55). Quintilian disliked *qu* (XII, 10, 30). The author *Ad Herennium* (IV, 18) criticizes Ennius for a line in one of his plays:

quoiquam quicquam quemquam, quemque quisque conveniat, neget.

Often the assonance is increased automatically by the favourite figures of anaphora and repetition:

> cedant carminibus reges regumque triumphi,
> cedat et auriferi ripa benigna Tagi;
> vilia miretur vulgus, mihi flavus Apollo
> pocula Castalia plena ministret aqua.[1]

As with alliteration, there are remarkable assonances in the *opening* lines of some of Horace's *Odes*; for instance,

> quem tu, Melpomene, semel...,

or

> qualem ministrum fulminis alitem...,

an almost perfect chiasmus of sound.[2] There is also sometimes a noticeable assonance in the equally important end-position, as in

> ter pede terram,

and

> dulce ridentem Lalagen amabo,
> dulce loquentem,

and

> et mihi Delphica
> lauro cinge volens, Melpomene, comam.[3]

Under the Empire the taste for assonance increased. One has only to think of the chiastic refrain of the *Pervigilium Veneris* (a poem full of ornamental anaphora also),

> cras amet qui nunquam amavit quique amavit cras amet.

It also plays a prominent part in the prose of Apuleius.[4] In the Middle Ages it became a regular feature of poetry, as in the *Chanson de Roland*, surviving longest in Spain, the last country in which it was entirely superseded by end-rhyme.*

---

* Keats, who loved to talk of 'the principle of melody in verse', employs assonantal pattern to a remarkable extent in his verse written between autumn 1818 and the end of June 1819— *Hyperion*, *The Eve of St Agnes*, the odes and many of the sonnets (W. J. Bate, *Styl. Devel. Keats* (1945), pp. 50–65). For similar effects in Valéry see Herescu, *Poésie* (1960), p. 165 n.

(e) Rhyme

A tendency to actual rhyme could hardly fail to occur in an inflected language, and it was promoted by the taste for parallelism.* παρίσωσις and ὁμοιοτέλευτον were both Gorgianic figures, and such rhyme as occurs in classical times is a chance by-product of rhetoric. In poetry it became commoner as caesuras became more regular, rhyme between caesura and end of the line being much more frequent than that between successive lines. Epithet and noun in particular were liable to rhyme in this position, and more so in pentameters than hexameters, since there the fixed caesura invited it. In Theognis one pentameter in seven exhibits it, and in the remains of Hellenistic elegy the proportion is higher; in the long fragment we have of Hermesianax it is found in no fewer than 26 pentameters out of 49—more than half.[1] This may have been due to an increasing taste for separating noun and epithet, a device with which Gorgias had experimented—τοὺς πρώτους τῶν πρώτων Ἕλληνας Ἑλλήνων, κ.τ.λ.[2]

Here again, as with alliteration and assonance, we have a feature which was indigenous to Latin, independent of the influence of Greek oratory or poetry. The jingle of rustic incantations like

huat hauat huat ista pista sista,

quoted by Cato,[3] might take the form of rhyme, as in

terra pestem teneto: salus hic maneto,[4]

or

de Tebeste usque ad Tergeste liget sibi collum de reste,[5]

or in the spell uttered by Virgil's rustic,

limus ut hic durescit et haec ut cera liquescit.[6]

Again it is a feature of proverbs, oracles, prophecies, etc.,† as well as a plaything of Plautus. And again it is found in Ennius.

In literature there was one reason for its going further in Latin than Greek. Whereas Gorgias' experiment with the separation of substantive

---

* For an excellent account of the history of rhyme see Norden, *Kunstprosa*, pp. 810–908. Rhyme differs from simple *homoeoteleuton*, as occurring between the ends of verses in poetry, of symmetrical members in prose. I should also recognize rhyme between main caesura and end of verse.

† See also R. G. Austin's interpretation of the remarkable sound-patterns in the fourth *Eclogue*, C.Q. (1927), pp. 100–5.

and epithet did not really catch on, this feature proved more congenial
to Latin, in which word-order was more flexible, so far as can be deduced
from comparison of Latin poets with the Greek Anthology, our best
surviving representative in the almost total loss of Hellenistic elegy.[1]
The Hermesianax fragment may be a freak. Certainly Propertius II, 34
is, where there are 38 examples of caesura-to-end rhyme (hexameters
and pentameters) in 94 lines, including six in succession (85–90).[*]
Marouzeau has noted a similar succession in the Asclepiads of Horace's
first Ode.[†]

terrarum dominos	evehit ad deos
hunc, si mobilium	turba Quiritium
certat tergeminis	tollere honoribus
illum si proprio	condidit horreo
quicquid de Libycis	verritur areis.

But this is a by-product of the Horatian love of separating substantive
and epithet, and probably no more sought as rhyme than his

> non satis est pulchra esse poemata: dulcia *sunto*
> et quocumque volent animum auditoris *agunto*.[‡]

(I understand that the parallelism of Hebrew poetry produces similarly
a fortuitous effect.) In elegy there are cases in which rhyme could easily
have been secured by a change of word-order if it had been sufficiently
desired, as in

> caeruleis Triton per mare curret equis,

where priority was perhaps given to beginning with a dactyl.[§] Ovid
actually eliminates a rhyme in adapting from Propertius: he changes

> haec erit a lacrim*is* facta litura me*is*

---

[*] About 44% of the hexameters in Propertius I and 30% in IV have an epithet before the
caesura with its substantive at the end of the line (Tibullus I, 13%; Ovid, *A.A.* I, 12%). Internal
rhyme occurs in nearly two-thirds of the Propertian samples, rather more than half in the Tibullus
and Ovid. (D. R. Shackleton Bailey, *Propertiana* (1955), p. 57 n. Full analysis for Propertius by
B. O. Foster, *T.A.P.A.* (1909), pp. 32 ff. He thinks the effects intentional.)

[†] *Quelques aspects* (1949), pp. 198–9. Full analysis in Herescu, *Poésie* (1960), pp. 163–5. Line 6,
terrarum dominos...probably begins a new sentence, instead of ending the previous one (Rutgers).
A tendency to such 'leonine' rhyme in Catullus before him has been noted by K. P. Harrington,
Proc. A.P.A. (1903), p. xxix.

[‡] *A.P.* 99–100. Marouzeau, *op. cit.*, thinks that the rhyme here emphasizes the imperative
character of the precepts. This seems rather fanciful to me. The rhymes at *S.* I, 6, 10–11 also seem
to me fortuitous. There are about 30 such pairs in the *Aeneid*. Herescu, *Poésie* (1960), p. 173.

[§] Ovid, *Her.* VII, 50; cf. VIII, 94; IX, 60; 148. Prop. IV, 3, 4; Ov. *Tr.* I, 1, 14. See further
M. Platnauer, *Latin Elegiac Verse* (1951), p. 49. Herescu, *Poésie* (1960), ch. v, distinguishes
assonance from rhyme as repetition of the final 'tonic' vowel (? = vowel with ictus), and he

to
>de lacrimis fac*tas* sentiat esse me*is*.

In the hexameter, too, rhyme between the caesura and the end seems not to have been sought in classical times. Indeed there are two cases in Virgil in which a normal gender seems to have been changed on purpose to avoid it,

>cum canibus timid*i* venient ad pocula dammae

and

>aut oculis cap*ti* fodere cubilia talpae.[1]

Lines like Ovid's

>quot caelum *stellas*, tot habet tua Roma *puellas*[2]

strike us now the more forcibly because we have become used to the regular 'Leonine' hexameters of this type introduced by Gottschalk in the ninth century, which became so popular in the Middle Ages. The ninth century also saw the adoption of regular rhyme by the new lyric poetry of the nascent Romance languages.[3] But by then it had been for five centuries a feature of Latin lyric, notably of Christian hymns. No doubt it was introduced to compensate for the loss of quantitative metre when verse was becoming accentual. Its mnemonic value would commend it especially to hymn-singers, for whom the old measures would also be inseparable from pagan thoughts;[4] and in any case we have seen that assonance is naturally associated with religious utterances.

III. THE REALITY OF VERBAL MUSIC

Mr Bateson (who may be quoted as an extreme champion of the preponderance of meaning in poetry) believes that the uses of metre, alliteration and rhyme can be reduced to three general modes of semantic reinforcement:

(i) The main function of metre is simply to provide a recurrent pattern in the background of the poem, which will act as a continual reassurance to the reader.... (ii) In alliteration, assonance and rhyme the repetition of sounds

---

finds many cases of it in Catullus and other Roman poets. In isolation they are striking, and I would not deny that sometimes, e.g. in Cicero, they may have been 'intended', whether consciously or subconsciously. The question is, do they occur in a greater degree than chance would produce, given the nature of Latin terminations? To prove or disprove the proposition would require linguistic and statistical calculations of appalling complexity.

provides a semantic pointer, emphasising contrasts and underlining connections.... (iii) Vowel quantity and accumulation of consonants serve as a kind
of punctuation, accelerating or slowing down the reading of the poem.[1]

These uses may be genuine by-products, but to anyone sensitive to the
sounds and rhythms of poetry they are ludicrously inadequate as main
explanations. Metre may well have arisen from dancing: at any rate, it
gives the heart of the reader a sympathetic pleasure akin to that of
dancing, though it be only a vestigial shadow. The other effects are
patently used again and again where they can have no such purpose as
is here alleged. What semantic significance could the rhymes in *Epipsy-
chidion* have had for Shelley, seeing that (as his manuscript reveals) his
original draft left some lines blank except for the rhymes? They may
have *suggested* connections but can hardly be said to have *underlined*
them.[2] Schiller and Swinburne both testified that the tune of words or
musical mood or rhythm was often in their head before the meaning.[3]

This is not to deny that the so-called music or melody of poetry is an
elusive thing, and that many of the evidences for it can be impugned.
There are indeed stories enough of people being enchanted by the sound
of speech they do not understand, as the young Augustine by the
speech of St Ambrose, the young Petrarch by the periods of Cicero, the
young Auden by a reading from *Beowulf*.[4] And further instances have
been reported of children guessing quite nearly the subject of a passage
from Homer recited to them.[5] Mr Bateson however, following Bradley, supposes that in such cases some suggestion of the meaning has
seeped through because the reciter understood what he was saying, and
the language was cognate to that of the hearer.[6]

Again, we know indeed that Schliemann's lifelong passion for ancient
Greece was first kindled by his hearing a drunken miller recite Homer;[7]
and Edmund Gosse recalled that when, at the age of eleven, he heard
his father recite the first Eclogue of Virgil, 'all my inner being used to
ring out with the sound of

> formosam resonare doces Amaryllida silvas'.[8]

Says Miramont in Beaumont and Fletcher,[9]

> Though I can speak no Greek, I love the sound on't:
> It goes so thundering as it conjured devils.

But to what garbled pronunciation were these three responding? I have heard Aeschylus' *Agamemnon* performed at Cambridge both in the old English and in the reformed pronunciation. On both occasions there were Greekless members of the audience who, with obvious sincerity, professed themselves enchanted by the sound. The sceptic may say that this only goes to show that they were deluded, but I suspect that a genuine pleasure arose in part at least from the facts that Greek, like Italian, abounds in open vowels and is largely free from agglomerations of consonants, and that its range of vowel-sounds is increased by a generous array of diphthongs. But it is not so easy to divorce sound and sense.

Ezra Pound, in a well-known passage, advised the budding poet 'to fill his mind with the finest cadences he can discover, preferably in a foreign language, so that the meaning of the words may be less likely to divert his attention from the rhythm'.[1] It may be that a poet can cultivate his ear in this way, but Eliot is probably right when he says, 'The music of poetry is not something which exists apart from the meaning. Otherwise, we could have poetry of great musical beauty which made no sense, and I have never come across such poetry. The apparent exceptions only show a difference of degree: there are poems in which we are moved by the music and take the sense for granted, just as there are poems in which we attend to the sense and are moved by the music without knowing it.'[2] Horace alluded to this difference of degree more bluntly from a partisan standpoint:

> interdum speciosa locis morataque recte
> fabula nullius veneris, sine pondere et arte,
> valdius oblectat populum meliusque moratur
> quam versus inopes rerum nugaeque canorae.

'Sometimes a play which has fine set-pieces and good character, though it lack charm, grandeur and art, pleases the people more intensely and is more worth their while than verses poor in subject-matter and melodious trifles.'[3] He was being prompted in this passage, it seems, by his source, the Hellenistic treatise of Neoptolemus of Parium, who had taken his stand against one Heracleodorus, representative of the idea that poetry consisted solely in beautiful sounds. (There were such pure aestheticians more than two thousand years before Poe and the French

Symbolists and Edith Sitwell's *Façade*, and their quarrels with the defenders of the primacy of meaning can be half-overheard through the fragments of Philodemus' book *On Verse*.)[1] But he may also have had in mind the artistic, Alexandrianizing, 'modernist' poets of the previous generation, the 'chanters of Euphorion' (*cantores Euphorionis*) as they were called by Cicero, whose phrase about poets being more addicted to sound than sense I have already had occasion to quote.[2]

If ever a poet anticipated Pound's advice to 'fill his mind with the finest cadences he could discover, preferably in a foreign language', it was Virgil when he was studying to become the Roman Theocritus. The subject-matter of some of the *Eclogues*, especially the earlier ones, is not of prime importance; we distort them if we seek to intensify it by too much allegorical or other serious interpretation. Virgil was at this age still under the spell of the 'Neoteroi': he was making music. And even when a deeper meaning crept in (and I do myself believe that Daphnis in v is meant to suggest Julius Caesar), he was still intent also on producing a transposition of Theocritean melody and rhythm:

> Candidus insuetum miratur limen Olympi
> sub pedibusque videt nubes et sidera Daphnis.
> ergo alacris silvas et cetera rura voluptas
> Panaque pastoresque tenet Dryadasque puellas.
> nec lupus insidias pecori nec retia cervis
> ulla dolum meditantur; amat bonus otia Daphnis.
> ipsi laetitia voces ad sidera iactant
> intonsi montes; ipsae iam carmina rupes,
> ipsa sonant arbusta: deus, deus ille, Menalca!
> sis bonus o felixque tuis! en quattuor aras;
> ecce duas tibi, Daphni, duas altaria Phoebo.
> pocula bina novo spumantia lacte quotannis
> craterasque duo statuam tibi pinguis olivi,
> et multo in primis hilarans convivia Baccho,
> ante focum, si frigus erit, si messis, in umbra,
> vina novum fundam calathis Ariusia nectar.[3]

The theme of the first two lines here is ethereal, of the rest, idyllic: the ideas are pleasing. But can we not also detect a special care in the manipulation of entrancing sounds and rhythms?

Another passage in Virgil which strikes me as particularly musical, is the *epyllion* of Aristaeus at the end of the fourth *Georgic*, with the story of Orpheus and Eurydice inset.[1] Here again one may reasonably suppose that Virgil was lavishing all his artistic powers. It was his last gesture to the Hellenistic poetry of the Neoteroi, the fashion in which he had been reared, before he turned to his national epic; and in it he has shown that mythological story-telling could also rise to be sublime poetry in the hands of a great artist.

> Pastor Aristaeus fugiens Peneïa Tempe....

What a lovely line to begin with!—ruined if the varied vowel-sounds are reduced to a monotonous bleat, and the smoothness ruffled by a soft *g*, in the old English pronunciation:

> Păstor Aristeeus fujiens Peenee-e-a Tempee.

How exquisitely in sound the names of the nymphs are disposed, to enhance the beauty of the subaqueous world!

> At mater sonitum thalamo sub fluminis alto
> sensit. eam circum Milesia vellera Nymphae
> carpebant, hyali saturo fucata colore,
> Drymoque Xanthoque Ligaeaque Phyllodoceque,
> caesariem effusae nitidam per candida colla,
> Cydippeque et flava Lycorias, altera virgo
> altera tum primos Lucinae experta labores,
> Clioque et Beroë soror, Oceanitides ambae,
> ambae auro, pictis incinctae pellibus ambae,
> atque Ephyre atque Opis et Asia Deïopeia,
> et tandem positis velox Arethusa sagittis.

If need be, we can isolate some of the elements of this harmony. The names and the little details must have been selected primarily for beauty —what other motive can have been at work? There is the blending of Greek with Latin—*thalamo, Milesia, nymphae, hyali;*[2] the interlinear hiatus, and the concurrent vowels within the names—*Clio, Beroë, Oceanitides,* and Marouzeau's *Deïopeia.*[3] There is alliteration—*caesariem ...candida colla, Cydippeque,* and the assonance of anaphora—*altera... altera, ambae, ambae...ambae*; and the crowning line, rounding off the whole description, devoted to Arethusa alone. And there is the variation of sound and rhythm whose effect no analysis can convey. And so the episode goes on till its lovely close:

Tum quoque marmorea caput a cervice revolsum
gurgite cum medio portans Oeagrius Hebrus
volveret: 'Eurydicen' vox ipsa et frigida lingua,
'a miseram Eurydicen!' anima fugiente vocabat:
'Eurydicen' toto referebant flumine ripae.

I find a similar distinction in the two wedding-songs of Catullus[1] (and their descendants, Spenser's *Prothalamion* and *Epithalamion*). The poet's main object must have been to distil beauty, by sounds as well as associations:

Cinge tempora floribus
suave olentis amaraci;
flammeum cape laetus, huc
huc veni, niveo gerens
luteum pede soccum.

Open the temple gates unto my love,
Open them wide that she may enter in,
And all the posts adorne as doth behove,
And all the pillars deck with girlands trim,
For to receive this Saynt with honour dew,
That commeth in to you.

Dionysius, apparently following Aristoxenus, thought that the difference between music and oratory was simply one of degree. Greek, of course, had a pitch accent. 'There is a kind of melody in speech', says Aristoxenus, 'which depends upon the accent of words, as the voice in speaking rises and sinks by a natural law.'[2] And although Dionysius indicates clearly that when words were set to music (he gives an instance from a chorus of Euripides) the pitch-accent might be overridden by the melody, in the Delphic Hymns of which the notation has survived there is remarkable correspondence between the musical notes and the word-accents. This is naturally liable to happen when the poet is also composer—something of the kind has been detected in Campion's songs, for instance.[3] The difference was that in Greek speech the pitch rose or fell gradually, whereas in music it jumped from one note to another.[4]

In spoken Latin, on the other hand, intonation was presumably in part a matter of personal taste.* Cicero refers to this as 'etiam in dicendo

* Unless those are right who think that the fixed accent of Latin also was one of pitch. (See p. 91.)

quidam cantus obscurior'—'a sort of tune of a less pronounced kind'. Tune, in the form of 'vocis moderatio', had been transferred to oratory from music as far as was compatible with the restraint of that medium.[1] He warned against its being allowed to become monotonous, and told the strange story of the emotional Gaius Gracchus, who when orating had a servant concealed behind him with an ivory pitch-pipe to give him his note from time to time.* The Asiatic orators were inclined to ululate, especially in their perorations, which were almost intoned, and there were Romans who incurred censure for doing the same.[2] Though Quintilian thought that poetry should not be read in the same voice as prose, but in one combining *gravitas* with a certain *suavitas*, he quotes with approval the remark of the boy Caesar to someone who was reciting in an effeminate sing-song: 'If you're trying to sing, you're singing badly; if you're trying to read, you're singing.'[3]

But is there really such a thing as the *music* even of poetry? Is the term more than a metaphor? There are many who believe passionately that it is. Katharine Wilson, for example, is even ready to write out the musical notation of poems.† There is some evidence that vowels at least do vary in their intrinsic pitch, but the differentiation seems hardly sufficient to permit of pleasurable music being made, though minute subtleties of variation in texture may compensate partly for limitation of range.[4] There is also, concurrently (in many languages, including English and probably Latin), the more widely ranging pitch-line introduced by intonation; but this line may be quite different for several perfectly valid and satisfying renderings of a poem.[5] Alternatively there may be imposed a still more widely wavering line, that of melody, if the poem is set to music. When people speak of 'verbal music', they generally seem to mean the first of these, the subtle texture of vowel-values as modified by consonants. And here we come up against the awkward fact that there have been poets enough whose ear for poetry is adequate or even particularly admired, who have yet been indifferent to real music, or even tone-deaf. Though Browning and Hopkins for

---

* It is clear from the succeeding paragraphs in Cicero, and from Quintilian (I, 10, 27), that the 'fistula' (τονάριον) was to give the note, not merely to warn him that he was speaking too loud or too softly (Cic. *De Or.* III, 225–7 as against Gellius, *N.A.* I, 11, 10).

† In her lively book *Sound and Meaning in English Poetry* (1930), which may serve as an extreme expression of the view opposed to that of Bateson.

instance were very musical,* those who were not include Victor Hugo, Tennyson, Yeats, Housman—and, of all people, Swinburne.[1]

Let us follow traditional usage, however, and call this texture of vowel and consonant sounds 'verbal music'.† Is this a myth, as Bateson contends? If so, it is an extraordinarily widespread and pertinacious one. All sorts of analyses have been made, with recordings and so forth, yet the quality remains indefinable—as what artistic quality is not? It is a matter of τὸ ἄλογον τῆς ἀκοῆς πάθος.[2] Cacophony we can often agree in recognizing; but euphony, especially diffused over a long passage or poem, is a more subtle, not to say subjective, matter. We do, however, think of some poets as more musical in general than others, or some poems (for example *Lycidas, pace* Dr Johnson) as signally euphonious. Collins's *Ode to Evening* is a case in point. Swinburne considered that Collins had 'a note of pure lyric song', and we may reasonably suppose that on this occasion he was 'all ears'; for he was daring to write a lyric poem without the aid of rhyme, as few had done at all, let alone success-fully, for centuries. In a sensitive analysis James Sutherland has shown how well he wove his poem out of alliteration, assonance, and the words and ideas they partly suggested.[3]

I would say myself that there is such a thing as 'verbal music', as distinct from the music of pitch-accent and intonation, and that its ingredients probably include what so many critics, ancient and modern, of widely differing tongues and often independently, have felt them to be. They are such phenomena as we have been discussing—sonorous vowels, vowels subtly modified by consonants, concurrence of vowels, avoidance of cacophonies, smoothness, ease of utterance, variation of sounds, and on the other hand alliteration, assonance and rhyme.‡ There are also the phenomena of rhythm, which I shall discuss later. It follows

---

* Keats fancied that, if he had studied music, he might have been able so to combine sounds as to produce something as original as his poetry. Mallarmé aimed at 'un art d'achever la transposi-tion, au livre, de la symphonie'. Edith Sitwell has said that her *Façade* might be regarded as the poetic equivalent of Liszt's *Transcendental Exercises.* W. J. Bate, *Styl. Devel. Keats* (1945), p. 51; J. Press, *Fire and Fountain* (1955), pp. 96, 98.

† Wellek and Warren would have us abandon it for the Russian term 'orchestration' (*Theory of Lit.* (1949), p. 160), but it is really too late.

‡ Cf. Rosamund E. Deutsch, *The Pattern of Sound in Lucretius* (Bryn Mawr, 1939): 'Read aloud, accustom your ear to the music of this language, hear the alliterations, assonances, rhymes, the similarities and contrasts of words, be it in a single verse or in two, or spread over five or fifteen or fifty, and you will then have an experience to be equalled with few other poems at least in European literature.'

that our pronunciation should try, as far as our knowledge permits, to reproduce the music intended by the ancient authors. (And if English were a dead language which one learnt in order to read Shakespeare and his contemporaries, I should be in favour of learning to pronounce it as nearly as possible in the Elizabethan way.)

But—and herein lies the mystery—these elements cannot *of themselves* concert anything sufficiently melodious to give much pleasure independently of meaning. The music is only latent and potential. As Eliot puts it (for where a mystery is concerned, one had best appeal to the experience of critics who are also creators):[1] 'A musical poem is a poem which has a musical pattern of sound and a musical pattern of the secondary meanings of the words which compose it, and these two patterns are indissoluble and one.... The sound of a poem is as much an abstraction from the poem as is the sense.' Or in the words of Robert Bridges,[2] 'The great indefinable complication is that this euphony, especially in poetry, is fused with the meaning; and that this fusion of sound and sense is the magic of the greatest poetry.'

Those whose experience leads them to accept this belief (for it cannot be called an explanation) will not be disconcerted by arguments drawn from the effect that can result from very slight changes in the outward, letter-by-letter, make-up of a poem, whether, as in Press's amusing *jeu d'esprit*, a burlesque meaning is substituted,

> In Bakerloo did Aly Khan
> A stately Hippodrome decree,
> Where Alf, the bread-delivery man...,

or whether, as in I. A. Richards's experiment with Milton's *Ode on the Morning of Christ's Nativity*, the changes produce a meaningless rigmarole.[3] The fact that the alterations are in themselves small does not mean that their effect is not drastic. (In the church of S. Ignazio in Rome there is a baroque painted ceiling which is a masterpiece of perspective. It represents a worm's-eye view from a courtyard to the heavens, with tier upon tier of pillared balconies carrying the eye ever upwards. When you enter the church it looks an almost meaningless jumble, and it is only when you take your stand on a specially sited disc in the floor that the whole painting clicks into perspective.) And one can counter with Sutherland's question: would it then have been just as good if Shakespeare had written 'Full fathom six'?[1] It would scarcely have affected the sense. Nor does the fact that the sound of language without meaning can give but a faint pleasure imply that the sound as *evoked* by meaning is not of supreme importance; on the contrary, many people feel it to be for them the element that contributes most to their delight in poetry.

We have seen that the orators in the Isocratean tradition thought that oratory should, as far as possible, be composed of euphonious words. The corresponding view about poetry has also been widely held in most periods of literary history: it was not simply a fad of nineteenth-century romantics. Poetry has been expected to be beautiful not only when the subject-matter is positively pleasant, but when it is more or less neutral. We must remember, however, that (in the words I quoted before from Eliot) 'it would be a mistake to assume that all poetry ought to be melodious'. We have already had our ears suitably offended by Virgil's rustic piper, and ancient poets and critics were aware, like their modern counterparts, that in some contexts cacophony might be called for. When Homer is representing the Cyclops as dashing out the brains of Odysseus' companions, he uses a phrase unmistakably intended to be cacophonous and expressive, as Dionysius observed:

σύν τε δύω μάρψας ὥστε σκύλακας ποτὶ γαίη
κόπτ'· ἐκ δ' ἐγκέφαλος χαμάδις ῥέε, δεῦε δὲ γαῖαν.

How horribly vivid is the sound of κόπτ', and how unpleasant the struggle of the mouth to enunciate κόπτ'· ἐκ δ' ἐγκέφαλος![2] Robert Graves has put it thus:

'By judicious manipulation of vowels and consonants a line can be made to limp, crawl, scream, bellow, and make other ugly or sickening noises. Mr Eliot, though a master craftsman of musical verse, amuses himself by letting a line snuffle and clear its throat realistically:

> Madame Sosostris, famous clairvoyant,
> Had a bad cold, nevertheless
> Is known to be the wisest woman in Europe.*

* *Asphodel* (1949), p. 15. '*Back* is not pretty, but it gives the feeling of physical constraint which I want' (G. Manley Hopkins, *Letters to Robert Bridges*, 1935, I, p. 162; J. Press, *Fire and Fountain* (1955), p. 105. 'Longinus' was surely wrong to criticize Herodotus for cacophonous sigmatism in the appropriate-sounding phrase, ζεσάσης τῆς θαλάσσης (XLIII): cf. Virgil, *A.* v, 866: 'Tum rauca assiduo longe sale saxa sonabant.'

The idea that writing should be beautiful has been in conflict down the ages with the idea that it should be expressive, sound and rhythm waiting upon every whim of sense, and leaving no neutral tracts for beauty to cultivate. The Greeks called this principle τὸ πρέπον, propriety, for which Cicero introduced the Latin term *decorum*. It was part of an all-embracing doctrine which concerned life as well as art and literature. Cicero speaks of it in the *De Officiis* and *Orator* as a topic widely discussed as to ethics by philosophers, as to poetics by *grammatici*.[1] On the literary side Aristotle had had a short chapter in the *Rhetoric*[2] broadly concerned with making style appropriate to the speaker, the audience and the subject. It is interesting to observe however that, when treating of metaphor in an earlier chapter of the same book,[3] he has tacitly disregarded this principle in saying that 'metaphors should be taken from beautiful things, beauty of a word residing either in the sound or the meaning, as Licymnius says, and ugliness likewise' (a few lines later he enlarges the concept to include appeal to the inward eye and the other senses). This would today be called the romantic heresy: in the present phase of poetry no metaphor is avoided because of ugly sound or associations, provided it is vivid and expressive.* The fact is, that Aristotle was treating metaphor as an *adornment*, and as such it continued to be treated by rhetoricians.

For a full application of the principle of propriety to diction we must wait for another golden chapter of Dionysius, *De Compositione*, xx. He has previously given, as the four chief contributors to charm and beauty of style, melody, rhythm, variety and the propriety that attends on these three (xi), and he now continues:

All the other ornaments of speech must be associated with what is appropriate; indeed, if any other quality whatever fails to attain this, it fails to attain the main essential—perhaps fails altogether.... Keeping an eye on this principle, the good poet and the orator should be ready to imitate the things of which he is giving a verbal description and to imitate them not only in the choice of words but also in the composition.[4]

---

* One may disagree with Aristotle in not requiring metaphor to be beautiful, and yet agree with the view that a metaphor should not positively distress us by unpleasant associations: 'I dislike hearing that the death of Africanus castrated the state, or that Glaucia was the excrement of the Senate' (Cicero, *De Or.* III, 164. Cf. Ar. *Rhet.* III, 2, 13; *Rhet. ad Her.* IV, 45; Quint. VIII, 6, 14–15).

And he proceeds to analyse in detail the passage in the *Odyssey* about Sisyphus and the stone. Yet even he is in two minds: for he has previously said (XVI) that if it were possible that all the parts of speech by which a given subject is to be expressed should be euphonious and elegant, it would be madness to seek out inferior ones.

But we have already trespassed several times on the next subject of our inquiry—expressiveness.

3

EXPRESSIVENESS

I. EXPRESSIVE WORDS

At the beginning of Plato's *Cratylus* we are plunged into an argument about language which was part of the grand debate in the Sophistic age between nature (φύσις) and convention (νόμος).* Cratylus argues for the natural basis of language against Hermogenes, and appeals to Socrates. Socrates begins by supporting him, and imagines an original word-coiner at work.[1] He found certain letters useful for expressing certain ideas—ρ for motion or rapidity, ι (*ee*) for penetration or subtlety, φ, ψ, σ, ζ for breathless activity, δ, τ for binding or inactivity, λ for gliding or liquidity, γλ for glutinousness, ν for inwardness, α for greatness, η for length, ο for rotundity. An analogous list may be found in one of the most influential critical works of the Renaissance, the *Poetics* (1561) of the elder Scaliger, who gives *a* (*ah*) for breadth, *u* for obscurity, *i* (*ee*) for length, *l* for softness, *o* for greatness.[2] The discrepancies between the two lists are at once apparent, but these do not really discredit them, since the same sound can *potentially* reinforce a wide range of meanings.†
It is also easy to point to words obviously intended to be onomatopoeic which differ from one language to another; but often these differences are due to variations in degree of success. Thus our 'ding-dong' is surely a better imitation of a bell's resonance than Italian 'din-din' or German 'bim-bam'.

Socrates qualifies his naturalism by conceding that words have often been insensitively coined (Poe's poem *The Bells* could hardly have been written round the word 'cloche'), and that original words often become distorted in the interests of euphony, or by mere lapse of time; and further, that in the latter stages of development convention plays a large

---

* The idea that words were φύσει μιμητικὰ τῶν πραγμάτων stems from the Heraclitean Logos. Hippias wrote περὶ γραμμάτων δυνάμεως καὶ συλλαβῶν καὶ ἁρμονιῶν (Plato, *Hipp. Maj.* 285D). E. Norden, *Aeneis VI*, 413–14[3].

† Thus Marouzeau quotes passages from Latin in which the use of *r* reinforces the idea of vibration, tearing, rolling, grinding (objectively), and anger, terror (subjectively) (*Traité* (1954), pp. 27–8).

part.[1] The debate continued throughout antiquity. Thus Cicero derided the Stoics for thinking that every word had some natural origin though it might now be undetectable.[2] We do not know what he thought of Nigidius Figulus, who alleged that *vos*, *tu* and *tibi* were expressive because in uttering them we shoot out our lips and breath, whereas in *nos*, *ego* and *mihi* we keep them more to ourselves.[3] To some extent the controversy is still alive today. We no longer dream of intoning the music of the universe, as some did in the seventeenth century, but there have been naive enthusiasts who have fancied they detected onomatopoeic elements ubiquitously in language. These have provoked others to extravagant denials. Burke declared roundly that 'words undoubtedly have no sort of resemblance to the ideas for which they stand'.* But what else could we expect from one who committed himself to the opinion, 'so little does poetry depend for its effect on the power of raising sensible images, that I am convinced it would lose a very considerable part of its energy, if this were the necessary result of all description'?† As usual, a middle view is the most plausible. We all recognize that there are 'good words' and 'bad words' for things and actions. Thus the name of Jacob Schweppe has, at least since the invention of the siphon, proved a providential asset to his successors in the manufacture of soda-water. For it is not only primitive words that are onomatopoeic; indeed the creation and use of onomatopoeic words seems to have been on the increase in historical times. 'Match' originally denoted a wick; yet how admirably it catches the scrape of sulphurated stick on emery, as contrasted with 'allumette', 'Streichholz' or 'fiammifero'! Indeed, popular usage will pervert the original meaning of a word to what it 'sounds like'. Take 'buxom'. By origin it means 'bending' (Ger. *beugsam*), 'pliant', 'obedient'. In a pre-Reformation marriage-service the bride promised to be 'obedient and buxom in bed and at board'.[4] But ask anyone today, and he will probably give what is the fourth meaning in *O.E.D.*: 'plump and

---

* *The Sublime and the Beautiful* (1767), p. 333. 'Inner and essential connection between idea and word...there is none, in any language upon earth' (W. D. Whitney, *Language*, 1868, p. 32). 'With the exception of the small group of onomatopoeic words ("murmur", "tomtom", "bomb", "cuckoo" etc.) there is no umbilical cord which connects sounds and meanings' (Bateson, *English Poetry*, 1950, p. 31).

† *Ibid.* p. 328. Contrast Dryden's view, that 'beautiful descriptions and images are the spirit and life of poetry' (*Essay on the Georgics*).

comely'. I believe this has come about because 'that is what it sounds like'.

It seems going rather far to judge someone by the name his parents gave him, as Augustine asserted that, even if you knew nothing about them, you would deduce that Artaxerxes was a harsh man and Euryalus a mild![1] Walter de la Mare remarked that many words have missed their vocation: Linoleum, for instance, ought to be a charming old Mediterranean seaport.* On the other hand words may arise by chance and stick because they satisfy. The Irish place-name of Ballyhooly seems to have lent itself not only to 'bally-hoo', but also to 'hullaballoo', as 'bunkum' arose (owing to an unfortunate Congressman) from Buncombe County in North Carolina.[2] The whole matter of sound-symbolism is discussed with admirable good sense by Otto Jespersen in chapter xx of his authoritative book *Language*.

It will be noticed that in Socrates' list it is not so much the objective sound of the letter as the action or configuration of the mouth in uttering it which is expressive.† ρ represents motion because 'the tongue is least at rest and most agitated when pronouncing this letter'; the word-coiner felt likewise that 'the compression and pressure of the tongue in pronouncing δ and τ was naturally fitted to imitate the notion of binding or rest'. These are pertinent observations. Thus ᾠόν uttered with the mouth rotund well represents the shell egg, while 'egg', a word which momentarily impedes utterance, suggests its glutinous interior. Sir Richard Paget went so far as to advocate the view that

human speech arose out of generalized unconscious pantomimic gesture language...which became specialized in gestures of the organs of articulation, owing to the human hands (and eyes) becoming continuously occupied with the use of tools. The gestures of the organs of articulation were recognized by the hearer because the hearer unconsciously reproduced in his mind the actual gesture which had produced the sound.[3]

---

* This has prompted a delightful series of poems: see *New Statesman Competitions*, ed. Arthur Marshall (1955), pp. 19–20: 'Sweet Hernia on the heights of Plasticine...', etc.

† 'But inasmuch as there are things which have no sound, for these the analogy of touch comes into play: if they touch the sense smoothly or roughly, smoothness or roughness of touch is heard in the letters, and so their names are produced': Augustine, Migne 32, col. 1412. Cf. M. Grammont, *Traité de phonétique* (1933), pp. 413–14. G. Gerber suggested that *m* was associated with darkness because it was uttered with the lips closed, labials with weakness because their pronunciation required little effort (*Die Sprache als Kunst*, 1871, I, 224–8).

As a theory of the *origin* of all language this may be partial and inadequate, but it is important as emphasizing that words may be expressive subjectively as well as objectively.

II. EXPRESSIVENESS IN LITERATURE

How is all this relevant to literature? Because the instinct which makes men try to coin words somehow corresponding to the things or actions they denote may also prompt a writer not merely to select such words,* but to combine in a similar way syllables from words which may not in themselves be semantically connected with the matter in hand. And the value of this lies in the vividness of presentation, as though we were being shown in colour what would otherwise be mere black and white.

If we do not adopt the reformed pronunciation, says Marouzeau, 'what will become of all the skilled imitative harmony on which the Latins prided themselves?'[1] This harmony is commonly called 'onomatopoeia', but that is an unsatisfactory word, because by etymology and generally by ancient usage it denotes merely the coinage of words to represent things or actions.[2] The phenomenon we are now going to consider is

something far more deeply interfused

and far more important. The French call it 'expressivité', and for want of a better word I will call it 'expressiveness'. It is an important, though not an essential, ingredient of much good writing that is not concerned with abstractions.[3]

I say 'much' rather than 'all' because we must recognize that writers as well as readers vary greatly in the value they assign to it. And indeed a writer may show more interest in it at one time than at another, as Johnson pointed out with reference to Milton.[4] James Sutherland, in his book *The Medium of Poetry*, contrasts Wordsworth and Keats as two types of poet. Wordsworth was intent on reviving, as completely as he could in words, his moments of intense emotional experience. The revisions that he made in his works are all in the direction of more

* 'Poetry is very likely to repeat the creative work of language on a different level': P. Friedländer, *A.J.P.* 1941, p. 29. F. E. Halliday makes the same point (*Shakespeare and his Critics*, 1949, p. 118). Conversely, 'Language is fossil poetry' (Emerson, 'The Poet'; *Essays*, p. 222 World's Classics edn.).

perfect presentation of a scene or event. With Keats poetry was far less *communication* and far more *making*. He revised to enrich and beautify. It is in poets of the Wordsworthian type that we shall expect to find the subtlest and most frequent examples of expressiveness. Their mind and ear are continually trying out words against the idea that is there to be expressed and selecting those that light it up.* When Mr Robert Graves describes how he redrafted one of his poems, he makes it clear that he was feeling both for better euphony and for more exact expressiveness.[1]

Before braving the charge of subjectivity by parading a selection of illustrative quotations, it may be well to see what the ancients themselves had to say about expressiveness, if only for the sake of reassuring ourselves that we have a *prima facie* justification for recognizing it in their literature.

The doctrine that style should be appropriate to subject-matter (πρέπον—*decorum*), a basic assumption of Greek music, was firmly established in classical criticism by Aristotle (see p. 44).[2] On appropriate diction the *locus classicus* seems again to have been Theophrastus' περὶ λέξεως. Dionysius of Halicarnassus has some interesting chapters on the subject in his *De Compositione Verborum* (14–20). 'The greatest poets and prose-writers', he says, '...often with curious and loving skill adapt the very syllables and letters to the emotions they wish to represent.'[3] They keep their eye on the object—πρὸς χρῆμα ὁρῶσιν. He adduces a considerable number of illustrations from Homer. (It must be confessed that some of these are not very convincing, though we must be duly humble about our disabilities as judges of Greek sound. Later writers assumed that Homer must exhibit features that had developed and become admired since.)[4] Plutarch has a passage in which he compares poetry and dancing. 'Dancing', he says, 'is a silent poetry and poetry a speaking dance'; and by dancing he meant, of course, mimetic ballet. He dwells at length on the value of expressiveness, giving instances from Euripides, Pindar and Homer, and after quoting from Simonides exclaims: 'These passages almost seem to invite the hands and feet, or rather to pull and guide the whole body with their music as with puppet-strings.'[5]

---

* Cf. Emerson, 'The Poet', p. 225: 'Poems are a corrupt version of some text in nature, with which they ought to be made to tally.' 'The poet', said Michelangelo, 'is a blind painter.'

Yet, as far as we can judge, this expressiveness is more characteristic of Latin than of Greek poetry. Hellenistic criticism made Roman writers conscious of its importance. Panaetius wrote of τὸ πρέπον in poetry as well as in conduct.[1] The idea 'runs like a red thread' throughout the *Ars Poetica* of Horace,[2] as it does, under the Ciceronian name of *decorum*, through the literary discussions of the Renaissance. To observe it is a critical canon as widely accepted as any, if not as invariably obeyed. Pope's exposition of it in his *Essay on Criticism* is well known (though Johnson was right in observing that as a piece of self-illustration it was only partially successful).[3] Walter Pater used to insist that 'the word, phrase, sentence should express perfectly the writer's perception, feeling, image or thought'.[4] Authorities could be cited *ad infinitum*.

People who disparage 'onomatopoeia' in literature probably have in mind instances so obvious as to seem childish, or so obtrusive as to distract attention from the matter in hand to the writer's exhibitionism. 'Onomatopoeia', says Cocteau, 'reduces us to the level of a parrot.'[5] Mr Bateson speaks of 'ingenious but fundamentally perverse attempts to transcend the natural limitations of the medium'.[6] (He uses 'onomatopoeia' only to denote what is literally an echo of the sense; for the subtler forms of expressiveness he uses Pound's word 'melopoeia'.) But there is every gradation of subtlety, as we shall see, and imitation of sounds is only a comparatively minor element in the exquisite art of *decorum*. Dr Johnson concluded that 'beauties of this kind are commonly fancied; and, when real, are technical and nugatory, not to be rejected and not to be solicited'.[7] But here he seems insensitive, and the matter is summed up more wisely by Wellek and Warren: 'There is still, within a given linguistic system, something like a "physiognomy" of words, a sound symbolism far more pervasive than mere onomatopoeia. There is no doubt that synaesthetic combinations and associations permeate all languages, and that these correspondences have been, quite rightly, exploited and elaborated by the poets.'[*] As for the pleasure we

---

[*] *Theory of Literature* (1949), p. 164. For thoroughgoing expositions of this view see, for example, for English, K. M. Wilson, *Sound and Meaning in English Poetry* (1930), book II, chs. III and V; for French, M. Grammont, *Les vers français* (1904), and *Traité de phonétique* (1933), part III; for German, G. Gerber, *Die Sprache als Kunst* (1871), I, 224–8; for Latin, E. Norden, *Aeneis VI*, Appendix VII; J. Marouzeau, *Traité de stylistique latine*[3] (1954), pp. 24–34. Marouzeau does not always indicate why he thinks the examples he gives should have the alleged effect.

can derive, this is surely analogous to that of metaphor, which no one disparages—indeed expressiveness is often itself a kind of metaphor, based on analogy between form and content. And as with metaphor, what pleases most is aptness combined with surprise, resulting in vivid presentation of images to the inward eye* and agile exercise of the mind.

But, as in the case of euphony and cacophony, one must emphasize that the effects are only latent and potential in the form; they can only illuminate appropriate subject-matter (see p. 42). In the words of an eminent French authority, Maurice Grammont:[1] 'En somme, tous les sons du langage, voyelles ou consonnes, peuvent prendre une valeur expressive lorsque le sens du mot dans lequel ils se trouvent s'y prête; si le sens n'est pas susceptible de les mettre en valeur, ils restent inexpressifs.' And for this reason it is, again, no refutation to point to cases where sounds or rhythms similar to those claimed as expressive in a particular passage have clearly no such effect,[2] or where words of similar meaning in another language use no such sounds,† or to make very slight alterations in the sounds which profoundly affect the meaning, as in J. C. Ransom's delightful example,

> And murdering of innumerable beeves,

for Tennyson's

> And murmuring of innumerable bees.

On the other hand it is important not to suggest, except in guarded terms, that sounds of themselves have particular expressive qualities. Lucretius has a famous description of primitive man living at the mercy of wild beasts and finally

> viva videns vivo sepeliri viscera busto.[3]
> *seeing his body buried alive in a living tomb.*

Munro comments '*v* often in alliteration expresses indignant pity'. Why on earth should it? And in any case surely the poet is here absorbed in envisaging the caveman's experience, not in conveying his

---

* τοῦτο γὰρ μεταφορὰ καὶ πρὸ ὀμμάτων (Arist. *Rhet.* III, 10, 7). 'Rei ante oculos ponendae causa' (Auct. ad Her. IV, 45, on metaphor).

† Jespersen characterizes Madvig's attempt to confute Humboldt by this method as 'a little cheap'. It is not suggested that there is only one way of expressing the same sense-perception, nor that all words are originally onomatopoeic (*Language*, p. 397).

own reaction. To me the line is indeed highly expressive, but that is because it conjures up a horribly vivid image of that maw wolfing another mouthful with every successive v $(= w)$, just as at V, 1056 Mr Friedländer feels the dog's lips moving in the m-sounds of

> canum cum primum magna Molossum
> mollia ricta fremunt*
> *when first the huge soft maws of Molossian hounds growl.*

Mr Jackson Knight ventures the following generalizations in his *Roman Vergil* (p. 247):

The sound of *a* is often tragic and sad at close range, actively, as in 'moriamur et in media arma ruamus'. The *a* may be diverted by other sounds in proximity to a more remote sadness, as in 'Parthenopaeus et Adrasti pallentis imago'. There the *ae*, *e* and *i* sounds have an effect. All are sad, *ae* bitterly, *e* richly, glowingly sad, with tears warm as afternoon light; the *i* is the most remote of all, the salt of tears fainting in mist.

This is a recognizable account of the sort of effect those two lines of Virgil might produce on an impressionable reader, and a plausible diagnosis of the means by which the sounds may have contributed to it; but the element of generalization, no less than the sentimentality, makes it a succulent prey for the unbeliever hungry to blaspheme.

III. VARIETIES OF EXPRESSIVE TECHNIQUE

Let us now try to differentiate, with a few illustrations, between various ways in which language can be expressive in literature. This is seldom done, though the differences are considerable. We must distinguish subjective expression of the speaker's emotion as reinforced by the sounds he uses, which may naturally be sought first in drama, from objective representation of things or actions. And within the latter we must distinguish simple echo of things which make sounds from imitation by sympathetic mouth-gesture. From this we pass to suggestion by association, and then to the whole range of phenomena which may

---

* *A.J.P.* (1941), p. 16. Festus (70) says that *h* was pronounced, at a time when it was ceasing to be sounded generally, in *helluo* (glutton), 'quo aviditas magis exprobretur'! N. I. Herescu has some interesting pages, *Poésie* (1960), pp. 117–22, on various reasons advanced by critics for the expressiveness of particular passages.

be classed as metaphorical, where the subtlest forms of expressiveness are found. I shall not necessarily be able to provide an example for each variety from Golden Latin literature.

(a) Subjective mouth-gesture

We may begin with a famous example. No one will deny that human beings, like geese, hiss when they are angry. When Euripides' Medea is venting her resentment against Jason, she reminds him

ἔσωσά σ’, ὡς ἴσασιν Ἑλλήνων, ὅσοι...

I saved you, as is known to every Greek...,

and many have found the line expressive.* Indeed it is hard to think of an actor missing such an opportunity for effective speech. Men also spit when they are angry, and it would be a poor Oedipus who did not make the most of his line denouncing Tiresias,

τυφλὸς τά τ’ ὦτα τόν τε νοῦν τά τ’ ὄμματ’ εῖ[1]

You are blind in ears, and mind, and eyes.

They pout in scorn—

Je ne prends point pour juge un peuple téméraire[2]—

they 'shoot out their lips', as the Psalmist has it; and all Agememnon's *hybris* goes into the line that describes the burning of Troy,

σποδὸς προπέμπει πίονας πλούτου πνοάς.†

the ashes send forth rich puffs of smoke.

---

* *Med.* 476. Plato the comic poet apparently had this line in mind, perhaps also *I.T.* 765, τὸ σῶμα σώσας τοὺς λόγους σώσεις ἐμοί, when he wrote (fr. 7 M.) ἔσωσας ἐκ τοῦ σῖγμα τῶν Εὐριπίδου. Cf. Eubulus (*Dionysius*, fr. 27 K.). The *I.T.* line is not scornful; and J. A. Scott has shown that Euripides is in fact no more sigmatic than the other dramatists (*A.J.P.* 1908, pp. 69–77). O. J. Todd (*C.Q.* 1942, pp. 33–9), apparently ignorant of Scott's work, demonstrates this again, and with immense but, in my submission, irrelevant labour collects instances of sigmatic lines which do not express scorn and asigmatic lines which do. Robert Bridges noted that when Milton's chorus find Samson asleep, 'This, this is he, softly awhile', the sibilants are hushing (*Milton's Prosody*, 1901, p. 62). Mr Bateson 'cannot see that sibilants are particularly "hushing"' (*English Poetry*, p. 26), but surely they are *here* and also in the whispering of that favourite line of Tennyson's,

Universal ocean softly washing all her warless isles.

On the other hand, when T. E. Page notes on *Aen.* VI, 354 ('deficeret tantis navis surgentibus undis') 'observe the sibilant character of the line expressive of the whistling of the wind', I cannot feel with him, as the line describes towering waves, not winds, and that is the image it raises in my mind.

† Aesch. *Ag.* 820. Professor Fraenkel sees in this line 'a true note of profound sympathy'; but surely it and the whole context are hybristic. It is easier to agree when he suggests that in l. 268, πῶς φής; πέφευγε τοῦπος ἐξ ἀπιστίας, 'the piling up of *p*-sounds is probably meant to express the

Is it fanciful to feel a break in the voice, a sobbing effect, in the *q*'s and *k*'s and elisions of Catullus' final pentameter about his faithless friend, which to some has seemed merely a shocking instance of technical incompetence?

> quam modo qui me unum atque unicum amicum habuit.*
> *than he who but now had me for his one and only friend.*

D. A. West has defended the elisions here as aiming at a special effect, the conveying of intense emotion, comparing 68, 89–90 and 76, where exceptional elision also characterizes passages of intense, indignant grief.[1] He might have added 91, 2,

> in misero hoc nostro, hoc perdito amore fore.
> *in this wretched, this desperate love of mine.*

Bateson finds it 'significant that there are next to no onomatopoeias in Shakespeare'.[2] But a dramatist is mainly concerned with making people express views and emotions, not with describing things objectively. Bateson himself cites Daniel Webb (1762) as observing that the breast actually labours to get through Hamlet's line

> And in this harsh world draw thy breath in pain.[3]

Shakespeare was no line-blotter, but had he no thought of the expressive effect of sound at Lear's entry—'Howl, howl'—or in Cassandra's echoing prophecies?—

> Cry, Trojans, cry! A Helen and a woe.
> Cry, cry! Troy burns, or else let Helen go.

Ennius achieved a similar effect, when his Andromache bewails the fate of Troy:

> haec omnia vidi inflammari,
> Priamo vi vitam evitari,
> Iovis aram sanguine turpari,
> Hectorem curro quadriiugo raptarier,
> Hectoris natum de moero iactarier,

breathless excitement of the questioner' (for stammering *p* see p. 26 above); and it is reassuring to find that so eminent a scholar, when he feels a phrase to be expressive, does not hesitate to say so (cf. his *Horace* (1957), pp. 76 n., 81 n., 104 n.).

On euphony and onomatopoeia in Aeschylus W. B. Stanford has some judicious pages (81–5) in *Aeschylus and his Style* (1942). He does not mention l. 820 however.

* 73, 6. 'Probably the most prosaic verse in Catullus' (Ellis); 'besonders ungeschickt' (Kroll); 'cas désespéré' (Herescu); 'cum horridus tum poeta indignus' (Nobbe).

and Cicero admired how the sound and rhythm here reinforced the wailing: 'praeclarum carmen; est enim et rebus *et verbis et modis* lugubre'.*

If anyone thinks that the old English pronunciation loses nothing in expressiveness, let him try to make the wailing of the nymphs heard through the following:

> At chorus eequaylis Dryadum claymorey supreemos
> impleerunt montees: fleerunt Rhodope-e-e arsees
> altaque Pangeea et Rheeseye Mayvorshia telleus,
> atque Jetee atque Heebrus et Actias Oreyethuya.[1]

(b) Objective imitation of sound

Quintilian felt that the invention of onomatopoeic words was particularly resisted by the Latin language, at any rate in its developed form; that if *balare*, to bleat, and *hinnire*, to whinny, had not been sanctioned by antiquity, Romans would hesitate to use them. 'We are not justified in coining entirely new words, having no resemblance to the words invented by primitive man.' Even new derivatives were by now scarcely acceptable: Latin had become fossilized.[2] In Homer we frequently come across words which we suspect of being invented by some bard for expressive purposes rather than taken from common usage. Ennius may do the same, but not Virgil. He will use any onomatopoeic words that are available, as in

> *balatu* pecorum et crebris *mugitibus* amnes—
> *with baaing of flocks and frequent mooing the rivers—*

or (twice)

> exoritur *clamorque* virum *clangorque* tubarum,
> *there arises the clamour of men and the blare of trumpets,*

but the effect is hardly worth comment.[3]

More interesting is the use of words to be expressive by sound independently of their individual meaning. Our onomatopoeic word 'trickle' is testimony that short *i*, *c* (*k*, *q*, *x*), and *l* are felt to be imitative

---

* *Tusc.* III, 45. 'Et rebus' shows that 'verbis' must refer to the sound, not the meaning, of the words. 'All this I saw set on fire, Priam deprived by violence of his life, Jove's altar defiled with blood, Hector dragged by the four-horsed chariot, Hector's son thrown headlong from the battlement.'

of running liquid. The Romans felt the same, and could use their long *i* (*ee*) as well.* Horace has (noted by the scholiast Porphyrion)

> mella cava manant ex ilice; montibus altis
> levis crepante lympha desilit pede;

honey flows from the hollow ilex; from the high hills with plashing foot the little rivulet leaps,

and again

> me dicente cavis impositam ilicem
> saxis unde loquaces
> lymphae desiliunt tuae.[1]

as I am telling of the ilex that grows above the hollowed rocks from which your chattering waters leap.

The recurrence of similar sounds in similar contexts is some guarantee that it is not merely subjective to find these lines expressive: and *lympha* is the only word that has any connection with water. The repetition of *ilex* and *desilire* puts beyond doubt the poet's intention.

Sometimes a *sight* may be described in words that express an accompanying *sound*. Theocritus has a line describing a beautiful stream:

> λάλλαι κρυστάλλῳ ἠδ' ἀργύρῳ ἰνδάλλοντο.

This means, 'the pebbles were like crystal and silver'. But the thrice repeated αλλ sound irresistibly suggests the babble of the brook—and indeed ancient critics associated λάλλη with λαλεῖν (to chatter) as an onomatopoeic word.[2]

In Tennyson's well-known *tour de force*

> Myriads of rivulets hurrying through the lawn,
> The moan of doves in immemorial elms,
> And murmuring of innumerable bees,†

the first line was probably suggested by Horace's

> et properantis aquae per amoenos ambitus agros
> *and the winding of rushing water through pleasant meadows,*

---

* In a fascinating paper O. Jespersen has attempted to show that *i*, especially in its narrow or thin form, also serves very often to indicate what is small, slight, insignificant or weak (*Linguistica*, 1933, pp. 283–303).

† For the bees cf. Leconte de Lisle's calculated vowel-monotony, 'Le murmure léger des abeilles fidèles'.

the second certainly by Virgil's

> nec gemere aërea cessabit turtur ab ulmo
> *nor will the dove cease to moan from the lofty elm.*[1]

If we give the *u*-sounds their full value, *turtur ab ulmo* remains unsurpassed as an echo of the cooing of doves. Fitzgerald said that so great a poem as his Wellington ode should have opened with broad, sonorous vowels, not 'Bury the great Duke'; but the muted vowels help to suggest the dull tramp of the funeral cortège, as Sir Charles Tennyson remarks.*

(c) Objective imitation of rhythm

Rhythms also can echo successions of sound that are a mixture of long and short, or stress and no-stress, such as galloping.† Tennyson speaks of

> The sound of many a heavily galloping hoof.

His Light Brigade moves to the same rhythm,

> Half-a-league, half-a-league, half-a-league onward.[2]

Homer's mules who cantered off to get wood for Patroclus' pyre—

> πολλὰ δ' ἄναντα κάταντα πάραντά τε δόχμιά τ' ἦλθον—

are as well known as the horse foaled by Virgil out of Ennius, who

> quadrupedante putrem sonitu quatit ungula campum.[3]

Virgil, indeed, seems to have felt an intrinsic affinity between his dactylic hexameters and galloping horses.

The Galliambic metre was invented to express a particular subject, the orgiastic dance to Cybele.

> Γάλλαι, μητρὸς ὀρείης φιλόθυρσοι δρομάδες
> αἷς ἔντεα παταγεῖται καὶ χάλκεα κρόταλα

The Gallae, thyrsus-mad whirlers of the mountain mother, with their clashing arms and rattles of bronze,

---

* *Six Tennyson Essays* (1954), p. 191. For 'das dumpfe *u*' in Latin see Norden, *Aeneis VI*, 417³ n. 2.

† καὶ ἵππων δὲ πορεία ῥυθμὸς ἐνομίσθη, [Longinus], Proleg. to Hephaestion, p. 84 Westphal. Many examples, mostly from Latin, are collected by A. S. Pease, *Cl. J.* (1925–6), pp. 625–8. Spondees on the other hand often express the trouble and difficulty of ship-manœuvres: ναυτιλίας τε καὶ εἰρεσίας καὶ τὰ χαλεπώτατα τῶν χειρωνακτικῶν ἔργων, Arist. Quint. *De Mus.* II, 4 (p. 41, 22 Jahn); Norden, *Aeneis VI*, 423³ and n. I.

is a specimen of the Greek form that Catullus and others adapted to Latin:

> Super alta vectus Attis celeri rate maria.

The essentials beneath the variations are the anapaestic tread of the wild dance and the short rattling syllables of the tambourine or castanets at the end.[1]

(d) Objective mouth-gesture

So far everything is obvious enough. We now come to mouth-gesture which is objective rather than subjective. Lessing remarked that Virgil's phrase

> tum fumida lumine fulvo
> involvi
> *then smokily was wrapped in lurid light*

was expressive because the thing it described was suggested by the rolling, tortuous movement of the tongue in pronouncing the words.[2] This is true, at least if the *v*-sounds are pronounced *w*, as they should be. Postgate, deploring the 'old' pronunciation, exclaimed, on another line of Virgil,

> quinquaginta atris immanis hiatibus Hydra,
> *the Hydra fearful with its fifty dark gapes,*

'What schoolboy, schoolmaster or hydra opens its mouth when it utters *eh*?'[3] Sir Charles Tennyson, quoting from his grandfather's *Oenone*

> The gorges, opening wide apart, reveal
> Troas, and Ilion's column'd citadel,
> The crown of Troas...,

comments, 'Here in the first line the vowels in the second, third, fourth and fifth words, which require a gradually wider opening of the mouth to pronounce them, suggest the gradual opening of the gorge, and the sharp, clear sound of "reveal" brings suddenly before the mind's eye the vision of the divinely built city of Ilion far away on the plain'.[4] I entirely agree. I have always found the expressive contrast between wide *a*-sounds and buried *u*-sounds effective in Horace's

> Te maris et terrae numeroque carentis arenae
> mensorem cohibent, Archyta,

> pulveris exigui prope litus parva Matinum
> munera.[1]

Thou, measurer of sea and land and sands without number, Archytas, art confined now by a little tribute of scanty dust near the Matine shore.

The momentary gasp caused by hiatus, especially when it is between identical vowels so that modulation is excluded, can be expressive. In a detailed and admirable analysis of the art by which Homer made vivid his description of Sisyphus rolling his stone Dionysius includes the gasp between ἄνω and ὤθεσκε—λᾶαν ἄνω ὤθεσκε ποτὶ λόφον, and other ancient commentators made the same point.[2] Pope, in his translation, sought to reproduce this effect of panting by a combination of monosyllables and alliterative aspirates (Johnson mentions the slowness, but apparently overlooked the aspirates):*

> With many a weary step and many a groan
> Up a *h*igh *h*ill *h*e *h*eaves a *h*uge round stone.

Hiatus between identical vowels is similarly used by Hérédia in his *Artémis* to express panting:

> Et bondis à travers *la h*aletante orgie.

On the other hand the expressive effect of Tennyson's couplet

> Music that gentlier on the spirit lies
> Than tired eyelids upon tired eyes

depends on the fact that 'tired', though a disyllable, is uttered with scarcely more energy than a monosyllable (the repetition is also soporific—the Lotus-eaters are too languid to think of fresh words).

(e) Association

It can also happen that a sound or rhythm is expressive by association of ideas. For instance, the foot consisting of two long syllables was called 'spondee' because it was used in the invocations that accompanied the pouring of a libation (perhaps seeming appropriate both because of the

---

* *Life of Pope.* Robert Graves is thus wrong in stating that the lines in the *Odyssey* do not mimic Sisyphus' breathlessness, though his criticism of Pope's next couplet is just (*Privilege*, 1955, p. 102, Pelican edn.).

60

solemnity of slowness and because the smooth regularity reflected the act of pouring).

σπένδωμεν ταῖς Μνάμας
παισὶν Μώσαις
καὶ τῷ Μωσάρχῳ
Λατοῦς υἱεῖ.[1]

It is thus (*pace* Leaf) surely no accident that the only completely spondaic line in our text of Homer is that in which Achilles is described as invoking the dead Patroclus with a libation,

ψυχὴν κικλήσκων Πατροκλῆος δειλοῖο.[2]

Heinze pointed out that Horace, anticipating the triumphal return of Augustus, contrived to introduce into the fixed Sapphic stanza a reminiscence of the septenarian metre used for the popular snatches shouted at triumphs (e.g. 'Gallos Caesar in triumphum ducit, idem in Curiam'):

> tum meae, si quid loquar audiendum
> vocis accedet bona pars, et '*o sol*
> *pulcher, o laudande*' canam, recepto
> Caesare felix.[3]

then, if I have anything to say worth hearing, I will add the best of my voice and sing 'Sun most glorious, we extol thee' for joy at Caesar's homecoming.

We have seen that in Latin assonance, approaching rhyme, was characteristic of solemn religious formulae, prophecies and so forth. The ten echoing *o*-sounds of Virgil's prophecy in the fourth *Eclogue* seem more than fortuitous:

> Ultima Cumaei venit iam carminis aetas;
> magnus ab integro saeclorum nascitur ordo
> iam redit et Virgo, redeunt Saturnia regna,
> iam nova progenies caelo demittitur alto.
> tu modo nascenti puero, quo ferrea primum
> desinet et toto surget gens aurea mundo
> casta fave Lucina: tuus iam regnat Apollo.

It has been suggested that we have here the influence of an element in Hebrew poetry working on Virgil through the Sibylline book he had before him;[4] but Roman tradition would be enough to account for his choice of sounds.

Association of this kind leads on to the whole range of phenomena which can be classed as metaphorical, in which the sound or form of the word, or the arrangement of words, or the rhythm or verse-technique, is analogous to the thing or action described. The subtlest and most effective forms of expressiveness are in this class.

(f) Appropriate euphony and cacophony

I have touched on this in the previous chapter (p. 14). Milton with his melodious fountains and his scrannel pipes was echoing actual sounds. But when euphony or cacophony are used to express things which are beautiful or ugly in a sense which is not auditory, they become metaphorical. Is it fanciful to suppose that in the following lines Virgil was intentionally pursuing euphony to describe a lovely scene?—

> at Venus Ascanio placidam per membra quietem
> inrigat, et fotum gremio dea tollit in altos
> Idaliae lucos, ubi mollis amaracus illum
> floribus et dulci adspirans complectitur umbra.*

Did Horace's sensitive ear merely desert him when he left eleven sibilants in one stanza about the hideous dropsy?—

> crescit indulgens sibi dirus hydrops
> nec sitim pellit nisi causa morbi
> fugerit uenis et aquosus albo
> corpore languor.†

I think he meant this to sound ugly.

(g) Appropriate configuration of words

The length or shape of a word can be metaphorically expressive. A scholiast remarked that in Homer's line

> λίγξε βιός, νευρὴ δὲ μέγ᾽ ἴαχεν, ἆλτο δ᾽ ὀιστός
> *the bow twanged, the string rang out, and leapt the arrow*

the use of the contracted form ἆλτο for ἄλλετο emphasized the speed of the discharge.[1] In Tennyson's line

> By the long wash of Australasian seas

---

* A. I, 691–4. Note the double *l*-sounds, which Demetrius found beautiful (see p. 11).

† Odes, II, 2, 13–16. Grammont gives a number of instances of sibilant lines in Racine which describe unpleasant things liable to evoke a *frisson* or *sifflement* (*Traité de phonétique*, 1933, pp. 410–11).

the effect of length is increased by the use of the word 'Australasian' for the more familiar 'Australian' (while the sibilants echo the wash). Length of time can also be so expressed—'*innumerabilis* annorum series', '*dolentis insolabiliter*', 'cras ingens *iterabimus* aequor'.[1] Bradley attributed the magic of Virgil's famous line

> tendebantque manus ripae ulterioris amore[2]
> *and were stretching out their hands in longing for the further shore*

to 'the long drawn sound of *tendebantque*, the time occupied by the five syllables, and therefore by the idea, of *ulterioris*, and the identity of the long sound "or" in the penultimate syllables of *ulterioris amore*'.* In-tensity is sought by the use of sesquipedalian forms, such as 'splendife-rous'; it was this that betrayed the unfortunate curate who preached on the *infinitesimal* love of God. Robert Bridges, quoting Virgil's

> fluminaque antiquos subterlabentia muros
> *and rivers gliding beneath ancient walls*

spoke of 'the long level *subterlabentia* with its two little gliding syllables at the end in quiet motion against the solid *muros*'.[3] That is exactly right. J. A. Platt subtly observed of his friend Housman's lines

> And like a sky-lit water stood
> The blue-bells in the azured wood,

that 'the magic effect is produced by repeating the syllable *like* inside the word *sky-lit*, but inverted as a reflection is inverted in water'.[4]

(h) *Metaphor from sound-values*

Quintilian remarked that long syllables represented *gravia, sublimia, ornata*, and that colloquial passages needed more short vowels; and further that *sublimia* and *ornata* called for clear vowels.[5] We have gone far beyond such simple notions of *decorum*. The idea behind Rimbaud's well-known *Sonnet des Voyelles* was anticipated by A. W. Schlegel and many others.[6] Grammont has elaborately analysed the expressive effect of various letters in French poetry;[7] and a poet's own feeling about the

---

* Surely the *sound* has much to do with it. Lamborn asked a Latinless boy what it suggested to him, and he guessed it was from the Psalm 'By the waters of Babylon we sat down and wept' (*Rudiments*, 1916, p. 20).

subtle metaphor of sound is revealed in the notes prefixed by Dame Edith Sitwell to her *Collected Poems* (1957). Some associations are through fortuitous assonances: thus Tuesday may have an aura of blue and Wednesday of red. Wellek and Warren sum up:

A poem such as Rimbaud's...which gives a one-to-one relationship between individual vowels and colors, though based on widespread tradition, may be purely wilful; but the fundamental associations between high vowels (*e* and *i*) and thin, quick, clear and bright objects and, again, between low vowels (*o* and *u*) and clumsy, slow, dull, and dark objects can be proved by acoustic experiments. The work of Carl Stumpf and Wolfgang Köhler shows also that consonants can be divided into dark (labials and velars) and bright (dentals and palatals). These are by no means mere metaphors, but associations based on indubitable similarities between sound and color observable especially in the structure of the respective systems.[1]

This is far from being pure fantasy, but surely 'mere metaphors' is an unfortunate phrase. Are not the associations in fact essentially metaphors? As such they cannot be 'mere': they are of fundamental importance. It would seem that *l* is the letter most connected with light, perhaps because in pronouncing it the tongue glides like light (or curls like flame) (cf. pp. 48, 59). It is hardly an exaggeration to say that most of the words concerned with it contain an *l*. Consider the following list:

φλέγω (φλόξ, *flagro, flamma, fulgeo, fulvus,* flame, flare, flash, flicker);
λύχνος (λευκός, *lux, lucerna, lumen, luna*);
στίλβω, λάμπω, *splendeo*;
ἥλιος, σέλας, σελήνη, *sol, stella, clarus, albus*;
glow, glare, gleam, glint, glimmer;
blaze, dazzle, kindle, sparkle, brilliant;
léoht, licht, light.

Some of these words may be interrelated where I have not so indicated. Some also may be derived from roots that have no *l* in them. But the facts remain that, once introduced into such words, the *l* has established itself firmly in popular favour, and that Anglo-Saxon words show a similar tendency to Greek and Latin. And we, in our unconsciously expressive choice of metaphors, say that flames 'leap' (not 'jump') and lick' (not 'gnaw').

A couple of examples may suffice to illustrate the use of metaphor from sound-values in poetry. Platt drew attention to a subtle vowel-play in Shelley's lines

> He will watch from dawn to gloom
> The lake-reflected sun illume
> The yellow bees in the ivy bloom.

'The enchantment', he said, 'greatly depends on the fact that the second syllable of "reflected" itself reflects in a weaker form the sound of the word "lake", as the water reflects in a weaker form the sun.'* And of the last two lines of Virgil's first Eclogue,

> et iam summa procul villarum culmina fumant
> maioresque cadunt altis de montibus umbrae

and now the roof-tops of the villas in the distance are smoking, and longer shadows are falling from the high mountains,

Professor Fraenkel has said: 'The long series of *u*-s helps, so it seems, to picture the darkening of the colours in the rich sub-alpine landscape that calls to mind backgrounds of paintings by Titian and Giorgione.'†

(i) *Metaphor from word-order*

Lucretius amuses himself with depicting by means of a topsy-turvy hyperbaton a man standing on his head,

> qui capite ipse sua in statuit vestigia sese[1]
> *who plants himself with his head in the place of his feet.*

The double nature of Achilles, half human half divine, is well suggested by the alternation of words in Horace's line,

> invicte mortalis dea nate puer Thetide[2]
> *unconquered, mortal goddess-born son of Thetis.*

The flexibility of Latin word-order lent itself to such effects. A. M. Young has drawn attention to Virgil's habit of 'representing pictorially in the arrangement of his words exactly what he relates'. For instance,

---

* *Nine Essays* (1927), p. 178. He says 'the bees', but this is surely a slip for 'the sun'.

† *Horace* (1957), p. 25 n. Note how the vowel-sounds modulate as the light fades in the series of words *glare, glimmer, gloaming, gloom* (cf. Jespersen, *Language* (1922), pp. 400–1). *Noon* is an unexpressive word (unless of deep blue sky); 'high noontide' would be a more expressive phrase. Edith Sitwell speaks of 'subtle variations of thickness and thinness (and consequently variations of darkness)' (*Collected Poems* (1957), p. xxiii).

when Rhoetus in the *Aeneid* tries to hide from Euryalus, the little word 'se' for him is tucked away in the middle of the line under cover of the huge bowl:

> sed magnum metuens se post cratera tegebat
> *but for fear was hiding himself behind a huge bowl,*

just as Cicero is snugly guarded in the phrase 'publico me praesidio'.[1] Akin to this, though not perhaps strictly metaphorical, is Virgil's way of representing sudden or violent action by setting the scene in a line or more and then striking with the first word of the succeeding line, as in:

> in segetem veluti cum flamma furentibus austris
> incidit
> *as when upon a corn-crop in a south-wind gale fire swoops.*

We have already seen Homer's Cyclops dashing Odysseus' companions to the ground in this way (p. 43):

> σύν τε δύω μάρψας ὥστε σκύλακας ποτὶ γαίη
> κόπτ'.

So Milton's Mulciber fell from Heaven:

> from morn
> To noon he fell, from noon to dewy eve
> A summer's day; and with the setting sun
> *Dropt...*[2]

('Dropt', of course, not 'dropped').* Among the devices by which the immense height is here indicated in terms of time is the repetition of 'from...to' and 'noon'; which brings us to our next topic.

(j) *Expressive repetition*

The various effects obtained by repetition of words or phrases are striking.[3] Homer uses it rarely, and perhaps only for expressive purposes (anaphora as a poetic ornament came in with the Alexandrians,

---

* Six examples from the *Aeneid* and two from Horace's *Odes* in Marouzeau, *Traité* (1954), pp. 307–8[3]. An instance from *Paradise Lost*, I, 22:

> What in me is dark
> Illumine.

'Shining out of the humble monosyllables and line-ending pause of "What in me is dark", the imperative enacts the miracle it invokes' (J. B. Broadbent, *Some Graver Subject* (1960), p. 69). For the same feature in Victor Hugo see L. M. Brandin and W. G. Hartog, *A Book of French Prosody* (1904), p. 34.

after the Gorgianic development of rhetoric).[1] Thus by the repeated ἐκ δέ at *Iliad* I, 436–9 he makes more vivid the action—disembarking item by item. When at II, 671–4 he repeats the name of Nireus three times, he is lingering lovingly over the name of the fairest of the Greeks after Achilles, as Milton lingers over that of his dead friend:

> For Lycidas is dead, dead ere his prime
> Young Lycidas, and hath not left his peer.

The very rarity of such repetitions makes doubly moving Hector's thought, as he shakes off delay and resolves to face Achilles, that he is not a lover dallying:

> οὐ μέν πως νῦν ἔστιν ἀπὸ δρυὸς οὐδ' ἀπὸ πέτρης
> τῷ ὀαριζέμεναι, ἅτε παρθένος ἠΐθεός τε,
> παρθένος ἠΐθεός τ' ὀαρίζετον ἀλλήλοιιν.[2]

This is no time to dally with him from oak-tree or rock, as a boy and girl dally, boy and girl with one another.

Donne used repetition in the same context:

> All day the same our postures were
> And we said nothing, all the day.

The effect of lingering is akin to that of stillness. At the crisis of the *Bath of Pallas*, before the young Tiresias unwittingly invades the privacy of the goddess and her nymph, Callimachus makes us feel the eerie hush of the southern noon (V, 71–4):

> ἵππω ἐπὶ κράνᾳ Ἑλικωνίδι καλὰ ῥεοίσᾳ
> λῶντο· μεσαμβρινὰ δ' εἶχ' ὄρος ἀσυχία.
> ἀμφότεραι λώοντο, μεσαμβριναὶ δ' ἔσαν ὧραι,
> πολλὰ δ' ἀσυχία τῆνο κατεῖχεν ὄρος.

In the fair-flowing spring of the Horse on Helicon they were bathing, and a noonday quiet held the hill; they were both bathing, and it was the noonday hour, and a deep quiet held that hill.

I suspect that Tennyson had these repetitions in mind when he wrote in *Oenone*,

> For now the noonday quiet holds the hill:
> The grasshopper is silent in the grass:
> The lizard with his shadow on the stone,
> Rests like a shadow, and the winds are dead.

Repetition can also emphasize extension of space—

> Water, water everywhere,
> And all the boards did shrink,
> Water, water everywhere
> Nor any drop to drink;

or of time—

> Day after day, day after day,
> We stuck, nor breath nor motion,
> As idle as a painted ship,
> Upon a painted ocean;[1]

or on the other hand of effort, as when Dionysus draws down the fatal pine for Pentheus—

> κατῆγεν, ἦγεν, ἦγεν ἐς μέλαν πέδον—[2]

or Satan struggles on through the elements—

> So he with difficulty and labour hard
> mov'd on, with difficulty and labour he.[3]

From lingering we have come round to effort. The discrepancy between these two ideas does not discredit the assertion that a description of both can be reinforced by the same device (cf. p. 52).

(k) Metaphor from rhythm

'Violent themes', says Quintilian, 'should be expressed in violent rhythms, to enable the audience to share the horror felt by the speaker.'[4] To call a rhythm 'violent' is to use a metaphor. Spondees are 'slow' metaphorically, and dactyls swift (as getting more into the same time). So do the Gauls in Ennius creep up the Capitol at dead of night, then suddenly set upon the guard and butcher it:

> qua Galli furtim noctu summa arcis adorti
> moenia concubia vigilesque repente trucidant.[5]

Spondees are restful, dactyls restless. Aeneas sleeps sound with a quiet mind once he has decided to tear himself away from Carthage:

> Aeneas celsa in puppi iam certus eundi
> carpebat somnos rebus iam rite paratis.*

---

* *A.* IV, 554–5. Cf. *A.* XII, 18: olli *sedato* respondit corde Latinus; *A.* IX, 30–1: ceu septem surgens *sedatis* amnibus altus...Ganges. The Greeks used spondees in passages about sleep (Norden, *Aeneis VI*, 424, 434³).

Spondees are heavy, dactyls light. And 'heaviness' in turn is a metaphor for boredom or misery. We may take it that when a poet normally so light and dactylic as Ovid wrote

> non me verbosas leges ediscere, non me
> ingrato vocem prostituisse foro,[1]

that I do not learn wordy laws by heart, nor prostitute my voice in the thankless forum,

he meant his spondees to emphasize how bored he would be by the career recommended to him. Spenser achieves a very beautiful contrast by having a struggling line full of emphatic monosyllables followed by one of reposeful regularity:

> Is not short pain well borne that brings long ease
> And lays the soul to sleep in quiet grave?

and again:

> Being with Thy dear blood clean wash'd from sin
> May live for ever in felicity.[2]

The hexameter, which is capable of no fewer than thirty-two variations even apart from synaloepha, gives particular scope for expressive rhythm. But Horace is also very skilful in adapting the fixed metres of his lyric to the matter in hand*—the love-sick poet setting out firmly for home but soon straying irresolutely to his mistress' door,

> iussus abire domum   ferebar incerto pede;

or the stamping of feet in rustic dance

> gaudet invisam pepulisse fossor
> *ter* pede *terram,*

or the sea-waves beating vainly on a rocky shore,

> quae nunc oppositis debilitat pumicibus mare.[3]

Whereas choriambs ($-\smile\smile-$) here have the appropriate pounding effect, anapaests served Tennyson for the storm at sea which closes *The Revenge,*

---

* Sometimes he uses a licence so rare as to confirm our impression that an expressive effect is intended. In *Epode* 2 the trembling hare (*pavidumque leporem,* l. 35) occasions the only resolution of the first foot in the 297 trimeters of the *Epodes,* and one of only two instances of successive resolutions; the hurrying sheep (*properantes,* l. 62) occasion one of only two instances of resolution in 228 dimeters. (Norden, *Aeneis VI,* 425[a] n. 1.)

And a wave like the wave that is rais'd by an earthquake grew,
Till it smote on their hulls and their sails and their masts and their flags
And the whole sea plunged and fell on the shot-shattered navy of Spain.*

(*l*) *Metaphor from verse-technique*

Sometimes the metrical feature involved is more technical than such expressive rhythm as any reader can recognize. Here a slightly larger number of illustrations may not come amiss.

Non quivis videt immodulata poëmata iudex
not every critic detects inharmonious verses,

says Horace,[1] slily omitting a caesura to test the reader. He has just referred to the verses of Ennius' plays as

in scaenam missos cum magno pondere versus
verses sent on to the stage with great weight.

This line is expressive not only because of the weighty spondees (Wickham), but because of the hammering coincidence of ictus and accent in the last three feet: unlike Ennius, a polished Augustan would have written

magno cum pondere versus,

thus avoiding coincidence in the fourth foot.† Horace's rustic on the river-bank waits for the caesura, the break when he can cross, and it never comes:

rusticus expectat dum defluat amnis, at ille
labitur et labetur in omne volubilis aevum
like a rustic who waits till the river has flowed by, but it glides and will glide rolling on for all time;

and Virgil similarly slips a caesura when a chariot gets out of control:

fertur equis auriga neque audit currus habenas
the charioteer is carried away by the horses and the car heeds not the reins.

---

* On Pindar, *O.* 6, 100 f., ἀγαθαὶ δὲ πέλοντ' ἐν χειμερίᾳ νυκτὶ θοᾶς ἐκ ναὸς ἀπεσκίμφθαι δύ' ἄγκυραι, Norden notes that the moment when the anchors are secure is expressed by the doubled syncope of the ditrochee (*Aeneis VI*, 423³ n. 2).

† According to their practice as observed by G. Cortius early in the eighteenth century (cf. Munro, *Lucretius*, II, p. 105). Cicero has *magno cum pondere* at *Arat.* 132, possibly altering an Ennian phrase.

Again, Virgil's metre, generally marked by reliable caesuras, loses its way in the Labyrinth,

> frangeret indeprensus et inremeabilis error.[1]

So Milton lets his metre break down into disorder to emphasize the demoralization of Samson:

> O change beyond report, thought or belief!
> See how he lies at random, *carelessly diffus'd.*[*]

In Tennyson's expressive line

> Slipping down horrible precipices

the iambic basis of the decasyllable has completely given way (and in those *i*, *l* and *p* sounds I seem to hear the simultaneous slithering of shale).

The running together of words in Latin elision (synaloepha) can help to represent continuity of space as in Horace's

> quo pinus ingens albaque populus
> umbram hospitalem consociare amant
> ramis?[2]

To what end do the large pine and white poplar love to concert a hospitable shade with their branches?,

or of relentless process, as at the close of the same poem,

> et nos in aetern(um)
> exilium impositura cymbae
> *and will set us aboard the ferry for eternal exile,*

where the rare synaloepha between lines by 'hypermeter' increases the effect—there is no pause for reprieve. Hypermeter, causing the voice to slur or die away at the end of the line, goes with the faltering tongue in

> cur facunda parum decor(o)
> inter verba cadit lingua silentio?[3]

Why does my eloquent tongue lapse into awkward silence while I am speaking?

---

* *S.A.* 117–18. He is reproducing in English the effect of Greek choral rhythms, but this line is nevertheless striking, for it was most unusual to have more than two short syllables together in any English verse, until Hopkins introduced his 'sprung' rhythm.

The cutting off of the last syllable expresses the cutting off of the flower at the meadow's edge by the passing plough in Catullus'

> qui illius culpa cecidit velut prat(i)
> ultimi flos praetereunte postquam
> tactus aratro est.[1]

In Dido's curse, 'may they fight, themselves and their grandsons', 'pugnent ipsique nepotesque' (*Aen.* IV, 629), the hypermetric *-que*, trailing on even beyond a full stop, helps to suggest interminable strife.

Coincidence of ictus and accent can help to represent smooth motion, as in Ennius'

> lábitur úncta carína per aéquora cána celócis[2]
> *smooth glides the well-greased keel of the cutter over the white sea-foam,*

or repose untroubled by conflict, as in Virgil's melodiously narcotic verse

> spárgens úmida mélla sopóriferúmque papáver*
> *sprinkling liquid honey and soporific poppy-seed.*

Again, Platt observed of Mary Coleridge's lines,

> Over the blue sea goes the wind complaining
> And the blue sea turns purple as he goes,

'How beautifully there the change of colour is echoed by the changing accent of the two words "blue sea"!'† Conversely Tennyson noted, on the first rhyme in *The Lotus Eaters*,

> 'Courage!' he said, and pointed toward the land,
> 'This mounting wave will roll us onward soon.'
> In the afternoon they came unto a land
> In which it seemed always afternoon,

'"the *strand*" was, I think, my first reading, but the no-rhyme of "land" was lazier'.[3] We may think this pernickety or imperceptible, but it does show what the poet was trying to do, and to what lengths he would go;

---

* *A.* IV, 486. That this metrical effect was intended is shown by other instances where it is used of sleep—*A.* v, 856: 'tempora, cunctantique natantia lumina solvit'; *A.* IV, 81:'...suadentque cadentia sidera somnos'.

† Platt, *Nine Essays*, p. 177. Though Greek poets, following Homer (Ἄρες, Ἄρες) occasionally repeated a word, even adjacently, with altered quantity, it may be that when Theocritus (VI, 19) wrote τὰ μὴ κᾱλὰ κᾱλὰ πέφανται, he meant to reinforce the meaning, 'foul seems fair'.

and notice again the drowsy effect of repetition—*afternoon, afternoon* (cf. p. 67), for of course there are cases in which more than one element contributes to the expressiveness.

(m) *Compound effects*

When Horace describes the tyrant's fear of a revolution,

> neu populus frequens
> ad arma cessantes, ad arma
> concitet imperiumque frangat,
>
> *lest the crowding mob arouse to arms the waverers, to arms, and break his sway,*

we have rhythm and repetition functioning together. '"Aux armes, citoyens!" cries the mob, but the moderates, the solid molossus of "cessantes", hold it back at first, till with a second cry, it sweeps them along in a torrent of dactyls.'[1] When he describes the breeze fanning the unshorn locks of Apollo,

> intonsosque agitaret Apollinis aura capillos,

we have a steady, undulating motion caused by the coincidence of ictus and accent, combined with a gentle effect of floating or hovering caused by the lingering double *l*'s (which incidentally impart an appropriate euphony to the line: see p. 11).[2]

In the famous Homeric line in which Sisyphus' stone careers down the mountain again,

> αὖτις ἔπειτα πέδονδε κυλίνδετο λᾶας ἀναιδής
> *downward anon to the valley the boulder remorselessly bounded,*[3]

the effect is due to the dactylic metre (rocks rolling down an uneven incline strike heavily less often than lightly, and this is stylized into dactyls, as in our onomatopoeic word 'bumpity'), but also to the sharp thud of the dentals; as in Tennyson's

> the spires
> Prick'd with incredible pinnacles into heaven

the expressive effect is due partly to the sharp *i*-sounds and consonants, partly to the 'jagged', irregular rhythm.

IV. EXPRESSIVENESS IN VIRGIL, 'GEORGICS', I, 43–392

These few examples may suffice to indicate the sorts of effect we may find. Instead of multiplying them, let us examine one extended specimen of poetry. For this purpose I have chosen an ostensibly didactic portion of the first *Georgic* (ll. 43–392). A Georgic, in Dryden's words,[1] is 'some part of the science of husbandry put into a pleasing dress, and set off with all the beauties and embellishments of poetry'. 'It raises in our minds a pleasing variety of scenes and landskips, whilst it teaches us; and makes the driest of its precepts look like a description.' In fact, the *Georgics* are not didactic, but pseudo-didactic: in essence they are the first descriptive poem in literature. They give abundant opportunities for 'those beautiful descriptions and images which are the spirit of life and poetry'. Virgil indeed could afford to neglect nothing which would impart this quality to his miscellaneous and work-a-day subject-matter. We should expect to find him alert to make his language expressive, and can guess what occupied him for at least part of that process of revision during those afternoons and evenings in which the lines hastily brought forth in the morning were licked into shape.[2] There could be no better illustration of what was said above (p. 8) about the two types of reader than a comparison between the commentaries of Conington and of Page. The former never mentions such phenomena, while the latter shows a keen sensitivity sometimes verging on the fanciful.

(45) depresso incipiat iam tum mihi taurus aratro
   ingemere

   let the ox begin right now to groan over the deep-driven plough.

The sense of effort comes from the alliteration in *túm mihi taúrus*, which coincides with the metrical ictus. There is no such effect in the lines of Lucretius which Virgil probably had in mind (v, 209–10):

   ...valido consueta bidenti
   ingemere, et terram pressis proscindere aratris.

(65) fortes invertant tauri

   let your strong oxen turn up (the rich soil).

The heaviness of spondees helps to express steady labour. It is thrown into relief by the fact that the 11 preceding lines begin with a dactyl, and there is no other line in the paragraph (28 lines) which begins with two spondees.

(74) siliqua quassante legumen

 the bean with rattling pod.

'siliqua quassante' echoes the sound.

(76) sustuleris fragiles calamos silvamque sonantem

 pick up the brittle halm and rustling undergrowth.

The light dactyls, light vowels (*a, i, u*) and sibilants combine to suggest the rustling to which *sonantem* draws attention.

(78) urunt Lethaeo perfusa papavera somno

 poppies steeped in the sleep of oblivion burn it.

Spondees for sleep (see p. 68).

(80) ne saturare fimo pingui pudeat sola, neve...

 don't be afraid to saturate the soil with rich manure.

The break at the fifth arsis, not preceded by a monosyllable, 'pudeat sola neve', is very rare. But I confess that I find Page's explanation fanciful here (though interesting as recognition of what I have called 'metaphor from verse-technique'). He says: 'With quiet humour Virgil gives this homely precept in a line the rhythm of which is peculiarly homely and rugged.' The expressive mare's nest is the last refuge of the metrist cornered by an anomaly. On the other hand I do think that the impression of a snake's coil-and-dart motion is helped by the rhythm of *G.* II, 153:

 nec rapit immensos orbes *per humum neque tanto.*

And if so, there is an interesting parallel in Demetrius' remark,[1] that at *Il.* XII, 208 Homer wrote

Τρῶες δ' ἐρρίγησαν ὅπως ἴδον αἰόλον ὄφιν
but the Trojans shuddered when they saw the wriggling snake,

harshly lengthening the first syllable of ὄφιν, instead of writing smoothly ὅπως ὄφιν αἰόλον εἶδον, for expressive effect. Certainly the metre does shuffle at the end.

(84–5) saepe etiam sterilis incendere profuit agros
        atque levem stipulam crepitantibus urere flammis

*often too it pays to set fire to the barren fields, and burn the light
stubble with crackling flames.*

Here the swift spreading of the flames is well expressed by the dactylic
rhythm, and the crackling of the flames by the light vowels (only one
ō, one ū) and the sharp *p* and *t* sounds. *Crepitantibus* draws attention to
the sound, and indeed the second line is otiose except as contributing to
this effect.

(107–9) . . . ecce supercilio clivosi tramitis undam
        elicit: illa cadens raucum per levia murmur
        saxa ciet, scatebrisque arentia temperat arva.

*(the man who makes runnels through parched fields) : look,
from the brow of the sloping channel he entices the water; in its
fall it stirs a hoarse murmur amid the pebbles, and cools with its
gushing the arid land.*

This *tour de force* is a paraphrase of an expressive passage in Homer
(*Il.* XXI, 260–2):

τοῦ μέν τε προρέοντος ὑπὸ ψηφῖδες ἅπασαι
ὀχλεῦνται· τὸ δέ τ᾿ ὦκα κατειβόμενον κελαρύζει
χώρῳ ἔνι προαλεῖ.

The effect here is enhanced by the sound of ὀχλεῦνται ('are rolled')
and the onomatopoeic word κελαρύζει ('babbles'), the *k*-sounds of
ὦκα κατ-, and the hurrying dactyls of the second half. Virgil's version
should be compared with Horace's passages about running water
already cited (p. 57). Like Horace, he imports the trickling *i, c* and *l*
sounds in words that have nothing to do with water: *ecce, supercilio,
clivosi, elicit, illa, cadens, saxa, ciet*, to join the onomatopoeic *scatebrisque*.
Having (again with the operative verb held up till the next line)
trickled over the barrier as it follows the ditcher's mattock, the water
becomes a purling, babbling runnel (*raucum murmur* draws attention to
the sound), refreshing the dried-up fields. The combination of *a* and *r*,

if I am not mistaken, has a 'dry' sound (cf. 'crackle', 'barren', 'arid', 'parched', *harena*).

> I chatter over stony ways
> In little sharps and trebles,
> I bubble into eddying bays,
> I babble on the pebbles.

Tennyson's *Brook* is like an elaborate variation on a theme by Virgil.

(114) collectum umorem

gathered moisture.

The spondees give a pent-up effect which is enhanced by the gathering together of *-um um-* by synaloepha.

(133) ut varias usus meditándo extúnderet artes

so that practice by taking thought should hammer out the various crafts.

The hammering effect which our metaphor recognizes is enhanced by the syllables *tand- tund-* coinciding with metrical ictus (cf. *tum- tau-* at l. 45).

Catullus uses such sounds to echo the pounding of sea on shore,

> litus ut longe resonante Eoa
> *tund*itur *unda*.[1]

(201) non aliter quam qui adverso vix flumine lembum
      remigio subigit

just as a man rowing who scarce propels his boat against the current.

Norden thought that Virgil used a spondaic rhythm here to represent effort, pointing it by the word *vix*.[2] (But I doubt if it is sufficiently exceptional, the first foot being a dactyl.)

(224) invitae properes anni spem credere terrae

(before you) hasten to entrust the year's hope to the unwilling soil.

The burial of the little word *spem* in the middle of the line, as the little seed is buried in the earth, is one of A. M. Young's examples of 'pictorial arrangement' (see p. 65). It may be appreciable, but we are on the borders of the fanciful.

77

(281–4) ter sunt conati imponere Pelio Ossam
scilicet, atque Ossae frondosum involvere Olympum:
ter Pater exstructos disiecit fulmine montes.

thrice they attempted to set Ossa on Pelion indeed, and upon Ossa
to roll leafy Olympus: thrice the Father struck down the piled-up
mountains with his thunderbolt.

A classic instance. (Conington merely says that in 281 the non-elision and shortening of -*o* are in imitation of Greek rhythm, and appropriate because the subject is Greek.) In line 281 we have two instances of gasping hiatus between identical vowels (these were probably suggested by the ἄνω ὤθεσκε of Sisyphus' effort and what critics like Dionysius said of that—see p. 60; but Homer's lines describing the Giants' attempt at *Od.* XI, 314–15 are lightly dactylic, with nothing of the expressiveness here introduced by Virgil). The spondees also help to suggest effort. Line 282 has three examples of slurring synaloepha, suggesting the rolling of something ponderous that cannot for a moment be lifted. 283, on the other hand, is an effortless line without elision or hiatus, firmly based on the fulcrum of *disiecit*.

(295) aut dulcis musti volcano decoquit umor(em).

or boils down the liquid of sweet must over the fire.

The -*em* of *umorem* is elided before *et* at the beginning of the next line. (This licence is rare except with -*que*.) Page comments: 'Notice the hypermetric line suggesting the boiling over of the must.' But does it boil *over*? Virgil does not say so. It is being *reduced* in volume. On the other hand the Tiber really is overflowing in Horace's overflowing line

sinistra
labitur ripa Iove non probante u-
xorius amnis.[1]

(311–34) This is a showpiece expressive of stormy weather.

(313) cum ruit imbriferum ver

when spring comes down in showers.

The exceptional and startling use of a single heavy monosyllable at the end suggests the suddenness of the downpour. Nettleship (not Conington) compared *Aen.* II, 250, 'ruit oceano nox'.

(319–21) quae gravidam late segetem ab radicibus imis
    sublimem expulsam eruerent: ita turbine nigro
    ferret hiemps culmumque levem stipulasque volantes.

*(the battling winds,) far and wide to tear up the well-filled corn by
the very roots and whirl it high in air, then in a dark whirlwind
the storm sweeps along the light stalks and flying straw.*

Here the flexibility of Latin word-order enables the data to be given
in one line, for the violent action to burst out at the beginning of the
next (see p. 66). The wind gives three tugs, expressed by the stress-
accents on *sublímem expúlsam erúerent*, then sweeps off the uprooted
corn in a whirling rhythm.

(322–34) Now comes Virgil's most elaborate picture.
    Saepe etiam immensum caelo venit agmen aquarum
    et foedam glomerant tempestatem imbribus atris
    collectae ex alto nubes.

*Often too a huge mass of water advances across the sky, and
clouds gathered from on high roll up a storm ugly with dark rain.*

Here again (after the first line) spondees with synaloepha suggest
gathering of pent-up masses (cf. I, 114). The *o*-sounds are heavy, dark and
ominous.   ruit arduus aether
    et pluvia ingenti sata laeta boumque labores
    diluit; implentur fossae et cava flumina crescunt
    cum sonitu fervetque fretis spirantibus aequor.

*Sheer drops the sky, and with mighty rain washes away the glad
crops and the oxen's toil; the ditches are filled, rivers rise in their
hollow beds with a roar, and the sea is in ferment with seething friths.*

The suddenness of 'ruit' speaks for itself; so does the swift metre of
what follows; and again the violent verb (*diluit*) is held up, to burst out
at the beginning of the next line. The spirants (*f* and *s*) in the next two
lines echo the hissing of the downpour, especially on the sea's surface.

    ipse Pater media nimborum in nocte corusca
    fulmina molitur dextra: quo maxima motu
    terra tremet, fugere ferae et mortalia corda
    per gentis humilis stravit pavor.

The Father himself in the midst of the night of clouds wields his thunderbolt with brandished right arm; at that shock the mighty earth trembles, the wild beasts are fled, and throughout the world human hearts cower in terror.

In the first two lines the *ō* and *ū* sounds darken the ominous scene, especially those that coincide with metrical ictus (*nimborum, nocte, corusca, fulmina, molitur, motu*). The alliterative *m*'s intensify the gloom (see p. 48 n.). In the next two lines the eight shivering *r*-sounds express the terror of men,* and the pause after the fourth foot ('bucolic diaeresis') is the hush before the thunder.

> ille flagranti
> aut Athon aut Rhodopen aut alta Ceraunia telo
> deicit: ingeminant Austri et densissimus imber;
> nunc nemora ingenti vento, nunc litora plangunt.

He with his flashing bolt strikes down Athos or Rhodope or the high Ceraunia; the blasts redouble and the densest rain; now the woods wail with the great wind, now the shores.

With the *l*-sounds of *ille flagranti* comes the lightning flash (cf. p. 64); then a line brilliantly adapted from Theocritus'

> ἢ Ἄθω ἢ Ῥοδόπαν ἢ Καύκασον ἐσχατόεντα,

as the thunder crackles round the sky in *a* and *au* sounds combined with sharp *t*'s, to end in the roar of 'Ceraunia'. Grammont praises Vigny's rival line

> Roulaient et redoublaient les foudres de l'orage;[1]

but surely the roar of *orage* should come before the rumbling of *roulaient, redoublaient* and *foudres*. Virgil is the master. Again he holds up the operative verb to burst in the next line—*deicit*. As after a thunderclap, the wind redoubles, and the hissing rain (*densissimus imber*), and the series of gusts is felt in the three successive accented *e*'s—*nunc némora ingénti vénto*.† And so the storm blows itself out.

---

* *R* is of course the letter of trembling or shivering: it can be set vibrating by the gusts of breath forced out by fear; as in the *Aeneid* (i, 296),

> furor...fremit horridus ore cruento;

or in Racine,   tu frémiras d'horreur si je romps le silence

(Grammont, *Traité*, 1933, p. 409).

† Compare the *u*-sounds coinciding with the pulse of the metre at *Aen.* i, 85: '*u*na Eur*u*sque Not*u*sque ru*u*nt' (N. I. Herescu, *Poésie*, 1960, p. 110).

(341–2) tum pingues agni, et tum mollissima vina;
   tum somni dulces densaeque in montibus umbrae.

   Then lambs are fat, and then is wine most mellow; then sleep is
   sweet, and deep the shadows on the mountain sides.

After the turmoil of the storms, when spring is now fine (*iam vere*
sereno) come the lazy enjoyments which these sleepy spondaic lines
express.

(350) det motus incompositos et carmina dicat

   (*let your rustic youth*) *tread artless measures and render songs.*

Incompositos runs over the caesura there should strictly be at the third
trochee, *incompos*‖. It is the word Horace uses to describe the un-
polished metre of Lucilius.[1] Like his *immodulata* (p. 70), the word
makes the metre here metaphorical of the subject-matter. Compare
Homer's enormous word for an enormous object,

   κολλητὸν βλήτροισι, δυωκαιεικοσίπηχυ[2]
   fitted together with hoops, twenty-two cubits long,

and Milton's sea-monsters,

      Wallowing unwieldy, enormous in their gait.[3]

(356–9) Continuo, ventis surgentibus, aut freta ponti
   incipiunt agitata tumescere et aridus altis
   montibus audiri fragor, aut resonantia late
   litora misceri et nemorum increbrescere murmur.

   Straightway, as the winds rise, either the sea-friths begin to swell
   choppily and a dry cracking sound to be heard in the high moun-
   tains, or the shores to send a confused sound afar and the mur-
   muring of the wood to increase.

Stormy weather again. With the sibilants of *ventis surgentibus* the
winds begin to stir. The agitation of the waves is reflected in the undulating rhythm of the second line with its missing caesura at *tumesc*‖
and the choppy *t*-sounds in *-unt agitata tum-*.* The dry cracking sound

* Virgil uses similar *t*-sounds and rhythms at 464–5, when the storm of civil war is rising, as
Mr L. A. S. Jermyn has pointed out to me:
         ille etiam caecos instare tumultus
      saepe monet fraudemque et operta tumescere bella.
The repetition of *tumescere* suggests that in writing the second passage he had the first at least
subconsciously in mind.

of pine forests is echoed in the *a* and *r* sounds of 'altis aridus audiri fragor' (cf. Lucretius VI, 119: 'aridus unde auris terget sonus'), and the murmuring of the wind in the woods in the muffled *m*'s, thick consonants and slurred synaloephas of 'misceri et nemorum increbrescere murmur'.

(361) cum medio celeres revolant ex aequore mergi

when the gulls fly swiftly back from mid-ocean.

This rhythm, a succession of three anapaestic words unblurred by synaloepha, is extremely rare. The 'medio celeres revolant' helps to suggest the regular beating of wings, just as dactyls help to suggest the pounding of horses' hooves. Although it only occurs four other times in the 2188 lines of the *Georgics* (and there is less than an average of one instance per book in the *Aeneid*),* we meet it again at line 383 when birds are again the subject—'iam varias pelagi volucres'. It makes itself felt in Propertius (one case out of five in over 2000 hexameters) in another line about birds,

> et Veneris dominae volucres, mea turba, columbae[1]
> *and the birds of my lady Venus, my flock, the doves....*

(366) praecipites labi caelo

headlong glide down the sky.

The sudden appearance and smooth motion of the shooting star is conveyed by the dactyl followed by two spondees and the lubricating *l*'s.

(369) aut summa nantis in aqua colludere plumas

or skimming feathers play together in the surface of the water.

The little twirl of *in aqua* amid the spondees delightfully suggests what we see so often, two feathers intertwined on the surface of water suddenly waltzing round in the breeze.

---

* The others are: *G.* II, 213; III, 165, 410. *A.* III, 259, 606 (but comma and hiatus); IV, 403; V, 605, 822 (? expressive of plunging sea-monsters); VII, 479; IX, 156, 554 (? expressive); X, 390 (but commas), 568. The *Eclogues* have two instances in 835 lines: I, 22; VIII, 28 (? expressive). τῶν ὀρνίθων τὰ πτερυγίσματα is given as an example of wordless rhythm by [Longinus], Proleg. to Hephaestion's handbook (p. 84 Westphal).

(377) aut argúta lacus circúmvolitavit hirúndo

or a darting swallow has flitted round the pools.

The incessant flight of the long word *circumvolitavit* is articulated by the four swoops of the repeated *u*-sounds coinciding with the pulse of the metre, three of them also accented.*

(378) et veterem in limo ranae cecinere querelam

and frogs in the slime have chanted their agelong complaint.

As we all know, frogs go βρεκεκεκὲξ κοάξ κοάξ (pronounced something like 'quarx'). Ovid brilliantly echoed their κοάξ in his line about the Lycians turned into frogs—

quamvis sunt *sub aqua sub aqua* maledicere tentant.[1]

though they are under the water, under the water they still try to revile.

Virgil echoes their βρεκεκεκέξ with his *cecinere querelam.*

(388–9) tum cornix plena pluviam vocat improba voce

et sola in sicca secum spatiatur harena.

Then does the unconscionable raven call full-throatedly for rain,

and stalk alone by herself along the dry sand.

The alliteration in these two lines seems more than fortuitous. Page calls it 'imitative', but I cannot see what it is supposed to imitate. It is clearly meant to be slightly comic, somehow enhancing the burlesque dignity of the bird. But more than that I would not venture to suggest.

V. EXPRESSIVENESS IN SOME OTHER POETS

These examples, set out in order thus, may suggest that Virgil was too much preoccupied with expressiveness, as Tennyson sometimes seems to be; and no doubt I have overlooked what some may feel to be signal instances. But if the section is read as a whole, I do not think that will be the conclusion. In fact Virgil represents a mean in this respect. One cannot do more than give an impression of relative interest and proficiency in this art among poets unless one sets out all the examples one

* N. I. Herescu, *Poésie* (1960), p. 110. The similar image of a sea-bird swooping hither and thither over shore and rock-pools is enhanced by a repeated *circum* at *Aen.* IV, 254–5: '. . .quae circum litora, circum piscosos scopulos. . .' (*ibid.* pp. 114–15).

can discover, and in any case what shall count is a matter of degree as well as personal feeling. I can only say that I am surprised at one or two of the verdicts of Eduard Norden, great connoisseur though he was. 'In Lucretius', he says, 'the pictorial aim is not conspicuous (*zurück-tritt*), in conformity with the character of the didactic poem.'[1] But Lucretius' didactic technique consisted largely in embellishing Epicurus' precepts with vivid illustrations. Moreover he was a great admirer of Ennius' poetry, and Ennius had a taste for devising expressive effects which was almost childish. I should have thought that Lucretius provided quite a large number of instances, some of them rather obvious and playful *tours de force*, some of them brilliantly contributive to poetic effect.

Catullus' short poems (apart from the *Attis*) strike one only occasionally as expressive, as in the stammering effect in Septimius' protestations to Acme (see p. 26). In his long epyllion he had plenty of opportunities, but he gives a Keatsian impression of being more intent on richness and beauty. (The one exception is the description of Bacchus' band:

> plangebant aliae proceris tympana palmis
> aut tereti tenuis tinnitus aere ciebant;
> multis raucisonos efflabant cornua bombos
> barbaraque horribili stridebat tibia cantu.

This is rather overdone, in the Lucretian manner. And indeed the same subject is similarly rendered by Lucretius at II, 618 ff. and by Varro in his Menippean Satires, 131 f., so that here Catullus may simply have been lured into emulation.) There seems reason to suppose that generally the Neoteroi, in this as in other respects, were reacting fastidiously from the earthy Ennian tradition.[2]

That Norden should have thought that Horace was relatively abstemious in alliteration and expressiveness* I do indeed find astonishing, as will be clear from illustrations I have already given. Numerous examples spring to mind from the *Sermones*, with their free rhythm: but even in the more or less fixed metres of the *Odes* there are examples beyond those I have already cited. He can be called abstemious

* *Aeneis VI*, 416[3]; 421[3] ('in diesen Dingen sonst recht zurückhaltend', citing *Epode* 16, 48); 425[3] n. ('viel zurückhaltender als Vergil sind mit Ornamenten dieser Art Horaz und Ovidius gewesen'). J. Marouzeau adduces many examples from him, *Quelques aspects* (1949), pp. 193–201.

among Golden Latin writers only in comparison with Virgil, who himself however, in this as in other respects, represents a mean between Ennius and the Neoteroi. Virgil's tact is perfect. He is the great master —a Wordsworth, one might say, rather than a Tennyson.

Elegiac poetry, with its invariable dactylic rhythm in the second half of every other line, did not lend itself so easily to expressive rhythm as hexameters. Moreover it developed away from the free Catullan form in the direction of lightness and neatness—fewer spondees, fewer elisions.* Ovid, when he turned from elegiacs to hexameters in the *Metamorphoses*, still pursued these same qualities, and this may partly account for my feeling that, although the poem is highly descriptive, there is *comparatively* little use in it of expressive effects, though he shows from time to time what a master of them he can be.†

I have often quoted in this Part writers who have shown by their attitude that they find euphony and expressiveness to be important for their appreciation of literature. I have done this at the risk of being accused of merely using scissors and paste, instead of simply giving my own experience and opinion, because this is a matter of feeling rather than argument, so that one needs the support of a crowd of witnesses. The arguments, indeed, are mostly on the other side, such as they are. But do they weigh much against the avowed intentions of so many poets and the strong apperceptions of so many readers, in widely different lands throughout two and a half millennia? Let us test similar arguments in another sphere. A woman may appear beautiful to one man, but not to another; she may attract a number of men who nevertheless allege different reasons for their feeling; she may be generally admired in England, but unnoticed in Pekin; a slight accident to an eye or an operation on her nose may completely destroy her charm. But should we for such reasons deny the reality or the importance of feminine beauty?

---

* As to sound, it might be thought that Propertius' line about Hylas falling into the stream (I, 20, 48),   *tum* soni*tum* rapto corpore fecit Hylas,

was meant to be expressive. But it becomes less so when one remembers that syllables ending in -*m* were probably nasalized in Latin.

† T. F. Higham produces good examples (*C.R.* 1957, p. 41), but it is a question of *relative* frequency in a poem of over 12,000 lines. See L. P. Wilkinson, *Ovid Recalled* (1955), pp. 236–7.

PART II

RHYTHMS

4

VERSE RHYTHM

I. ACCENT, QUANTITY, ICTUS

What is rhythm? Cicero gave an answer which at least has the merit of elasticity: 'whatever can be somehow measured by the ear'.* (Not necessarily the ear: Goethe professed to have tapped out rhythms on the bare back of his mistress—but let that pass.) *What is Rhythm?* E. A. Sonnenschein wrote a book with that title, and essayed a more exact definition: 'Rhythm is that property of a sequence of events in time which produces on the mind of the observer the impression of proportion between the durations of the several events or groups of events of which the sequence is composed.'[1] Note the concession to subjectivity: 'mind of the observer', 'impression'. Even this did not allow of sufficient looseness, and he added, 'without asserting or implying that the sequence is itself proportioned with mathematical or metronomic exactitude; some sequences may be so proportioned, some not'. Cicero says elsewhere that rhythm consists in *distinctio* (that is, the way in which a sentence is divided up) and in the beat (*percussio*) set up by equal *or often varied* intervals.[2] Even the verse of Mr Ogden Nash might be said to have a rhythm because, however unpredictable the metre or the length of the line, the expectation of rhyme is always richly rewarded.

Nature has its own rhythms, often quite elaborate, as in the songs of some birds. Certain rhythms affect the nervous system in particular ways. Thus the sequence ... — ... — keyed up Sophocles' audience for the murder of Clytemnestra,

ἴδεθ' ὅπου προνέμεται τὸ δυσέριστον αἷμα φυσῶν Ἄρης.[3]

It suggested the opening of Beethoven's Fifth Symphony as the symbol of Allied revenge approaching, to harass the nerves of the Nazi: 'Fate knocking at the door.' The rhythms of poetry probably developed from

* *Or. 67*: 'quicquid...sub aurium mensuram aliquam cadit'.

89

dancing, marching, spinning, grinding, etc., along with those of music. *
There is surely a parallel between the popularity of dactylic verse in
ancient Greece and of the waltz in modern Europe. I have heard the
sprung rhythm of Gerard Manley Hopkins criticized on the ground that
the mind cannot comfortably dance it, with all those unemphatic
syllables to trip over.[1]

Rhythm can be differentiated either by loudness, as in the beating of
drums—in poetry this is produced by force of expiration, that is, stress
accent; or by length, as in skating—to which length of vowels corresponds in quantitative verse; or simply by numbers, as of syllables.
Which of these elements come into play in Latin verse? That is one of
the thorniest questions in classical scholarship.†

Greek had a tonic or pitch accent. We have seen (p. 39) that it might
sometimes affect musical setting, but it does not appear to have influenced verse or prose rhythm. The accentual signs familiar to us were
said to have been invented by Aristophanes of Byzantium, the great
Alexandrian scholar who flourished at the turn of the third and second
centuries B.C. The early literary papyri and Homeric scholia suggest
that these were originally intended only to help the inexperienced to
distinguish between words otherwise identical, such as θέα and θεά: we
cannot deduce that by Aristophanes' time Greek was losing its accent.
What does seem to have happened is that the pitch-accent gradually
yielded to stress-accent on the same syllable. Stress seems to have become
dominant by the second century A.D., and it remains so (to most ears)
in modern Greek.[2]

As to Latin of the classical period, the rule for word-accent is clear
and simple: it was bound to the penultimate syllable if this was long, to
the antepenultimate if the penultimate was short (e.g. *domórum*, but
dómibus).‡ This causes no difficulty to an English-speaking boy: indeed

---

* The trochaic septenarius was suited to olive-grinding (Servius on *G.* II, 519). See also Robert
Graves's suggestive, if fantastic, Lecture 4, 'Harp, Anvil, Oar', in *The Crowning Privilege* (1955).

† I shall avoid the terms 'thesis' and 'arsis', because they actually exchanged meanings in
antiquity, and are only confusing (W. Beare, *Latin Verse and European Song*, 1957, p. 60). I shall
also avoid using 'rhythmic' to distinguish any particular kind of verse, keeping its meaning as
wide as possible. (It was Bede who started the practice of calling 'rhythmic' the new poetry of
his day which took no account of quantity. *G.L.* VII, 258K.)

‡ Monosyllables were generally accented, except prepositions. It is inferred (though disputed)
that two-foot polysyllables had a secondary accent further back, for example *tèmperátus*, *tèm-
pestátibus*, *còmmemoráre*, *cùpidínibus* (see H. D. Broadhead, *Rhythm*, 1922, pp. 50-3). I am now

he is seldom even told what the rule is.* In primitive Italic dialects, however, and in early Latin the accent is believed to have fallen on the first syllable, as in Hungarian.[1]

But what sort of accent was it? Our authorities in the classical period —Cicero, Varro, Nigidius—all use language which points unmistakably to pitch, at least as predominating.[2] But did these Romans understand what they were talking about? They were not trained phoneticians, and in the theory of accentuation, as in other matters, they were liable to follow Greek instructors blindly. Atticus got hold of a treatise about it by Tyrannio, and was wittily teased for this by Cicero: 'I'm glad you were so deeply impressed by this very subtle science...but I can't help asking what bearing that acute and grave study has on the *summum bonum*.'[3] The Latin technical terms *accentus, gravis, acutus, circumflexus* are mere 'calques' of the Greek προσῳδία, βαρεῖα, ὀξεῖα, περισπωμένη. Even the Greeks went on applying βαρεῖα and ὀξεῖα to their own accent long after, as all agree, it had become predominantly one of stress, and talking of 'rough' breathing when there was no longer any such thing to be heard. The Germans use *Betonung* of an accent which is one of stress, not tone. If we look at the Latin language itself, we find that it displays markedly a feature characteristic of languages that have an accent of stress, not pitch: the tendency of short vowels to drop out after a stressed syllable (syncope). We say 'med'cine, 'choc'late'. An American thinks it affected not to say 'Soph'more', just as Augustus told Gaius Caesar it was affected to say 'cálidum' instead of 'cal'dum'.† Or if the syllable did not drop out, it might be 'weakened'—'facit', but 'efficit.

To some extent the two kinds of accent are inseparable, as many have suspected and experimental phoneticians have now demonstrated;[4] and the Romans, prompted by the Greeks, may have been more *conscious* of

inclined to agree with Broadhead, that words with ᴗ ᴗ before the main accent (for example *videatur*) had no secondary accent. Enclitic particles like *-que*, parts of *sum* when auxiliary, personal, possessive and demonstrative pronouns when unemphatic, had no accent. A preposition coalesced with a following noun, for example *circum-lítora*.

* In English we sometimes swallow syllables, for example in the terminations *-t(o)ry* or *-abl(e)*; but it is surprising how many people contrive to swallow two and say 'láboratory' for 'labóratory'. Is this an unconscious echo of 'lavatory', or is it an attempt to fall in with the abbreviation 'lab.'? 'Récondite' is also surely a solecism, perhaps induced by 'reckon'.

† Quint. I, 6, 19. The stress was so strong, in early times at least, that it could shorten a long syllable in a Greek loanword. Βαλανεῖον (bath) was introduced when accent still fell on the first syllable in Latin, hence 'bálineum', which later became alternatively 'bálneum' by syncope.

the pitch than the stress. But the question remains, which was dominant in Latin of the classical age? And it is a sobering thought that the answer given is so much prejudiced by the critic's own linguistic nurture. In general Frenchmen, having no stress-accent in their own language, take their stand on what the ancients said and deny any appreciable stress to Latin, whereas Englishmen, Americans and Germans, for instance, maintain on the evidence of the language's development that stress was the sole or dominant factor.* If I follow my native prejudice, it is because I believe (as will emerge) that accent sometimes affected versification in classical Latin, whereas those who believe that it was solely one of pitch do not.

Quantity was also an essential feature of the Latin language.[1] If the length† of syllables had not been generally felt and agreed, the Rule of the Penultimate for accentuation could never have established itself, nor could Greek metres have been introduced so easily for even un-lettered theatre-audiences. As in Greek, any long syllable counted as equivalent to two shorts, though the strict scrutiny of a tape-recording might have revealed considerable variations within these classes. But what role, if any, did accent play in Latin versification? That is the great corollary to the dispute over the nature of the accent.

Before attempting to deal with this question we must look at another term, 'ictus'. It is derived from the beating of time with foot or finger by the performer or accompanist.‡ In quantitative metres it falls on the first long syllable of each foot. In any metre that is not merely a matter of number of syllables, and in some that are, there is a fundamental pulse. Originally it is emphasized by regularity.

> From jigging veins of rhyming mother-wits,
> And such conceits as clownage keeps in pay,
> We'll lead you to the stately tent of war,
> Where you shall hear the Scythian Tamburlaine

---

* There are, of course, exceptions. Postgate held that pitch-accent could equally well produce the phenomenon of syncope (*Cl. Ph.* 1908, pp. 99–100). Beare comes down on the side of pitch (*Latin Verse*, p. 54). All I would claim is that the element of stress was sufficient to affect versification sometimes.

† More properly called 'weight', as Professor W. S. Allen insists.

‡ Quint. IX, 4, 51. It is unlikely that there was a conductor in antiquity who beat time for a choir. Horace's thumb at *Odes*, IV, 6, 36 was plucking the strings of an imaginary lyre. (E. Reisch, *R.E.* III, 2382.28 ff.; E. Fraenkel, *Horace*, 1957, pp. 403–4.)

Threatening the world with high astounding terms
And scourging kingdoms with his conquering sword.

Marlowe's audience was put in no doubt about the metre. The only variations here are the lifting of the stress on 'to' in line 3 and the inversion of it in the first two syllables of lines 4 and 5. But when a metre has become familiar, it is freely overlaid with pleasing variations, as a waltz may be without the dancers' faltering, so that even the intrusion of a totally exceptional line such as

Never, never, never, never, never

or

The lost Traveller's Dream under the Hill

is accepted, and felt as particularly effective in its place. It is only when the opening lines do not make clear what metre is being used, or when the metre gets lost in a continued orgy of exceptions, that the pulse is felt no more and the inward ear gives up.

But no reader of English verse would stress the pulse and say

We'll lead you to the stately tent of war

or

Of man's first disobedience and the fruit.

Similarly in Latin it is distorting to say

Ac veluti magno in populo

or

Hoc Ithacus velit et magno mercentur Atridae.

That is what Bentley called reading 'ut pueri in scholis'.[1] But unfortunately he adopted the same symbol (') to mark ictus and word-accent. This was disastrous. It encouraged those who were disposed to stress the ictus in utterance, as seems to be common practice in Germany and some other countries. Beare himself has said: 'In reading Latin verse no doubt most of us do stress the metre: Italiam fato profugus.'[2] Most of us? If we do, we lose a subtle and continual pleasure of interplay, to which Cecil Day Lewis has referred as 'that most desirable of rhythmical effects, the counterpoint of the line spoken according to the natural rhythm of the words, working in contrast to the strict beat of the metre'.[3]

The same phenomenon is found in other languages. In German poetry it occurs only to a limited extent.[1] In Russian of the syllabic-accentual type the natural word-stress may not conflict with the metrical pulse except in the first foot; but variety became progressively sought by the use of words which have no stress—proclitics, enclitics and certain other words—or long words (for Russian has no secondary accent). 'There is a marked difference between the metrical scheme and the (accentual) rhythmic pattern.' 'Individual rhythms in no way destroy the metrical scheme, which is present, though hidden, in the verse.'[2] Again, 'this conflict between rhythm and metre is found in Spanish poetry as well as in Latin; the flow of a Spanish verse is a combination of two accents, a resultant of two forces'.[3] Conflict of accent and pulse is said to occur in Greek popular poetry.[4] If we find something similar in Latin, it can hardly be denied that it answers to an aesthetic desire which has made itself felt independently in widely differing literatures. And in fact there is both positive and negative evidence in the Latin grammarians that they assumed verse to be read in normal speech-rhythm.[5]

And here I must record my gratitude that, after I had learnt how Latin verse is scanned, I was taught (by A. L. Irvine) to read it as though it were natural speech (as one reads English verse), and to let the now familiar metre make itself felt as an undercurrent; and not only for the sake of the interplay I have been discussing, but because only so can the words be uttered as though they meant what they say, since the stress will generally fall on the stem, much less often on a mere termination.[6]

Herescu quotes a number of instances from the Roman poets in which a word, especially a proper name, is repeated in such a way that its relation to the pulse of the verse is different: here the stem, there the termination, coincides with the pulse.[7] He sees in this a device for enhancing *variety*. But in some of the examples he gives the repetition is clearly designed for *emphasis*: it is reinforcement, not variety, that is needed. The effect is dissipated if the verse is read, as he indicates, by metrical ictus, enhanced if it is read accentually. Consider the following cases. Should we read

> Grais ingenium, Grais dedit ore rotundo
> Musa loqui

94

or
> *Grais* ingenium, *Grais* dedit ore rotundo
> Musa loqui;
>
> Ve*ster*, Camenae, *vester* in arduos
> tollor Sabinos

or
> Ve*ster*, Camenae, *vester* in arduos
> tollor Sabinos?

There can surely be no doubt that the semantic advantage of the second method outweighs any purely aesthetic merit there may be in the first.

The effect of reading by natural stress is as much superior to that of reading by metre as is that of chanting the English Psalms in 'speech rhythm' to the old 'wor-orms and featherèd fowls' style of pointing. And it derives support from certain Latin texts. Why could Horace take the beginning of a septenarius in Terence, *hinc illae lacrimae* and make it the beginning of a dactylic hexameter *hinc illae lacrimae*? Why could he take another whole septenarius from him,

> exclusit; revocat; redeam? non si m(e) obsecret,

and make it a hexameter by the minimum of alteration—

> exclusit; revocat; redeam? non s(i) obsecret. ecce?[1]

Presumably because in either poet the verse was uttered as natural speech, the rhythm established by the preceding lines being still felt as an undercurrent. For comedy, indeed, Cicero says as much: 'the senarii of the comic poets, through their similarity to everyday talk, are often "thrown away", so that sometimes the fact that they are verse and rhythm can hardly be perceived.'[2] (The same is true of Shakespeare's blank verse as spoken on our stage.) We need not worry about possible effects of music; for it seems that, whereas Plautus' *cantica* had musical accompaniment, his iambic dialogue had not.* The argument that we must not expect from Latin verse the same effects as from English can be reversed: the two may share a feature just because, as I have said, it answers to a universal aesthetic desire.

Beare is therefore surely right when he insists that ictus was not expiratory: 'It is not something heard or seen: it is expectation.' Expecta-

---

* In the *Stichus*, at l. 758, the metre changes from trochaic septenarii to iambic senarii while the flute-player is drinking. On all this see W. Beare, *The Roman Stage* (1950), pp. 211–15.

tion of a stressed syllable in accentual verse, of a heavy syllable in quanti-tative verse.* But to deduce from this that no such thing could be felt as coincidence or conflict between ictus and accent would be mistaken. We are never unconscious of the *pulse* (I shall use this term instead of ictus, because it suggests something subtly felt, something that can con-flict with stress-accent without causing chaos). No wonder critics object to those who *stress* 'ictus' that they must choose between that and word-accent, on the ground that both cannot co-operate in the same verse. Nevertheless the term refers to something which regulates the life-blood of poetry: it is not a mere will-o'-the-wisp—or 'ictus fictus', as Axelson has dubbed it.[1]

II. CAESURA

A caesura is best defined as a break between words within a verse which divides it into members. Caesuras cut across feet, because otherwise 'the listener gets the impression of a chain, the links of which are placed side by side without being actually joined',[2] as in Ennius' notorious line that was a joke already to Lucilius,

sparsis | hastis | longis | campus | splendet et | horret.

Their function is, not so much to give the reader a rest, as to divide the line into sections which the mind can take in at once without effort. As a psychological investigator has put it, 'we can take in without thought the time during which a clock strikes two or three, not eleven or twelve'.[3] A line as long as a Greater Asclepiad, or a dactylic hexa-meter which has no strong ($2\frac{1}{2}$) caesura, may require two. The members so created become artistic units. They tend to be responsive in sense, as in

parcere subiectis ‖ et debellare superbos;

and their identity may be emphasized by anaphora, as in

sic oculos ‖ *sic* ille manus ‖ *sic* ora gerebat,

---

* *Hermathena* (1953), p. 40. P. Barkas uses the phrase 'Subjective Ictus' (*A Critique of Modern English Prosody*, 1934, pp. 13–14). E. Kalinka says, 'We must not feel the ictus as loud hammer-strokes, but as the gentle steps of light-footed Muses dancing away over the meadows' (*Jahres-bericht*, 1937, p. 100). F. W. Shipley, who is admirable on all this, calls it 'more of an abstraction than a reality' (*T.A.P.A.* 1938, p. 135).

or by internal alliteration or assonance, as in

Marsa *manus* ‖ Paeligna cohors ‖ *Vestina virum vis.*[1]

Punctuation also tends to coincide with such caesuras as well as with the end of the line, unless this is consciously avoided.

Further, the incidence of caesuras in the hexameter is such that the aesthetic principle of increasing members is satisfied:*

> arma virumque cano
> Troiae qui primus ab oris

or

> inde toro
> pater Aeneas
> sic orsus ab alto.

This pleasing effect may be enhanced by the size of the words involved:

> Phillyrides Chiron
> Amythaoniusque Melampus.

The same is true in the case of the commoner, masculine caesura in iambics and choliambics:

> phaselus ille
> quem videtis, hospites,

or

> paene insularum,
> Sirmio, insularumque;

but not where the caesura is feminine:

> quis hoc potest videre
> quis potest pati?

nor in some lyric metres:

> lugete, O Veneres,
> Cupidinesque;

nor in the trochaic tetrameter:

> Gallias Caesar subegit
> Nicomedes Caesarem,

except where the tripartite division is contrived:

> Salva Roma,
> Salva patria,
> Salvus est Germanicus.

* De Groot, *Mnemosyne* (1935), p. 106. For the principle see part III, p. 175.

III. POPULAR VERSE

Livius invoked the Latin Camena at the beginning of his *Odyssey*:

> Virum mihi, *Camena,* insece versutum.

But Ennius, the half-Greek from the heel of Italy, turned to the Hellenic Muses at the beginning of his *Annals*:

> *Musae* quae pedibus magnum pulsatis Olympum.

This resounding line signalized a revolution. In future all classical poetry in Latin would be quantitative and based on Greek metres. Ennius had only patronizing disdain for his uncouth predecessor who wrote 'in verse such as the Fauns and seers of old used to sing, before anyone had climbed the cliffs of the Muses or taken care over language'.[1] More than two thousand years later an English schoolboy set to write quantitative Latin verse could still be told, 'If you do not take more pains, how can you expect to write good longs and shorts? If you do not write good longs and shorts, how can you be a man of taste? If you are not a man of taste, how can you be of use in the world?'[2]

It is often said that, while this quantitative metre introduced from Greece proved acceptable to the educated, the common man preferred measures which catered for his speech-accent. Now the popular measure *par excellence* was the trochaic septenarius, heir to the oldest Greek metre after hexameters. It was used, for instance, by children for a game:

> rex eris si recte facies; si non facies, non eris
> *You'll be king if you be kingly; not if you unkingly be.*

It was used by ribald soldiers to chaff their general Caesar as they marched behind him in his triumph:

> urbani, servate uxores, moechum calvum adducimus
> *Romans, keep your wives in safety: here the baldhead lecher comes;*

or for political lampoons:

> postquam Crassus carbo factus, Carbo crassus factus est.
> *Crassus being reduced to ashes, Carbo straightway put on fat.**

> * Crassus means 'fat', Carbo 'ash'.

This was basically a line of seven-and-a-half trochees (– ◡), with a diaeresis after the fourth; but any long syllable except the last could be resolved into two shorts. The Greeks allowed a spondee (– –) to take the place of a trochee in the *even* feet; but the Romans allowed this in *any* foot except the last (as in the line just quoted), Plautus as freely as the soldiers.* Latin has more long syllables proportionately than Greek, so this was very convenient. But, we may well ask, how could Romans take so much licence and not lose the lilting rhythm? What had they that the Greeks had not? 'Stress-accent' is a possible answer: the reciter was conscious of an accentual rhythm as well:

> póstquam Crássus cárbo fáctus, Cárbo crássus fáctus ést.†

IV. LYRIC VERSE

(a) Catullus

The Plautine *cantica* in lyric quantitative metres borrowed from the Greek show no urge to make accent coincide with pulse. They were recitative accompanied by music, and the music probably emphasized the metre. ('Lesbium servate pedem'—'keep to the Lesbian feet'— Horace imagines himself as saying to the choir of boys and girls that sang his *Carmen Saeculare*.)[1] In any case, musical settings notoriously tend to disregard normal speech rhythms.

It is a great pity that nearly all Alexandrian lyric, which was no doubt as accomplished as Alexandrian epigram, has perished. The scanty fragments of Callimachus are particularly tantalizing; and the names of two metres that struck deep roots in Latin, the Phalaecian hendecasyllable of Catullus and the Asclepiads of Horace, are reminders of two Hellenistic

---

* Similarly Ennius and his successors in hexameter verse allowed the fourth foot to be a spondee coinciding with word-end, a rhythm disliked by Homer and almost forbidden by the Alexandrians.

† Beare, however (*Latin Verse*, p. 17), rightly rejects any suggestion that the metre was *basically* accentual, like its English counterpart (*Locksley Hall*, etc.):

> 'Cómrades, leáve me hére a líttle, whíle as yét 'tis éarly mórn.'

If the basis had been accent, the legionaries would have sung, not 'Gallias Caesar subegit...' but

> Cáesar Gállias subégit, Nicomédes Caesárem.

Cf. J. Vendryes, *L'intensité initiale en Latin* (1902), p. 98.

poets.* One Latin poet of whom we would wish to know more is Laevius, who, if indeed he lived at the turn of the second and first centuries, was a forerunner of the Alexandrianizing school of the 'Neoterics' ('Modernists'). His *Erotopaegnia* (short, playful poems on love in various metres) were, to judge from the half-dozen fragments, among the precursors of the *nugae* ('trifles') of Catullus.

Mea Vatiena, amabo...

he begins a poem, as Catullus was to begin one

Amabo, mea dulcis Ipsithilla....[1]

One of his metres was the Phalaecian, later a favourite of Catullus, the metre of

Lugete, O Veneres Cupidinesque.

A more important figure in the history of Latin verse is the encyclopaedic scholar, Cicero's friend, M. Terentius Varro. In his Menippean Satires, of whose 150 books nearly 600 small fragments remain, he ranged widely in prose and verse. And the specimens we have show that, as Cicero politely says to him in a dialogue, he 'wrote varied and elegant poems in almost every metre'.[2] He wrote archaic hexameters like those of Ennius and Lucilius, and archaic senarii, septenarii and octonarii like those of Plautus and Accius. But he also indulged in the lyric polymetry of the Neoterics, with Phalaecians, Choliambics, Glyconics, Sotadeans, Anapaestic dimeters and Galliambics, and discussed their natures too.[3] Since he did not merely imitate Menippus (for he uses metres that came in after him), and since he also uses metres which to the best of our knowledge had long been defunct, it has been supposed that he followed a handbook.[4] The Menippeans were mostly composed between 81 and 67 B.C., when Catullus was still a boy.[5] We have to remember that when Catullus wrote the *Attis* he had before him such lines as Varro's

spatul(a) eviravit omnes Veneri vaga pueros.[6]

Catullus too enjoyed improvising in various metres, as on that evening he spent with his friend Calvus of which we have a souvenir

* Phalaecus, who apparently flourished in the fourth century B.C. (Wilamowitz, *Hellenistische Dichtung*, 1924, I, 134), and Asclepiades of Samos, famous as an epigrammatist (fl. *c.* 270).

in the poem he scribbled for him, still excited, the next morning (50: *Hesterno, Licini*).* In general he seems to have modelled himself on the Hellenistic lyric poets. For instance, his one piece in the iambic septenarius (25: *Cinaede Thalle*) follows them, not the Roman dramatists, in avoiding a spondee except in the first foot. His skill is particularly shown in the case of *Phaselus ille* (4) and *Quis hoc potest videre* (29),† in which, for 27 and 24 lines respectively, he writes pure iambics—a considerable feat in Latin with its high percentage of long syllables, though one accomplished with equal facility by whoever wrote the brilliant parody of the former in the Virgilian *Catalepton* (10: *Sabinus ille*), and also (a fact liable to escape notice) by the young Horace in the 33 trimeters that alternate with elisionless hexameters in *Epode* 16 (*Altera iam teritur*).[1]

Catullus was particularly happy in the graceful Glyconic strophes of the Hymn to Diana (34) and the first Wedding Poem (61: *Collis O Heliconii*). And rightly disregarding the pedantic convention which bound certain metres to traditional subject-matter, he perceived, for instance, that the ideal metre for a relaxed poem about sinking exhausted into the blissful repose of Sirmio (31) was the 'lame' iambic (Choliambic) with a spondee at the end, which was generally associated with the lampoons of Hipponax—

$$\text{desideratoque acquiescimus l\bar{e}ct\bar{o}.}$$

His *tour de force* in Galliambics, the *Attis* (63), has already been mentioned (p. 58). In Phalaecians it is noteworthy that, while he sometimes begins a line with a trochee, as in

$$\text{\bar{a}rid\breve{o} modo pumice expolitum,}$$

or an iambus, as in

$$\text{m\breve{e}\bar{a}s esse aliquid putare nugas,}$$

he intensified the Hellenistic tendency to begin this metre with a spondee,

---

* Among the scanty fragments of Calvus are Phalaecian, Choliambic and Glyconic lines, as well as dactylic hexameters and elegiacs. The same metres appear in the fragments of other Neoterics, Cinna and Ticidas (*Frag. Poet. Lat.* ed. Morel).

† It is questionable whether l. 20 can have begun with *nunc*. Kroll prints this, though he has said (p. xi) that the poem is in pure iambics. Mynors prints *nunc* with a footnote 'repugnantibus tamen numeris'.

a trait which endows even the gaiety of no. 5 (*Vivamus, mea Lesbia*) with a touch of Roman *gravitas*:

> sōlēs occidere et redire possunt:
> nōbīs, cum semel occidit brevis lux,
> nox ēst perpetua una dormienda.

This tendency foreshadows the greatest of Roman metrists, Horace.*

(i) *General*   (b) *Horace*[1]

The eight extant fragments of Maecenas, two of them addressed to Horace, include Phalaecians, Galliambics and one in the jaunty Priapean metre Catullus had used for his poem (17)

> O colonia quae cupis ponte ludere longo.

He was, it seems, a follower of the Neoteric fashion. But Horace himself had other ideas. He left aside Alexandrian models, and went back to Archilochus and Hipponax, perhaps because they were more congenial to him in his bitter, disillusioned mood after Philippi. The Archilochian metres he introduced to Rome—

> Parios ego primus iambos
> ostendi Latio[2]

—were either iambic or composed of alternating dactylic and iambic rhythms. In fact Horace definitely turned away from the Neoterics, who 'had learnt no song beyond Calvus and Catullus'. His *carmina* were of a different genus from κατὰ λεπτόν, παίγνια, *nugae* ('trifles'). Perhaps the most Horatian poem in Catullus is the graceful hymn in six stanzas, each of three Glyconics and a Pherecratean (34):

> Dianae sumus in fide
> puellae et pueri integri;
> Dianam pueri integri
> puellaeque canamus.

Yet Horace never used this stanza,† though Anacreon had done so. His parallel ode (I, 21),

> Dianam tenerae dicite virgines,

---

* For a useful account of Horace's metres see W. R. Hardie, *Res Metrica* (1920), ch. III.

† Avoiding Catullus' tracks? Hardie, *ibid.* p. 255. In Catullus' *Epithalamium* (61) the stanza has an extra Glyconic. The metre was specially associated with wedding-poems (cf. Calvus, fr. 4, Ticidas, fr. 1).

is in the Fifth Asclepiad stanza. Nor did he ever use the Phalaecian. In fact, the only poems of Catullus that connect up metrically with Horace are no. 30, in Greater Asclepiads, and the two poems in Sapphic stanzas, 11 and 51, to which we shall come later.

Even when taking his cue from a poem in non-Lesbian metre, Horace moulds the theme to a Lesbian one. One might have expected an ode which arose out of Anacreon's fr. 43 to be in the same Anacreontic metre, but he converts it into Alcaics (1, 27),

> Natis in usum laetitiae scyphis
> pugnare Thracum est.

The stereotyped metre of the first ten Epodes,

> Beatus ille qui procul negotiis,
> ut prisca gens mortalium,

was all very well for some purposes, and for an imitator of Archilochus. But Horace experimented with other combinations of lines. Those complacent, tripping little couplets could not have expressed the restless lover's discontent in no. 11 (*Petti, nihil me*), nor the indignant scorn of no. 15 (*Nox erat*):

> heu, heu, translatos alio maerebis amores
> ast ego vicissim risero;

still less the tossing storm of no. 13:

> Horrida tempestas caelum contraxit, et imbres
> nivesque deducunt Iovem; nunc mare, nunc siluae
> Threicio Aquilone sonant.

As his poetic spirit grew, he needed a wider range of media, new metres and new sources of inspiration. The iambic element could be an encumbrance. In his new mood of positive enthusiasms, engendered by Maecenas' favour and gift of the Sabine farm and quickened by the Caesarian victory at Actium in 31, he collected in book form the iambics and the hexameter *sermones* he had in his desk, and published them as what we call the *Epodes* and *Satires* II, then turned, still fixing his eyes on the dawn of Greek personal lyric, to the Lesbians, Alcaeus and Sappho.

His exultation at mastering their metres found vent in the little Alcaic poem 1, 26, *Musis amicus*; and seven years later, in the Epilogue to *Odes*, I–III, his pride was, that he would be recorded as the first man to have composed Aeolic 'song' to Italian 'music'.* Again, in *Epistles*, I, 19 he boasted of having been the first Latin poet to make Alcaeus known. But he did not merely copy the Lesbians' metres. He observed a number of rules unknown to them: notably, he normalized certain caesuras, and made certain feet, particularly at the beginning of lines, which had allowed of variations before, invariably spondaic.† What led him to do so? In 1868 Wilhelm Christ put forward an explanation which held the field for fifty years.[1] This was based on what is called the 'Derivation-theory' of the origin of lyric verse-forms, traces of which he found in Varro: that they are composed of two limbs or 'cola', and that each colon is derived from a longer metre—is part of a dactylic hexameter, iambic trimeter or trochaic tetrameter. This theory was criticized in an article by P. Maas in 1911,[2] which inspired an entirely new and more satisfactory analysis published by R. Heinze in 1918.[3]‡ Heinze concluded that Horace did not use a handbook or follow any metrical theory. He merely normalized what had been preferences and tendencies in his predecessors as to caesuras and other positions where word-ends fell, and as to long syllables. So far from

* 'princeps Aeolium carmen ad Italos deduxisse modos.' The word *deducere* is regularly used of composing poetry, probably as a metaphor from spinning; and *ad* is the preposition corresponding to our 'to' with a musical accompaniment. The whole phrase is a metaphor—rather an odd one: we should expect him to say, 'compose *Italian* songs to *Aeolic* music' (cf. Prop. III, 1, 4, 'Itala per Graios orgia ferre choros'). It would be forcing the Latin to take *deducere* to mean 'adapt', with Sturtevant (*T.A.P.A.* 1939, p. 296).

Were Horace's odes sung? Poets 'singing' had become a mere conventional cliché by then, as it has remained; otherwise we might assume they were sung, taking various passages at their face value. Most recent scholars have assumed not (for example, O. Seel, *Philologus*, 1959, pp. 250–1); but Lenchantin thinks they were chanted as *recitative*, perhaps with use of the tuning-flute (τονάριον, *tibia contionatoria*—see p. 40), and that the regularization of caesuras may have been in aid of this (*Athenaeum*, 1944–5, pp. 84 ff.). Other recent writers on this side are N. A. Bonavia-Hunt, *Horace the Minstrel* (1954), pp. 10–12; J. Perret, *Horace* (1959), pp. 102–3. Since the *Carmen Saeculare* was sung, there is no *a priori* reason why some others, for example III, 9, *Donec gratus eram tibi*, should not have been. But many, for example those in the form of private letters, seem quite unsuitable for this.

† Exceptions are very few, fewer than has sometimes been assumed. Thus at I, 15, 36, *ignis Iliacas domos*, considerations of style would suggest that *Iliacas* was borrowed by a scribe from *Ilio* above to replace a reading beginning with a consonant which he could not recognize (as the unmetrical *Apuliae* at III, 4, 10 was apparently borrowed from *Apulo* above by a scribe unfamiliar with the name *Pullia*). The most plausible conjecture is that of Jones (1736): the true reading was *barbaricas* (quite natural as = Trojan, cf. Sen. *Tro.* 782), which became by haplography the unmetrical and unintelligible *baricas*. By using *urgent* at l. 23 instead of the more natural *urget* Horace seems to be carefully avoiding the use of a short syllable in the second position (Housman).

‡ The 'Derivation-theory' is still expounded in Hardie's *Res Metrica*, published two years later, p. 244. No doubt wartime conditions precluded his knowing of Heinze's work.

conceiving of his verses as made up of parts of dactylic, iambic and trochaic lines, his guiding principle was to avoid misleading the hearer by
rhythms that might recall such lines. In the case of Sapphics we can
particularly trace the growing tendency, because we have a Hellenistic
specimen in Melinno's five-stanza hymn to Rome, probably dating
from the early second century.[1] From Sappho (and Alcaeus), through
Melinno and Catullus (11 and 51), we can see the movement towards
Horace's norm—the caesura after the fifth (occasionally sixth) syllable,
and the fixing of the fourth syllable as long. Catullus'

$$\text{seu Sacas sag\breve{\i}ttiferosque Parthos}$$

was old-fashioned;

$$\text{sive trans \bar{a}ltas} \parallel \text{gradietur Alpes}$$

was the type of the future.

But this is not a technical treatise: our concern is with literary effects.
Horace may have been merely carrying tendencies to their logical conclusion; but he must also have realized that he was thereby creating
media particularly suited both to the genius of the Latin language and
to his own temperament. Those long syllables imparted strength and
calm dignity, at some sacrifice of flexibility and grace. Ionic, so to speak,
had been converted to Doric. And those regular breaks marked off
blocks of syllables which could be built into monumental wholes. (Instinctively one thinks of Horatian odes in terms of architecture.) But
by whatever process Horace arrived at his norms, it is difficult to believe
that he thought thereafter in terms of *feet*, any more than a musical
composer thinks in bars. Like modern composers in his metres, he
would have at the back of his mind various successions of longs and
shorts, lines, or possibly members in the case of those divided by
caesura, rhythms become instinctive to which his thoughts would
frame themselves.* Discussion of origins and analysis in terms of feet
is thus apt to be irrelevant and pedantic. To take a clear instance, it
would appear that the Greeks thought of the iambic line of their drama
as having been originally a trimeter, the dipody $\unlhd - \cup -$ occurring three
times; but nothing can have been further from the minds of the
classical poets who composed in such lines; the caesura imparted an

---

* F. W. Shipley, prompted by a study of the unfinished lines in the *Aeneid*, makes the same
point as to Virgil's method of composition (*T.A.P.A.* 1938, p. 134).

entirely different and more variable movement, and was probably meant to do so.

Let us now look at Horace's metres individually, taking the Sapphic first, for a reason which will appear.

(ii) *Sapphics*

The first poem of Sappho in our texts begins,

ποικιλόθρον᾽ ἀθάνατ᾽ ᾽Αφρόδιτα,
παῖ Δίος δολόπλοκε, λίσσομαί σε. . . .

Both these lines have a short syllable in the fourth place, and neither has a caesura after the fifth or even the sixth syllable. The third stanza ends with an Adonic (– ∪ ∪ – ⌣) which is not differentiated from the Phalaecian that precedes it, as we see from

πύκνα δίννεντες πτέρ᾽ ἀπ᾽ ὠράνωῖθε-
ρος διὰ μέσσω.

All these traits have almost vanished in Horace.* About half of the 28 lines end in a short syllable, where Horace much preferred a long. Of the seven stanzas three run on into the next without a break in the sentence; whereas of 204 such stanzas in Horace only 62 run on. Clearly the effect of the metre has changed fundamentally.

> Non enim gazae neque consularis
> summovet lictor miseros tumultus
> mentis et curas laqueata circum
>   tecta volantis

('For neither treasures nor the consular lictor can clear away the wretched disturbances of the mind and the cares that flit round coffered ceilings': II, 16, 9–12). The grave, collected, reasonable metre is well suited to gnomic utterances of this kind. The Adonic at the end has a certain finality about it which seems to preclude further argument; it is also useful for underlining a mildly epigrammatic point—'risit Apollo', 'palluit audax'—especially at the end of a poem—'te duce, Caesar', 'ter pede terram';[1] or for tailing off, as with an afterthought, into a 'dying

---

* Exceptions to the fifth-syllable caesura rule will be considered later. The lines (I, 2, 19)

> labitur ripa Iove non probante u-
> xorius amnis

are clearly designed as expressive of the overflowing of the Tiber. Two other exceptions occur, at I, 25, 11; II, 16, 7.

fall'—'dulce loquentem', 'Mercuriusque', 'consule Planco', 'cetera fulvus';[1] or simply for signing off, 'vatis amici', 'vatis Horati'.[2] A couple of these 'tight little stanzas' with the 'curling pig's tail at the end' can well reproduce the neat economy of the two-couplet Greek epigram, as in I, 30 ('O Venus, regina') and III, 22 ('Montium custos'). But although it may seem presumptuous to question Horace's judgement, I cannot feel that Sapphics come off so well in longer poems. No amount of enjambment can prevent the Adonic from reining us in as often as we get going. In I, 12 the stanzas may, as has been suggested, be grouped in triads to recall Pindar's strophic organization; but there is little else that is Pindaric in the *movement* of this poem, with its mechanically contrived lists leading up to Caesar; nor am I carried away by what is clearly intended to be the Pindaric sweep of the single five-stanza sentence early in IV, 2 ('monte decurrens…invidet Orco'). Nor, again, to my feeling, are Sapphics a quite happy medium for recounting myths, as of Hypermnestra in III, 11 and Europa in III, 27. For hymns, however, such as the *Carmen Saeculare*, they are well suited. The clearly marked stanzas and regular rhythm would make them easy to sing to a recurrent tune. Indeed Sapphics have been sung more often than other Horatian metres in modern times; and this brings me to a peculiarity of theirs which was my reason for considering them first.

As explained above, the reason why there was a tendency, normalized by Horace, to have a caesura after the fifth foot and a long syllable in the fourth position was probably a desire to avoid beginning $-\cup-\cup-\cup$, and so suggesting the familiar trochaic rhythm. (Perhaps for the same reason he preferred to begin the lines with a cretic word, for example *Persicos*, rather than a trochaic, for example *mitte*.)[3] But this caesura operated on the accentual Law of the Penultimate to generate a marked accentual rhythm;[4] thus:

> ´   ´   ´   ´
> sperat infestis, metuit secundis
> ´ʹ   ´   ´   `   ´
> alteram sortem bene praeparatum
> ´   ´   ´   ´
> pectus. informis hiemes reducit
> ´   ´
> Iuppiter, idem….

(The fourth syllable from the end of the line sometimes has a word-accent, or secondary accent, sometimes not.)

There is no question that, if the Latin accent was in any degree one of stress, such a rhythm might be perceptible. If proof is needed, we have only to observe what happened in the Dark and Middle Ages, when accent definitely became the basis of metre. In 814, when Louis the Pious visited Orléans, he was received by the Bishop, Theodulph, with a poem in correct quantitative Sapphics:

> En adest Caesar pius et benignus,
> orbe qui toto rutilat coruscus,
> atque prae cunctis bonitate pollet
> munere Christi.

Four years later, when he visited Tours, he was received with another Sapphic poem, written also perhaps by Theodulph and certainly by someone who knew the former one. It begins

> terra marique victor honorande
> Caesar Auguste Hludowice, Christi
> dogmate clarus, decus aevi nostri,
> spes quoque regni....

This is sheer accentual verse, with no regard for quantity.[1] Though discouraged in the classical revivals of the ninth and fifteenth centuries, this 'barbarous' rhythm (as Carducci called it) kept reasserting itself, and was naturalized in the vernacular languages. It was made widely familiar by hymns, such as J. Heermann's

> Herzliebster Jesu, was hast du verbrochen?

of the sixteenth century, and by musical settings such as ours for

> Now God be with us, for the night is closing.

It was even imposed on Horace's Latin itself, as in Flemming's well-known setting (1810) of *Integer vitae*. Indeed to many people the term 'Sapphics' denotes this rhythm, not the original quantitative metre.

But I cannot agree with those who have held that Horace *intended* to introduce it,[2] for the following reasons. First, we have already seen that there is another explanation for his fixing of this caesura, and one which has the advantage of applying to his other metres as well. Then there are little words, monosyllables which are unemphatic and unaccented, which have the effect of throwing the rhythm out of gear; and there are emphatic words which the rhythm leaves hopelessly unemphasized. One need only look at the first Sapphic poem we come to, I, 2. The keyword of the opening is *satis*: with the scansion *Iám satis térris* it is swallowed up. In line 22 the unaccented relative *quo* is made to bear the stress (cf. *quám Iocus* in 34, *quém iuvat* in 38). Line 33 turns, with an emphatic '*tu*', to Venus: *síve tu* is surely impossible. As for the final stanza, it hinges entirely on *hic*, and this too is robbed of its emphasis: *tóllat, hic mágnos*. Horace could never have meant to kill his meaning so. Again, the secondary accent (if those are right who assume one) is made to bear a main stress in lines like 15,

> ire deiectum *mónimenta* regis.

Another important clue is the incidence of caesura at the sixth syllable. This break, fairly common in Catullus, as in

> Ille mi par esse ‖ deo videtur,

occurs only seven times in *Odes*, I–III. Three of these examples occur in I, 10,

> Mercuri, facunde ‖ nepos Atlantis,

which is sufficiently near to its Aeolic model in Alcaeus for us to suppose it to have been one of Horace's earliest experiments. But of the four others two occur in the opening line of a poem (I, 12 and I, 30), just where a poet should be at pains to make clear what metre he intends; and they completely dislocate the accentual rhythm:

> Quém vírum aut heróa* lýra vel ácri...
> O Vénus, regína Cnidi Paphíque....

Further, when Horace came to compose the *Carmen Saeculare* he began with such a caesura,

> Phoébe sìlvarúmque ‖ potens Diána,

and one in three of its 57 lines has one. In the subsequent Book IV there are 22 instances in 105 lines. Why this reversal of trend (which inciden-

---

* Or perhaps 'héroa', as a Greek form (see Servius on Virgil, G. I, 59), or without stress. Even granted that the monosyllables *quem* and *O* in these lines may have weakened the accent on the pyrrhic word that follows them, the accentual metre is hopelessly out of gear.

tally was not followed by subsequent writers in this metre, such as Statius, or Seneca in his dramatic lyrics)?[1] Heinze merely says, 'One must be content with the explanation that Horace's ear changed as to this with the passing of years'.[2] But is it not possible that, having become aware, after the wider publication of the Odes in 23, that his audience were confused by this fortuitous by-product of a stress-metre, he took steps to counteract it, just as he took steps to stop up false trails of dactylic, iambic or trochaic quantitative rhythm? The need to do so would be particularly great in the case of the *Carmen Saeculare*, for the boys and girls could not be expected to find the Lesbian quantitative metre natural, for all the music could do: 'Lesbium servate pedem', he had to remind them. Their instinct would be to chant it with their normal speech accent.

Finally, his fixing of caesuras in the other Lesbian metres created no analogous accentual rhythm, so an explanation which applies only to Sapphics is hardly plausible.*

(iii) *Alcaics*

Horace's Alcaic stanza is a triumph. In spite of the regular lengthening of syllables which had been free in Alcaeus—the first (generally) and the fifth in the first three lines—and of the normalizing of caesura after the fifth, which tended to make it monumental, it could be successfully used for even a three-stanza poem such as I, 26, *Musis amicus*,† which achieves a spirited energy worthy of Alcaeus himself, galvanized by enjambment and by anaphora (*quis...quid, necte...necte, hunc...hunc, teque tuasque*). But it was the lengthening of the syllable in the middle of the third line that really transformed it. There is all the difference in the world between lines like

μέλιχρον, αὐτὰρ ἀμφὶ κόρσαι...

ἀκούσατ', ἐκ δὲ τῶνδε μόχθων...

---

* The same conclusion about Sapphics has been reached (independently, it seems, of my article in *C.R.* 1940, pp. 131–3) by O. Seel and E. Pöhlmann (*Philologus*, 1959, pp. 237–80). I have seen in typescript an attempt to extract an accentual rhythm from Horace's Alcaics, but it required so many licences that what emerged could hardly be recognized as a rhythm at all.

† W. Y. Sellar says, 'Perhaps Horace did not at first find out the true power and function of this metre' (*Horace*, p. 186). But one of the earliest examples is the great Cleopatra ode, I, 37; and his argument implies that the odes of Book I are earlier than those of Books II and III, a view which cannot be substantiated.

and

> clari Gigantéo triumpho...
> dulcem elaborábunt saporem....

This long syllable is the pivot of the stanza. It imparts to more spacious poems in this metre a succession of movements which I have characterized elsewhere as 'the gathering wave of the first two lines, the thundering fall of the third, and the rapid backwash of the fourth';[1] as in

> qui gurges aut quae flumina lugubris
> ignara belli? quod mare Dauniae
> non decolorávere caedes?
> quae caret ora cruore nostro?

Now Horace made certain restrictions in this line.[2] These were:

(1) That there should be no break after the fourth syllable unless it were a monosyllable. The only clear exception is in what seems to be one of the earliest Odes, I, 26:

> hunc Lesbio ‖ sacrare plectro.

(2) That there should be no break before the sixth syllable, unless it were a monosyllable. There are only ten exceptions to this in 317 such lines, one occurring in the same ode:

> gaudes, àpricos ‖ necte flores.

Heinze can give a reason which fits in with his general theory: Horace was anxious to avoid word-ends that would make the line seem to begin with a double iambus ($\smile - \smile -$) or end with a double trochee ($- \smile - \smile$). But has it been noticed that, as a doubtless unintentional result of the operation of the accentual Law of the Penultimate, these restrictions had the effect that in more than two cases out of three* what I have called the pivot-syllable is reinforced by bearing an accent? For they left the field largely to the types

> silvae laborántes geluque...
> deprome quadrímum Sabina...
> appone, nec dúlces amores....

* In 217 cases out of 317, by my reckoning.

III

The establishment of norms enabled special effects to be contrived by abnormalities. Thus in I, 29, 11, one of the ten exceptions mentioned above,

> quis neget arduis
> pronos relabi ‖ posse rivos
> montibus?...

who would deny that downward rivers can flow back up steep mountains?,

the rhythm changes and we feel the river turn from gliding down to mounting up.[1] Only twice does Horace elide a syllable at the end of an Alcaic line.* At II, 3, 25–8,

> omnes eodem cogimur, omnium
> versatur urna serius ocius
> sors exitur(a) et nos in aetern(um)
> exili(um) impositura cymbae,

the synaloephas and the running on of one line into the next help to convey the relentless compulsion of Fate's lottery (as in another Alcaic ode, III, 1, 16, the rare division of the fourth line between five disyllables,

> ′   ′′   ′   ′   ′
> omne capax movet urna nomen,

helps likewise to convey the constant movement of her urn).† And at III, 29, 34–6,

> nunc medio alveo
> cum pace delabentis Etrusc(um)
> in mare,

we feel the uninterrupted flow of the great river into the sea.

Gilbert Murray well characterized the nature of the Alcaic stanza in more abstract terms: quoting as an example

> Eheu fugaces, Postume, Postume,
> labuntur anni, nec pietas moram
> rugis et instanti senectae
> afferet indomitaeque morti,

---

* In the few fragments of Alcaeus we find one elided δέ here and three or four cases of overlap between the third and fourth lines (D. L. Page, *Sappho and Alcaeus*, 1955, p. 323).

† Two other cases: II, 13, 27,

> dura navis
> dura fugae mala, dura belli,

where the impression of regularly recurrent trouble is reinforced; and the compulsive line III, 3, 44,

> Roma ferox dare iura Medis.

he added: 'There is symmetry between 1 and 2, symmetry between 3 and 4; but 4 is the perfect rhythm, smooth and untroubled, at which 3 is an approximation or "attempt", and to which all three verses lead by a kind of progress. The last verse of an Alcaic is extraordinarily delightful in rhythm; but it would be nothing in particular if it were not reached by a struggle—and just the right kind of struggle.'[1]

(iv) *Asclepiads*

Of the Asclepiadic lines in Alcaeus, numbering about 50, nearly all have a break after the sixth (or less frequently the seventh) syllable, as in

> ἦλθες ἐκ περάτων ‖ γᾶς ἐλεφαντίναν...
> κτένναις ἄνδρα μαχάταν ‖ βασιληίων...
> Φίττακον πόλιος ‖ τὰς ἀχόλω καὶ βαρυδαίμονος
> ἐστάσαντο τύραννον ‖ μέγ᾽ ἐπαίνεντες ἀόλλεες.[2]

The first foot can be spondee, trochee or iambus, but a spondee seems to be preferred. In the Greater Asclepiads of Theocritus 28 and 29 there is a break after the sixth or, less than half as often, the seventh syllable, but hardly ever after neither, and two-thirds begin with a spondee.* Catullus 30 is Horace's only Latin predecessor:

> Alfene immemor atque unanimis false sodalibus.

Its twelve lines have no fixed caesuras, but each begins with a spondee. In Horace we find that both the spondaic opening and the caesura after the sixth syllable (as well as another after the tenth in the Greater Asclepiad) are almost binding:[3]

> Maecenas atavis ‖ edite regibus...
> Tu ne quaesieris ‖ (scire nefas) ‖ quem mihi, quem tibi....

Again he is making a rule of what had been a Hellenistic tendency.

The First Asclepiad metre,† consisting of Lesser Asclepiad lines in succession, is used only three times by Horace, on each occasion for a

---

* We do not know how Asclepiades, whom Theocritus admired (7, 40), deserved to have his name attached to this old metre.

† There seems to be no conformity in the numbering of the Asclepiad metres. I have adopted that used by Wickham, since this is a book for English readers (though T. E. Page differs from him). Here is a comparative table:

Wickham	I	II	III	IV	V
Page	I	V	II	III	IV
Klingner	I	V	IV	II	III

poem on his poetic achievement, for the prologue and epilogue to Books I–III, and the central poem of Book IV (8)—suitably, for it can be dignified and proud:

> sublimi feriam sidera vertice...
> exegi monumentum aere perennius...
> dignum laude virum Musa vetat mori...
> *My head will soar to strike the stars...*
> *I have fashioned me a monument more lasting than bronze...*
> *The man worthy of praise the Muse will not let die....*

The Second consists also of lines of one type (κατὰ στίχον), this time the Greater Asclepiad. Its salient feature in Horace is the choriamb (– ∪ ∪ –) in the middle, isolated as it is by the two caesuras he fixed. A succession of three choriambic words well expresses the resistance of rocks to repeated pounding from sea-waves in (I, 11, 5)

> quae nunc *oppositis debilitat pumicibus* mare
> Tyrrhenum.
> *which now makes the Tyrrhene sea spend its force on the barrier of rocks.*

The Third is capable of considerable energy, since the first line is followed by one which has the same beginning but seems to be carried on further by a sudden fresh impetus:

> – – – ∪ ∪– ∪ ∪
> in me tota ruens Venus
> – – –∪ ∪– – ∪∪ – ∪ –
> Cyprum deseruit, nec patitur Scythas
> – –∪ ∪ – ∪ –
> et versis animos(um) equis
> – – –∪ ∪– ∪ ∪ – ∪ –
> Parthum dicere, nec quae nihil attinent.

This is the metre that Horace chose for expressing the excitement of poetic success (IV, 3: *Quem tu, Melpomene, semel*), for Bacchic ecstasy (III, 25: *Quo me, Bacche, rapis tui*), and twice for the abandon of a wild party (I, 36: *Et ture et fidibus iuvat*, and III, 19: *Quantum distet ab Inacho*). The impetus can be increased by anaphora:

> *da* lunae propere novae,
> *da* noctis mediae, *da*, puer, auguris
> Murenae.

The Fourth Asclepiad metre, consisting of three Lesser Asclepiads followed by a Glyconic, is calm and sedate. Horace chose it for his ode

IV, 5 (*Divis orte bonis*) detailing the blessings of Augustus' rule. He counts them on his fingers, as it were, giving one line to each and avoiding the restlessness of enjambment:

> Tutus bos etenim rura perambulat;
> nutrit rura* Ceres almaque Faustitas;
> pacatum volitant per mare navitae;
>   culpari metuit fides;
>
> nullis polluitur casta domus stupris;
> mos et lex maculosum edomuit nefas;
> laudantur simili prole puerperae;
>   culpam poena premit comes.

For in safety the ox treads up and down the fields; Ceres nurtures the fields, and benign Prosperity; over a peaceful ocean the sailors fly; loyalty keeps clear of reproach; no scandal stains the chaste home; custom and law have purged away the taint of guilt; mothers are praised for children's likenesses; punishment treads on the heel of crime.

Only in a metre with practically equal lines could this effect of regularity and orderly peace have been obtained. It is the metre *par excellence* of idyllic rural contentment:

> dicunt in tenero gramine pinguium
> custodes ovium carmina fistula

(IV, 12, 9: 'the watchers of the fat flocks pipe their songs in the soft grass'); and again

> purae rivus aquae silvaque iugerum
> paucorum et segetis certa fides meae

(III, 16, 29: 'a stream of pure water, a wood of a few acres, and the safe promise of my harvest'). It can convey the Horatian precept of moderation in prosperity, as in this last poem (*Inclusam Danaën*), and also of resignation in grief, whether to Tibullus unhappy in love (I, 33: *Albi, ne doleas*) or to Virgil unhappy in bereavement (I, 24: *Quis desiderio*).

The Fifth Asclepiad is also a four-line stanza. It would be interesting to know why Horace decided to transpose into it his variation on Alcaeus' Ship-of-State allegory in Alcaics (I, 14: *O navis*). Perhaps he felt that only so could he escape the pull towards direct reproduction and

---

* This word has almost certainly been borrowed by a scribe from the line above, to replace a word that had become illegible or dropped out.

not tend to be 'desiliens imitator in artum'; for he was going to strike a different attitude, not merely expressing his own predicament like his predecessor, but shouting dramatic warnings to the ship itself:

> O navis, referent in mare te novi
> flatus! O quid agis? fortiter occupa
> portum! nonne vides ut
> nudum remigio latus...*

Ship, new blasts are sweeping you out to sea again! O what are you doing? Strenuously make port. Do you not see how your sides are stripped of oars....

The third line of this stanza, shorter than the others and ending like a dactylic hexameter, can pull it up with an effect of focusing, as in

> Quis multa gracilis te puer in rosa
> perfusus liquidis urget odoribus
> grato, Pyrrha, sub antro?

What slender boy drenched with perfume courts you amid all those roses, Pyrrha, in that pleasant grotto?,

or of coming, almost brusquely, to the point:

> O fons Bandusiae, splendidior vitro,
> dulci digne mero non sine floribus,
> cras donaberis haedo.

Spring of Bandusia, more glittering than glass, worthy of sweet wine and flowers too, tomorrow you shall be presented with a kid;

or more than brusquely:

> Audivere, Lyce, di mea vota, di
> audivere, Lyce; fis anus, et tamen
> vis formosa videri...

Lyce, the gods have heard my prayers, the gods have heard them, Lyce: you are aging, and yet you want to seem beautiful.

The above seven metres account for all but seven of the Odes. Two of the exceptions are in partly iambic metres, and would not have been out of place among the later *Epodes*: I, 4 (*Solvitur acris hiems*) and II, 18 (*Non ebur neque aureum*). Two (I, 7, *Laudabunt alii* and I, 28, *Te maris et terrae*) are in the same dactylic metre—hexameter alternating with

---

* I have printed *flatus* for the MS. *fluctus* to draw attention to Palmer's attractive and easy suggestion (*Hermathena*, 1942, p. 95). It makes better sense, and in Alcaeus it is the winds that are making trouble.

tetrameter—as *Epode* 12. These may be early experiments: so may III, 12 (*Miserarum est*), which is in a strange Ionic rhythm and imitated from Alcaeus.* I, 8 (*Lydia dic per omnes*) is in a metre that has similar potentialities to the Third Asclepiad, the metre of the companion-piece I, 12,

> Cum tu, Lydia, Telephi
> cervicem roseam, cerea Telephi...

which Horace seems to have come to prefer. And finally there is the dactylic metre of the beautiful IV, 7,

> Diffugere nives, redeunt iam gramina campis
> arboribusque comae.

It is reminiscent of elegiac couplets, but less of a canter, permitting the exquisite dying fall of

> vincula Pirithoö.

I have tentatively suggested reasons why Horace may have chosen a particular metre for a particular kind of subject. But there remains the probability that some poems arose out of a spontaneous phrase, a *vers donné*, that came into the poet's mind. Mr Robert Graves has laid down with his usual lucid extremism: 'A poet should not be conscious of the metrical pattern of a poem he is writing until the first three or four lines have appeared; he may even find himself in the eleventh line of fourteen before realizing that a sonnet is on the way.'[1] I cannot believe that Horace often worked like that. But might not, for example, 'carpe diem, quam minimum credula postero', the whole point of what he wanted to say to Leuconoë, have determined that I, 11 should be in Greater Asclepiads, or 'ergo Quintilium perpetuus sopor urget', his natural reaction to the news of his friend's death,† have made some Asclepiad metre inevitable for I, 24? Other possible generating phrases spring to the mind—'O matre pulchra filia pulchrior' (I, 16), 'Parcus deorum cultor et infrequens' (I, 34), 'Cur me querelis exanimas tuis?' (II, 17).

---

* In II, 18 gratitude for the Sabine farm is still dominant. I, 7 recalls *Epode* 13, with the speech at the end. I, 28 is imperfectly constructed. II, 12 is near Alcaeus, and most, if not all, odes that are so seem to be early. (See *Hermes*, 1957, p. 498.)

† Cf. *Sat.* II, 5, 101,

> ergo nunc Dama sodalis
> nusquam est.

'So my mate Dama is gone.'

I have dwelt far longer on Horace than on any other poet hitherto because he is so essentially what Ovid called him, *numerosus*, a master of many rhythms.

V. DACTYLIC VERSE

(a) Restrictive rules

The Latin hexameter, as introduced by Ennius, diverged from the Greek in two important respects. First, as many as 80 per cent of his lines have the 'strong' ('masculine') caesura in the third foot (I will call it '2½' for short), as in

Musae quae pedibus || magnum pulsatis Olympum.

The comparative scarcity in Latin of words with a trochaic ending like the Ionic genitives in -oio is not nearly sufficient cause for such over-whelming proportions.* Further, in nearly all the remaining 20 per cent he has the 'feminine' caesura, common in Greek, at the third trochee (2¾); and in 80 per cent of these cases it accompanies a masculine caesura in *both* the second and fourth feet (1½ and 4½), as in

Postilla || germana || soror || errare videbar.

Secondly, he showed some tendency, beyond the natural proportion of such words in Latin, to end his lines with a word of either two or three syllables.[1]

Already in the verse of Cicero, whom Plutarch credits with being the leading Roman poet of his day,[2] we find that these tendencies have almost become rules. In the more than 700 hexameters we have from him there are about fifty exceptional caesuras and only half a dozen exceptional endings not involving proper names. He is indeed more regular in these respects than Virgil, who introduced exceptions either for variety or for expressive effect.† In fact the Roman hexameter had put itself into a double strait-jacket. Why?

---

* In this section I have made free use of my article 'The Augustan Rules for Dactylic Verse' (*C.Q.* 1940, pp. 30–43), to which I must refer for more detailed discussion. I regret that, owing to the war, I had not then read F. W. Shipley's trenchant article, 'Problems of the Latin Hexameter' (*T.A.P.A.* 1938, pp. 134–60), with which I substantially agree.

† His poems were edited by W. W. Ewbank (1933): metrical analysis, pp. 40–71. Cicero followed the Greeks in requiring an auxiliary caesura after a strong one at 2½, either at 4½ or at 5,

The Roman pentameter eventually hastened, with almost panic acceleration, to put itself into an even more rigid strait-jacket. The statistics for disyllabic words at the end speak for themselves:

	%	Date
Catullus	39	(d. 54 B.C.)
Propertius I	61	c. 29–28
Tibullus I	93	c. 26
Propertius II	86	c. 25
Propertius III	95	c. 22
Tibullus II	92	(d. 19)
Propertius IV	98	? 16
Ovid, *Her.* 1–15	100	?

In fact in the middle twenties it became accepted that this restriction, though it greatly hampered freedom of expression and incidentally led to the closing of couplets, was unquestionably an improvement. (The idea that it was a quirk of *Ovid's* is quite contrary to the facts.)* But why?

These questions, which have been hotly debated for more than a hundred years, are of fundamental importance: they bear on the aesthetic appreciation of the verse; so discussion must not be avoided, though it is bound to be a little technical. To avoid confusion I will here give the explanation, generally known as the Ictus–Accent theory, which I still guardedly accept (though calling it Pulse–Accent for reasons already given). In Appendix I I deal with other explanations that have been advanced, and with detailed criticisms of this theory. It will there be seen that there is nothing like a single coherent and widely supported theory to set against it. Poets of the calibre of Virgil, Propertius, Tibullus and Ovid did not tie themselves up for no good reason at all. It is not enough for us, whose knowledge of Latin is so imperfect, to say with Meyer, 'Who could maintain that these rules were not mad?'[1]

and also in avoiding a break at the fourth trochee (only two exceptions), whereas Virgil has plenty of lines like

ipse manu quatiens ostendit || ab aethere nubem.

Winbolt gives the percentages of abnormal endings as: Ennius, 14, Lucretius I, 8½; Cicero, *Aratea*, 2½; Catullus, 2 (excluding 'hymenaeus'); Virgil, 3 (*Hexameter*, 1903, p. 127).

* F. Plessis abused poor Ovid (a boy of 17 in 26–25 B.C.) for his bad influence on Propertius! (*Le pentamètre dactylique*, 1885, p. 64). The misconception is still propagated by L. Nougaret, *Traité de métrique* (1948), section 146.

(b) The Pulse–Accent theory

(i) General statement

'I cannot help suspecting', says Mr T. S. Eliot, 'that to the cultivated audience of the age of Virgil part of the pleasure of the poetry arose from the presence in it of two metrical schemes in a kind of counterpoint, even though the audience may not have been able to analyse the experience.'[1] 'Scheme' is going much too far; but since we can hardly suspect him of 'acting innocent', we must assume that the Past President of the Virgil Society has been above the battle that has raged since Gottfried Hermann fired the first shot about the time of the Battle of Waterloo. This is therefore valuable testimony from a highly sensitive poet, that he feels in Virgil's rhythm something more subtly blended than the *dum-di-di-dum* of longs and shorts: Ritschl spoke of 'the secrets of the *Harmonious-Disharmony* of verse and word accent, on which the charm of ancient, and particularly Roman, versification so essentially depends.... The dactylic hexameter passes from clash of verse and word accent in the first part into the resolution of the conflict in the second.'* This appreciation is the more remarkable as coming from a German; for the classical metres introduced by Opitz and Klopstock into the German language and now well acclimatized have coincidence of pulse and accent throughout. Anglo-American readers have welcomed the theory because it finds in Latin poetry an element corresponding to one that is important in their own. As I have said, this does not put them out of court for prejudice: on the contrary, it gives them what every exponent of a metrical theory should have, a justification in terms of aesthetic principles.

Briefly stated, the Pulse–Accent theory is as follows: The differences between Greek and Roman practice in hexameters, already marked in Ennius and canonized before the Augustan age, when the pentameter also was regularized, are due to the most tangible prosodic difference between the languages, that of accentuation. To have operated in this way the accent must (unlike the Greek one at this period) have included

* G. Hermann, *Elementa Doctrinae Metricae* (1817), p. 217. F. Ritschl, *Opuscula* (1868), vol. II, Introd. p. xii. Hermann was developing the remarks of Bentley, *Schediasma* prefixed to his edition of Terence (1726), p. xvii. I do not know what ancient versification other than Latin dactylic Ritschl had in mind.

at least an appreciable element of stress, as many other indications would suggest. The Romans felt (as was especially natural when quantitative verse was a novelty to them) the ubiquitous desire that the basis of a verse should emerge clearly at the end. There should be a dactyl in the penultimate foot, no heavy elisions to blur the cadence, and no conflict of pulse and accent in the last two feet. But to avoid monotony they favoured caesuras likely to make conflict of pulse and accent balance or predominate in the first four feet.* Again this is in accord with an aesthetic principle.†

(ii) *Illustrations*

Let us have some illustrations, using the signs (.) for pulse, (′) for accent, (ˋ) for secondary accent,[1] (ˣ) for cases when accent or secondary accent does not coincide with pulse. (Lines with a monosyllable or synaloepha will be avoided for the moment, as conceivably involving doubt in some cases.)

(α) *Hexameter caesuras*

Caesura at 2½

Feet 1–4	Coinc.	Confl.
diva sol‖o fix‖os ‖ ocul‖os a‖versa tenebat	I	3
corpora ‖ nator‖um ‖ serp‖ens am‖plexus uterque	I	2
perfus‖us sani‖e ‖ vitt‖as atr‖oque veneno	O	3
diripi‖entque rat‖es ‖ ali‖i nav‖alibus. Ite	2 (1½)	2

Clearly this caesura produces more conflict than coincidence in the first four feet; hence its predominance in the Latin hexameter.

---

* E. H. Sturtevant, apparently unaware of such a principle, thought that the Romans 'made a virtue of necessity...in order to give their poetry the air of aloofness from common speech which was traditional in heroic verse' (*T.A.P.A.* 1923, p. 52; he gives elaborate statistics, pp. 57–63). T. O. J. Rönström, *Metri Vergiliani Recensio* (1892), p. 16, and J. Vendryes, *L'intensité initiale* (1902), p. 93, imagined that the predominance of conflict in the first four feet was an argument *against* the Pulse–Accent theory; so, apparently, does A. D. Leeman (reviewing Beare): *Mnemosyne* (1958), p. 181. But see now R. G. Tanner, *C.Q.* 1961, p. 223.

† Conflict emerging in harmony is a principle, for instance, of Elizabethan madrigal. Cf. Gilbert Murray on the Alcaic stanza (p. 113 above); J. B. Trend on Spanish poetry (*Rubén Darío* p. 23).

Caesura at 1½ *and* 4½

	Feet 1-4	Coinc.	Confl.

infánd|um, ‖ reg|ína iúb|es ‖ renóv|are dolorem   1   2

cúncta vír|i ‖ monu|ménta iúvat ‖ monstr|átque sacerdos   2   2

íamque vál|e; ‖ féror | ingént|i ‖ cír|cumdata nocte   1   3

Here again the Roman rule ensures more conflict than coincidence in the first four feet. But take away either of these caesuras, and you get lines in which coincidence predominates there, like

> mérsa|tur míss|úsque séc|úndo | defluit amni,

> lília | vérben|ásque prém|ens vésc|umque papaver.

Take away both, and you get full coincidence, as in

> dígnum | ménte dóm|óque lég|éntis hón|esta Neronis,

> témpora | cúnctant|íque nát|ántia | lumina solvit.

(β) *Hexameter endings*

> sídera | tóllit

> árma re|quírunt

> prae|séntia | dóna

> labe|fácta cad|ébant

Here coincidence is complete. But in the following it is not:

> equít|es trepíd|ábant

> lúc|et vía | lóngo.

Such endings were therefore practically excluded. (If you read *Odyssey*, I, 444 lines, with Latin accent, you get 63 conflicts with pulse in the fifth foot. In the whole of Virgil there are only 57 indisputable cases.)[1]

(γ) *Pentameter endings*[1]

These went unrestricted long after the hexameter endings were restricted. Catullus' percentage of disyllabic endings (39) is no greater, in all probability, than the relative frequency of such words in Latin would occasion. Since monosyllables were practically excluded, and hardly any other Latin words had an accent on the last syllable, it was inevitable that there should be a conflict at the end. The first four pentameters of Propertius' first elegy display four different forms:

$$\text{ante cup|idinib|us}$$

$$\text{pressit Am|or pedib|us}$$

$$\text{vivere | consili|o}$$

$$\text{cogor hab|ere de|os}$$

It will be seen that in the first two conflict predominates, in the third it is equal to coincidence, in the fourth alone, with its disyllabic end-word, coincidence predominates. Three years later hardly any pentameter was being written without a disyllable at the end.*

These facts are not disputed, nor are they seriously affected by the complications which monosyllables occasion or by synaloephas. 'All the great masters', said Munro, 'have with fine tact, the reasons for which we can feel if we cannot explain, given to the end this free open fall in opposition to the involution of rhythm which the caesura occasions in the middle of the verse.'[2] But the Pulse–Accent theory does explain most of the phenomena. It is not necessary to suppose that the preferences of Ennius, startling though they are, were dictated by conscious theory. Cicero, on the other hand, may have known why he subjected himself to strict rules about which Lucretius, passionately pressing his meaning into verse, did not bother so much. The opponents of the theory say that the accentual effects were a chance by-product,

---

* It is surely easier to suppose that the elegists were trying to treat the pentameter in a way analogous to the hexameter, not that they were *seeking* conflict at the end ('der Widerstreit also gesucht'—Wilamowitz, *Griechische Verskunst*, 1921, p. 5).

without value or significance, of rules introduced for other reasons. We see (in Appendix 1) how incoherent, and how weak for the most part, those alleged reasons are. And if it is a virtue 'rendre la chute des vers plus coulante', or 'that the flow of the rhythm should not be stemmed towards the end', then it should have been worth while to enhance this effect by avoiding conflict with accent, if accent is perceptible at all, in that area. Once Beare's thesis that ictus (pulse) is not a series of hammer-strokes, not something heard or seen, is accepted, much of his own case against the theory disappears.

(iii) *Further evidence for the Pulse–Accent theory*

Shipley has drawn attention to the possibly relevant fact, that the often uneducated writers of epitaphs, etc., collected in the *Carmina Latina Epigraphica* of Buecheler and Lommatsch are apt to write hexameters which have too many or too few syllables, and in fact are all at sea with the metre *except in the last two feet*, which are regular either quantitatively or accentually or both. The only plausible explanation of the distinction is that they read accentually, and did not understand the quantitative metre except where it coincided with accent.[1] And C. H. Moore adduced a papyrus published in 1912, dating from the fifth century A.D., which contains a few lines of *Aeneid*, IV (66–8, 99–102), as prepared apparently by a schoolmaster in Egypt for teaching Greek-speaking boys how to read Latin verse. What had to be marked was the *word-accents*, with (′), or (‾) in some cases when the vowel was long; for example,

quin] potius pacem aeternam pactosque hymenaeos
exerce]mus habes tota quot mente pe[tisti. ...

It is true that some Romans themselves were beginning to lose their grasp of quantitative metre at this time, but if pupils had been meant to read with emphasis on pulse, surely the schoolmaster would have marked the lines accordingly.[2] By the end of antiquity some were actually composing hexameters based on observation of where speech-accent had fallen in typical cases and not on quantity or pulse.*

* D. Norberg, *Versification latine médiévale* (1958), pp. 101–3, 106. He gives reasons for rejecting the idea that in the Middle Ages verses were read according to ictus rather than the ordinary word-accent (*Acta Conventus Romani*, 1959, p. 107).

(iv) *Expressive effects*

Conflict and coincidence give scope for effects of restraint, or struggle and release. The most elaborate study of this has been Mr W. F. Jackson Knight's *Accentual Symmetry in Virgil* (1939), of which more will be said later. Here it may be legitimate to cite in evidence a few cases in which accentual purpose might be acknowledged as such by a fair number of those who believe in its possibility.

Features which recur in similar contexts are best fitted to repel the charge of subjectivity. Norden, as we have seen (p. 68 n.), found spondees associated with repose, in Greek especially: 'dagegen' (no further comment) there were lines with feminine ($2\frac{3}{4}$) caesura which have similar associations, and these were strikingly dactylic:

spargens umida mella soporiferumque papaver   A. IV, 486

sprinkling liquid honey and soporific poppy-seed,

(tempora) cunctantique natantia lumina solvit   A. V, 856

and makes his swimming eyes relax their struggles,

(luna premit) suadentque cadentia sidera somnos   A. IV, 81

and the setting stars invite to sleep.

Though Norden is in favour of the Pulse–Accent theory, he explains the appropriateness of these rhythms as due to the weak caesura in the third foot, suggesting the *weakness* of slumber. Surely it is rather the almost complete absence of accent–pulse conflict (*facilitated* by this caesura), as shown by the accents I have added, that makes the lines so effortless and drowsy.[1] We may add two lines about sleep quoted by him previously[2] as obtaining the same effect from weak caesura in the fourth foot:

quam sedem somnia vulgo

vana tenere ferunt foliisque sub omnibus haerent   A. VI, 285

place where empty dreams dwell, they say, and cleave under all the leaves

and

dulcis et alta quies placidaeque simillima mortis.   A. VI, 523

pleasant and deep repose most like to peaceful death.

Here, then, are five separate lines on sleep, all with the 'released' movement imparted by coincidence in the fourth foot.

In a released movement the Simoïs sweeps away the debris of war,

> scuta virum galeasque et fortia corpora volvit; *A.* I, 101

in a released movement the stream sweeps down the ram that has been dipped:

> mersatur missusque secundo defluit amni. G. III, 447

Complete absence of accentual clash surely accounts, at least in part, for the expressive effect of Ennius' line (*Ann.* 478):

> labitur uncta carina per aequora cana celocis
>
> *the cutter's greased keel glides through the whitening water.*

On the other hand conflicting accent, falling successively on three *e*-sounds, helps to suggest buffeting gusts of wind at the end of Virgil's highly expressive description of a storm (see p. 80):

> nunc nemora ingenti vento nunc litora plangunt
>
> *now the woods, now the shores, howl with the huge blast;*

or indignant rejection where Sinon describes how the Greeks condemned Palamedes,

> insontem infando indicio, quia bella vetabat *A.* II, 84
>
> *innocent, on an unspeakable charge, because he opposed war;*

or shipwrecked men breaking the smooth surface of the sea dispersedly, in

> apparent rari nantes in gurgite summo *A.* I, 118
>
> *here and there appear men swimming on the surface of the deep.*

(v) *Summing up*

Let me try to sum up fairly as between the theory propounded above and the explanations and criticisms dealt with in Appendix I.

Against the Pulse–Accent theory

(1) The ancient writers speak of the accent in classical Latin in terms suggesting that it was one of pitch.

(2) There is little evidence that accent played much part in lyric verse, or in prose (though this is strongly disputed); and as to saturnians, trochaic septenarii and dramatic verse, its influence has been somewhat belittled of late.

(3) Some of the detailed phenomena are unexplained, or could be otherwise explained.

In favour of the Pulse–Accent theory

(1) The linguistic development of Latin suggests the operation of an accent which was appreciably one of stress.

(2) The Pulse–Accent theory explains the main divergences of Latin from Greek practice in dactylic verse as to caesuras, hexameter endings and pentameter endings. There is no other theory that does, or even attempts, all of these things together.

(3) The theory is consonant with aesthetic principles, observable in other spheres, and reveals telling effects in practice.

(4) To most of the questions on detailed phenomena it has at least some answer.

The balance seems to be distinctly on the side of the theory at present. Let me cite one witness who is not English or American, the great authority on prose rhythm and on Virgil, Eduard Norden: 'Until another satisfactory reason is found, I cannot help assuming (*pace* W. Meyer, with whom one is loth to disagree), that the avoidance of a separation of word and verse accent in cases like *pellit vada remis, supero dedit ore*, played a role, if perhaps only a secondary one.'[1] I should put it more strongly than that.

(c) Hexameter rhythm

Once the Pulse–Accent theory is accepted, subtleties of every kind can be perceived or fancied, in Virgil especially.[2] Mr Jackson Knight, borrowing a metaphor from radio, calls feet with conflict 'heterodyne', feet with coincidence 'homodyne'.[3] Occasionally he resorts to special pleading. When Neptune puts his head out of the water (*A.* 1, 127),

prospiciens summa placidum caput extulit unda

reared his calm head on the surface and looked forth,

he comments: 'Calmness is here rendered with heterodyne....The application of reluctance to render calm might be called indirect. The opposition in it is opposition to any interference, however hypothetical. The main point is speed. The heterodyne enables metrical means to reduce the speed of a passage, and so help the impression of calm....'[1] Surely calm is best rendered by *absence* of conflict, as in

> dulcis et alta quies placidaeque simillima mortis
> *pleasant and deep repose most like to quiet death.*

We must rather admit that in the line in question the rhythm does *not* support the meaning—unless it emphasizes a contrast with the surrounding waves.

Again, he rightly considers fourth feet particularly important in this respect, and he examines the *Aeneid* to see how the lines are disposed in respect of heterodyne and homodyne. In II, 402–15 he discovers: 'That is *b a b b b b a . a b b b b a b*—symmetrical about the full stop in the middle.' But leaving aside the fact that he chooses to end his sample where editors print a semi-colon, not a full stop, can we believe that Virgil's ear, even subconsciously, was yearning for such elaborate symmetry? If you analyse any poem of nearly 10,000 lines, will you not find some such patterns thrown up by chance? *Georgics*, II, 184–99 produce an even longer one, *b bababa a a ababab b*.[2] Accentual patterns related to meaning are vital. Short ones may even be pleasing in themselves. But long ones, though they may be symptomatic of a feeling after variety, can more easily be set out as such on the page than taken in by the ear. They exceed the 'psychische Presenszeit', and are probably fortuitous.

And yet, as in the case of sound-values (see p. 53), I believe that Mr Knight is courageously exploring territory that is important, even though he goes to lengths that invite counter-attack. There is indeed struggle and release in the rhythm, as in the sense, at Dido's death:

> omnis et una
> dilapsus calor, atque in ventos vita recessit.   *A.* IV, 705
> *and therewith all warmth went out of her, and her life departed to the winds.*

There is impetus in the rhythm of her famous outburst 'Dissimulare etiam...', in which eight of the first nine lines are homodyne in the fourth foot (*A.* IV, 303–13).* It is also true that Virgil, unlike his predecessors, tends to reserve lines with a strong, spondaic, homodyne fourth foot to round off periods, such as

Albanique patres atque altae moenia Romae,

especially favouring a monumental molossus-word (– – –) after the strong caesura:

tantae molis erat Romanam condere gentem.

This noble rhythm had been wasted in cloying excess by Cicero. Of the first nineteen lines of his *De Consulatu Suo* II, no fewer than ten have a molossus (*flammatus, conlustrat,* etc.) following a strong caesura. Catullus' *Peleus and Thetis* begins

Peliaco quondam *prognatae* vertice pinus
dicuntur liquidas *Neptuni* nasse per undas
Phasidos ad fluctus *et fines* Aeeteos,
cum lecti iuvenes, *Argivae* robora pubis....

Of the first 21 lines 12 have a molossus (or molossic combination) after a strong caesura; and five of the remaining nine have homodyne fourth foot (the proportion in the whole poem being over 61 per cent as against 36 per cent in the *Aeneid*).† Indeed no fewer than 146 out of the 408 lines have a molossian word in this position.‡ The rhythmic monotony is intolerable. In a later passage he has six lines (171–6) that fall naturally into three couplets, and in each the second line turns on the same sort of word:

Iuppiter omnipotens, utinam ne tempore primo
Gnosia Cecropiae *tetigissent* litora puppes,
indomito nec dira ferens stipendia tauro

* W. F. J. Knight, *Accentual Symmetry*, pp. 83, 46. Miss A. Woodward finds expressive effect in many cases where the fourth foot is an accented dactyl (*Phil. Qu.* 1936, p. 135).

† W. F. J. Knight, *ibid.* pp. 38–9. Sturtevant misstates what happened when he says 'Catullus tried with considerable success to extend the rule of harmony to the fourth foot, but this made the composition of the hexameter so difficult that other poets did not follow him' (*T.A.P.A.* 1923, p. 70). On the contrary, the latter went out of their way to avoid it except for special effect (see p. 70 above).

‡ In Horace's early sixteenth *Epode* seven of the last eight hexameters have a heavy verb in the middle—*circumgemit, mirabimur, urantur, contendit, torserunt, secrevit, duravit.* R. Lucot, surveying the verse of word-typology *dactyl, molossus, molossus, dactyl, spondee,* for example

levia substernens robusto bracchia collo,

finds it 'depourvu d'élan' (*Pallas,* Toulouse, 1955, pp. 29–39).

perfidus in Creta *religasset* navita funem,
nec malus hic celans dulci crudelia forma
consilia, in nostris *requiesset* sedibus hospes!

That is not Virgil's way. But we must not encroach here on structure, the subject of Part III.

A generation before Catullus all was clumsy. Look at what Lutatius Catulus made of a graceful epigram by Callimachus:

Aufugit mi animus; credo, ut solet, ad Theotimum
devenit. Sic est, perfugium illud habet.
quid, si non interdixem, ne illunc fugitivum
mitteret ad se intro sed magis eiceret?
ibimus quaesitum. verum ne ipsi teneamur
formido. quid ago? da, Venus, consilium.[1]

The hexameters here are as crude as the pentameters. Why was it that Catullus in his elegiacs achieved hexameters individually no less strict and mature than Virgil's, yet in his pentameters could tolerate (and often for no apparent expressive effect) such uncouth rhythms as

aut facere, haec a te dictaque factaque sunt.	76, 8
Corneli, et factum me esse puta Arpocratem.	102, 4
nuptarum laus ex laudibus eximiis.	111, 2
fertur, qui tot res in se habet egregias?	114, 2

I suspect the reason was simply this. The adaptation of Greek metres to Latin by means of special prohibitions was a much more formidable problem than we realize, familiar as we are with the finished Augustan product and with its rules which enable many a diligent schoolboy to be metrically polished. (A schoolboy likewise can learn instinctively to avoid breaking Porson's law, which Porson himself had broken three times in seventeen lines as winning candidate for the Craven Scholarship.)[2] The hexameter, however, came to Catullus with an advantage the pentameter had not: it had passed through the hands of a genius in the manipulation of words and rhythms, 'disertissimus Romuli nepotum', Marcus Tullius Cicero. It is not always realized that, apart from the neoteric mannerism of the *spondeiazon*, the norms of Catullus' hexameter differ little from the Ciceronian.*

---

* See p. 118 n. In the *Peleus and Thetis* there are 30 *spondeiazontes*, but none of these occurs between lines 120 and 250, though we find three in the next 14 lines (arrival of Bacchus). This may have some bearing on the order of composition.

With Virgil hexameter verse achieved its maximum of effectiveness both in variety without undue licence and in adaptability to subject-matter. To say that Ovid was 'a more polished and skillful versifier' (presumably because he used less elision and adhered more strictly to rules) is to misconceive.[1] His boyhood at Rome had seen the elegiac couplet transformed, by Tibullus in particular, into something smooth, neat and self-contained, in which blurring elisions were inappropriate; and the *Metamorphoses* is the work of one habituated to the movement of this elegy. Unlike the *Georgics* and *Aeneid*, it does not pursue expressiveness as a major virtue: it concentrates on speed—'always on the hand-gallop', as Dryden put it. 'A reader or hearer is not coaxed into reflection or any mature comparison between one passage or personality and another.'* So in general it prefers dactyls to spondees, elisions are fewer and easier,† and coincidence of ictus and accent (according to Mr Knight) is comparatively high. In general Ovid may have been right: his fantastic stories could only bear the lightest touch. Yet, on the rare occasions when we can make anything like a direct comparison between him and Virgil, we see at once what he sacrificed. Here is the opening of the story of Orpheus in the Underworld as told by Virgil in the *Georgics* (IV, 463–9):

> Ipse, cava solans aegrum testudine amorem
> te, dulcis coniunx, te solo in litore secum
> te veniente die, te decedente canebat.
> Taenarias etiam fauces, alta ostia Ditis
> et caligantem nigra formidine lucum
> ingressus Manesque adiit regemque tremendum
> nesciaque humanis precibus mansuescere corda.

And now Ovid in the *Metamorphoses* (x, 11–16):

> quam satis ad superas postquam Rhodopeïus auras
> deflevit vates, ne non temptaret et umbras,
> ad Styga Taenaria est ausus descendere porta,
> perque leves populos simulacraque functa sepulcro
> Persephonen adiit inamoenaque regna tenentem
> umbrarum dominum.

* So Mr W. F. J. Knight, who says the most that can be said for Ovidian expressiveness: 'Ovid's Metre and Rhythm', in *Ovidiana* (1938), pp. 110–12.

† 54·6 per cent of dactyls in the first four feet, to Virgil's 44·1 in the *Aeneid*; 15·6 elisions per 100 hexameters, to Virgil's 50·5. (R. B. Steele, *Ph. Qu.* 1926, pp. 212 ff.; A. G. Lee, *Metamorphoses* I (1953), 31–6; A. Siedow, *De elisionis usu in hexametris Latinis*, 1911, p. 55.)

9-2

The 7 lines of Virgil contain 15 dactyls and 5 elisions; whereas the 5½ lines of Ovid have 19 dactyls and no elisions beyond the negligible 'Taenaria 'st'. Virgil is concerned to create atmosphere by his rhythm, Ovid to get on with the story.

The movement of hexameter verse can be thrilling as a gallop or stately as a procession. So it seemed to Virgil. At the end of the Second *Georgic* he breaks off with,

> sed nos immensum spatiis confecimus aequor,
> et iam tempus equum fumantia solvere colla

But we have traversed an immense terrain in our course, and now it is time to unyoke the reeking necks of our horses.*

In the proem of the next book he develops this symbolism. He is fore-telling the national epic he hopes to write, in the guise of chief partici-pant and organizer of triumphal games.

> in medio mihi Caesar erit templumque tenebit.
> illi victor ego et Tyrio conspectus in ostro
> centum quadriiugos agitabo ad flumina currus.

In the midst I will have Caesar possessing the temple. In his honour, resplendent in Tyrian crimson, I will drive a hundred four-horsed chariots in triumph by the river.

The scene changes:

> ipse caput tonsae foliis ornatus olivae
> dona feram, iam nunc sollemnes ducere pompas
> ad delubra deum caesosque videre iuvencos...

I myself, my brow adorned with a wreath of olive-leaves, will bring gifts. It is my joy right now to lead solemn processions to the shrines and see the sacrifice of bullocks.

In any competition for '*stateliest* measure ever moulded by the lips of man' I should be inclined to put the French Alexandrine first (among those I know). But it has not the variety of the Virgilian hexameter: it cannot gallop.

---

* So Gray conceived of Dryden's chariot as borne over the fields of glory by
> Two coursers of ethereal race
> With necks in thunder cloth'd and loud-resounding pace

(*The Progress of Poesy*, stanza III, 2). Some Latinless children, hearing a passage of Virgil read aloud, guessed the subject to be a cavalry charge (E. A. G. Lamborn, *Rudiments*, 1916, p. 20).

(d) Elegiac rhythm

In hexameters there are (barring *spondeiazontes*) sixteen possible permutations of dactyls and spondees: in pentameters there are only four, since the principle that the basic rhythm (here the dactylic) should assert itself towards the end of the line stereotyped the latter half before the dawn of extant literature. Again, while the epic hexameter can have several combinations of caesura, the pentameter invariably has a strong caesura exactly in the middle. This was probably due originally to the exigencies of singing to a fixed tune. For even such hexameters as we find in Greek *lyric* poets—Sappho, Alcman and tragic choruses—are far more stereotyped than Homer's. They have only one caesura, nearly always in the third foot.[1] Moreover they are far more purely dactylic than Homer's. And the elegiac lines sung by the heroine in Euripides' *Andromache* (103–16) have all these features: their seven hexameters contain only three spondees, and they all have a strong caesura in the third foot. It has been concluded that epic was only intoned or chanted, whereas 'the lyrical hexameter was hampered by stricter rules because it was sung to a fixed tune'.[2] Elegy too was originally sung, to flute accompaniment and no doubt to a fixed tune, and it always retained habits derived from that fact.

Now the sophisticated sensibility of Augustan poets perceived that there was a fundamental hereditary difference of rhythmic potentiality between epic hexameters and elegiac couplets. The latter were severely restricted. Thus it came about that while Virgil was exploiting the variety of hexameters, the elegists turned to making a virtue of their medium's confinement. There was in any case a tendency for Augustan poets to tolerate fewer licences and irregularities in versification than the Greeks.[3] The elegists decided to make their metre even more regular than it was bound to be,* and to concentrate on neatness and lightness. The heavy elisions of Catullus were purged away: there should be few

* It is well known that Tibullus and Ovid (as distinct from Propertius) generally avoided, except for rhetorical effect, having a first half of pentameter dactylic with iambic end-word, such as could equally well be the second half. Sometimes a metrical restriction can be explained by desire not to mislead the ear by prematurely introducing what might be a close: but this explanation could hardly meet such an extreme case of fastidiousness, which remains a puzzle. Propertius' rhythms also tend to be heavier. His pentameters begin more often with two spondees than with two dactyls.

elisions at all, none at the caesura, and only the lightest, or better none, in the second half of the pentameter. The *spondeiazon* hexameter was eliminated,* no doubt because a spondee in the fifth foot slowed up the line so much as to impair the identity of the couplet. The hexameter became more dactylic.[1] And finally, the adoption of the disyllable-rule imparted to the end of all pentameters a rhythm not only less varied, but more marked through accentual reinforcement.

This last step had a further and far-reaching consequence: it marked off the couplets from one another in rhythm until the natural and logical thing was to make them self-contained in sense. (Rhyme exercised a similar influence in 'closing' the English heroic couplet, abetted by the study of Ovidian elegiacs, the potential effect of which is clearly discernible from Marlowe's line-for-line translation of the *Amores*.)[2] So elegy acquired increasingly a regular, undulating movement; as Ovid said:

> sex mihi *surgat* opus numeris, in quinque *residat*
> *Let my work rise in six feet and sink back in five.*[3]

Sometimes it may suggest to us, as to Schiller, a fountain that perpetually leaps up and falls back again, sometimes the flow and ebb of waves on the seashore, or of dancers.[4] But here again Propertius is exceptional: his pentameter often develops a climax or a new thought, and his couplets are less often self-contained.

---

* Catullus has ten, Tibullus none, Ovid only six in his vast corpus.

5

PROSE RHYTHM

(a) The legacy of Aristotle

The subject of classical prose rhythm was much discussed by Renaissance scholars, but it is only with Strabaeus in 1529 that we get a reasonably accurate account even of Ciceronian clausulae. Then from early in the seventeenth century to late in the nineteenth we hear little more of the subject, and what had been known became strangely forgotten.[1] Interest began to revive only about 1880. It received its greatest impulse from Zieliński (1904), and had more or less worked itself out, after immense labours largely misguided and leading to disputed conclusions, by 1929. In that year F. Novotný made a valuable report on the situation as to Latin prose rhythm (on which attention had mainly concentrated), distinguished for its courtesy and objectivity, especially as he was a partisan.[2]

The term 'rhythm', said to be used in some fifty different senses, must not be applied to prose without some definition. A. W. de Groot, whose works on the subject[3] are, it seems to me, the most scientific in method if also the most polemical, distinguishes under it:

(1) Metric—the arrangement of long and short syllables;

(2) Periodic—the arrangement of similar, sometimes corresponsive, parts of a sentence into a rhythmic whole, the 'period'.[4]

He uses 'rhythm' in the widest sense, that in which it can be applied even to the visual arts. In one work he says expansively: 'There is a rhythm of thoughts, and a rhythm in agreement between thought and language. This rhythm consists in a harmony which is generally recognizable only by means of intuition, and which cannot be grasped by statistics.'[5] I propose, however, to use the term only in the sense of 'metric', more usual in English at least, which brings it within this Part of my book: 'periodic' belongs to the next Part, and specimen

135

passages will generally be reserved for inclusion there, when periods can be surveyed in both aspects.

Indeed the connection between the two seems to me a historical accident:* both were introduced together at the time when prose was becoming consciously artistic, apparently by Thrasymachus (the fifth-century Sophist who in Plato's *Republic* maintains that justice is the interest of the stronger).[1] They are dealt with respectively in two consecutive chapters in Aristotle's *Rhetoric*, III, 8 and 9, which are the fountain-head of most subsequent discussion in antiquity. For Aristotle they have this in common: each introduces an element of ἀριθμός, of measure; and it is this element that redeems periodic prose from the discomfort always caused by the unlimited or formless, the ἀπέραντον.[2] Before going further with rhythm ('metric') I must quote the essential parts of chapter 8, using Jebb's translation.

The form of our composition should be neither metrical (ἔμμετρον), nor devoid of rhythm (ἄρρυθμον); the first is not persuasive, for it has an artificial air, and at the same time distracts the attention, for it makes us look for recurrence†. . . . On the other hand, that which has *no* rhythm is the illimitable (ἀπέραντον); and a limit we must have, but not a *metrical* limit (μὴ μέτρῳ); for the infinite, being beyond our grasp, is unpleasing.‡ It is number (ἀριθμῷ) which gives definiteness to all things; and that number which belongs to the form of composition is rhythm (ῥυθμός), of which metres (τὰ μέτρα) are sections.§ Prose must therefore have rhythm, but not metre—for then it will be poetry. The rhythm, however, must not be precise (μὴ ἀκριβῶς), and the precision will be avoided if it is carried only to a certain point (μέχρι του).

Aristotle then proceeds to consider various types of rhythm, in terms based on feet and borrowed from poetry.

One kind of rhythm is the heroic (= dactylic); this is grand, and remote from the measure (ἁρμονία) of common conversation.¶ The iambic, on the other

---

* Thus the symmetry characteristic of 'periodic' is found without 'metric' in early Latin prose. (Cic. *De Or.* III, 198; L. R. Palmer, *The Latin Language* (1954), pp. 132–3.)

† Here he agrees with, and perhaps follows, Isocrates, *Tech.* fr. 6 B.B.: ὅλως δὲ ὁ λόγος μὴ λόγος ἔστω· ξηρὸν γάρ· μηδὲ ἔμμετρος· καταφανὲς γάρ. But Isocrates adds: 'But let it be a mixture of all rhythms, especially iambic or trochaic'; which Aristotle would not accept.

‡ A basic Pythagorean–Platonic idea.

§ This seems a questionable definition, though not made haphazardly, since it occurs also at *Poetics*, IV, 7. If rhythm is not a precise, but only a general, loose conception (μέχρι του), sections of it will not necessarily be metres, which obey laws. Some of the confusion in later theory may arise from this aside of Aristotle's.

¶ That is, *too* grand. Cicero renders 'grandior' (*Or.* 192), Quintilian, 'amplior' (IX, 4, 88).

hand, is the very cadence of common talk; hence men use iambics in conversation more than any other kind of metre. But we must be impressive;* we must carry our hearers away. The trochee, again, is too much akin to the comic dance—as appears in the tetrameter, which has a tripping rhythm. There remains the paeon,† which rhetoricians began to use at the time of Thrasymachus, though without being able to say what it was....

The other rhythms, then, must be dismissed, for the reasons just given, as well as because they are metrical (μετρικοί); the paeon must be adopted, since it is the only one of the rhythms above-mentioned which does not constitute metre, and so it attracts least notice (λανθάνειν). At present the same form of paeon is used both at the beginning and the end of sentences; but the end ought to be distinguished from the beginning. And there are two opposite kinds of paeon, one of which suits the beginning, where the present usage places it; this is the type – ∪ ∪ ∪: Δαλογενές, | εἴτε Λυκίαν.... The other paeon, on the contrary, begins with three short syllables and ends with a long one: μετὰ δὲ γᾶν | ὕδατά τ' ὠ|κεανὸν ἠ|φάνισε νύξ.‡ And *this* paeon forms a conclusion; for the short syllable (*sc.* of the other one) mutilates the rhythm by its incompleteness. The period ought to be broken off by a long syllable, and the end ought to be marked, not merely by a copyist or a marginal note, but by the rhythm.

This last paragraph contains some important implications beyond the specific advice on the use of paeons:

(1) Rhythms that suggest metre must be avoided (though in view of the quotations from Simonides it is hard to see why the paeon is contrasted with the other feet as not constituting verse; perhaps he means that it is not the basis of one of the major verse-types familiar from epic, tragedy and comedy, and therefore not so *noticeably* metric).

(2) The rhythm of the end of a sentence (clausula) should be different from the beginning, and should have an air of finality.

(3) A long syllable is best for closing. (Cicero said that the final syllable was of indifferent length, though Quintilian disagreed.[1] Analysis has shown that there was a *preference* for a long syllable at the end,[2] as there was, more markedly, for example, in the Ovidian pentameter.)

* Jebb says 'have majesty' (for σεμνότης); but that is far too much, and weakens the force of the objection just made to the heroic metre.

† A paeon, he explains, is a foot of ratio 3:2, a long counting as two shorts, for example first paeon, – ∪ ∪ ∪; fourth paeon, ∪ ∪ ∪ –.

‡ Both quotations are from Simonides, fr. 26b, Bergk.

(4) A rhythmic clausula can perform the function of punctuation (παραγραφή, a short dash placed in antiquity below the first word in the line in which the sentence was *about to* close—which characteristically gave a *warning* to the reader, reading aloud, whereas our full stop presents him with a *fait accompli*).

Now I believe that a great deal of subsequent chaos was caused by the fact that Cicero, if not previous critics drawn on by him, confused the matter of these two chapters. Thus at *De Oratore*, III, 173 he makes Crassus say: 'The old Greek masters thought that in this prose style we ought to use something almost amounting to verses (*versus...propemodum*), that is, *numeros quosdam*. For they thought that in speeches the close of the period ought to come not when we are tired out, but where we take breath, and to be marked not by the copyist's punctuation mark, but by the arrangement of the words and thoughts.' The tell-tale words here are 'not when we are tired out, but where we take breath (*inspirationis, non defatigationis nostrae*)'; for these would be relevant to the organization of a period and its members as to length, not to the long and short syllables which are under discussion; in fact the reference to breathing, which does not occur in Aristotle's chapter 8, may well have been imported from his chapter 9, where it is said that a period, being ordered and εὐσύνοπτος, allows a speaker to keep an end in view, just as having a goal in view prevents a runner from *getting out of breath* and collapsing. Or again, at *De Oratore*, III, 182, he begins by talking about the greatest number of syllables that can be reeled off in one breath, but immediately continues: '*nam* cum sint numeri plures, *iambum et trochaeum...*'.[1]

I believe further that the confusion was aggravated by *patrii sermonis egestas*, by the lack of technical vocabulary in Latin for a subject which, so Cicero claims, no one had previously treated so fully.[2] What was the Latin for ἀριθμός, the most general term, which Aristotle applies both to metric in chapter 8, as we have seen, and to periodic in chapter 9?* *Numerus*. And what does Cicero use for ῥυθμός, which Aristotle expressly distinguishes from μέτρον?† *Numerus*.[3] And what does he use for μέτρον? A word used for it by Romans at least since Lucilius[4]—

---

* ἀριθμὸν ἔχει ἡ ἐν περιόδοις λέξις.

† ῥυθμὸν δεῖ ἔχειν τὸν λόγον, μέτρον δὲ μή. The normal Latin was *modus*. (*G.L.* VI, p. 610, 22 K.).

numerus (or *numeri*). He does in fact recognize that what is called *numerosum* in prose does not always arise from *numerus*, but sometimes from either the Gorgianic figures (*concinnitas*)* or the synthesis of the words (*constructio verborum*).[1] But the consequent terminological ambiguity seems to me to bedevil the section of the *De Oratore* which deals with rhythm, III, 173–98, and to a rather less extent the corresponding but larger section of the *Orator*, written a decade later, 168–236. Valiant efforts to vindicate Cicero have been made in the one full-scale work on his rhythm to appear recently, by Walter Schmid; but I must confess that I do not find his exegesis convincing.[2]

(b)   The comparative method

The theory of prose rhythm is a vast and varied jungle.

> Ahi quanto a dir qual era è cosa dura,
>   questa selva selvaggia ed aspra e forte!

In some areas at least it seems destined to be for ever impenetrable. But the Greek and Roman area is such that it was once reclaimed with a modicum of success. Aristotle made the first clearing, and from this paths were opened up by Theophrastus and his Peripatetic successors. Cicero and Quintilian kept these from getting overgrown, but introduced a labyrinthine quality by joining some of them together. Modern explorers, led by a track from the medieval area, rediscovered this long-lost network. Zieliński systematically surveyed large tracts and seemed, for a time at least, to have discovered a way of opening up the country; but his method had too much of the *a priori* and subjective, though many of his charts have been useful to subsequent explorers. Zander cut the largest swathe, but the further he went the clearer it became that it was based on a mistaken theory and led nowhere. Havet and Bornecque made a survey on quite different principles, but it did not fit in so well with the ancient tracks. Laurand was content with those tracks, and sceptical about the value of going beyond them, while Schmid believes they can be the starting-point for real and far-reaching discoveries. De Groot, on the other hand, thinks them negligible in the first instance, and liable only to mislead; for him there is no alternative

---

* So defined at 164.

initially to the laborious counting of trees and comparing of cultivated plantations with natural wildwood. Broadhead has a quite different principle of counting from de Groot. And here I must make it clear that I have done no pioneering work myself, nor followed all of these step by step, still less foot by foot, but only μέχρι του. Indeed I have for the most part only hovered over the jungle in a helicopter, obtaining certain impressions and drawing certain conclusions, which I give for what they are worth. (Some detailed remarks on modern theories will be found in Appendix II.)

To drop the metaphor: those are surely right who emphasize that these phenomena can only be studied on a comparative basis (whereas Zieliński, for instance, in his earlier work gave only absolute statistics). Some, such as Novotný, compare the endings with the rest of the sentence to see if a particular author has any which can be called preferred 'clausulae', but this method is open to criticism.[1] Others, such as de Groot, argue somewhat as follows. In any language there are certain natural rhythmic tendencies. What we have to do is to discover the natural norm and then compare, if we are to deduce the tendencies of sophisticated artists. In the tables for Latin authors which he gives at the end of his book *Der antike Prosarhythmus* he takes as norm the average between nineteenth-century translations of two Greek patristic treatises into Latin made by men unconscious of the tendencies which modern scholarship has since discovered. This is obviously a very rough-and-ready method; for the styles of the translators may have been unconsciously formed by ancient or ecclesiastical models; but *faute de mieux* it is the one used in the statistics given hereafter, which should not be treated with more respect than they deserve. In defence of these it should be said that they tally quite well with those extracted from the *Annals* of Tacitus, who is generally thought to have been indifferent to rhythmic art in his historical writing; and they have recently been corroborated in general by examination of different nineteenth-century texts.[2]

For amusement I have examined a set of sixteen Latin speeches made by Sir Richard Jebb as Orator of Cambridge University on 18 June 1874, a few years before the revival of interest in ancient rhythmic practice. The following table of percentages shows how his 99 sentence-clausulae compare with de Groot's 'normal' and with those of Cicero's speeches.

Type	'Normal'	Jebb	Cicero
– ⏑ – ⏓	17·2	15	25·3
– – – ⏓	23·5	15	6·4
– ⏑ – ⏑ ⏓	4·4	11	4·9
– – – – ⏑ ⏓	5·4	9	9·7
– ⏑ – – ⏓	7·4	9	16·2
– ⏑ – – ⏑ ⏓	2·9	7	8·3

These six types account for two-thirds of Jebb's clausulae. The remaining 33 are of 15 different types. One of them, – ⏑ ⏑ – – ⏓ (normal 2·2, Cicero 1·4), shows five examples, but four of these occur in one speech with seven clausulae! It seems that one can get a clausula, like a word, 'on the brain'. The tendencies that emerge seem haphazard. Jebb has a probably undesirable one towards iambic rhythm (and three of the ditrochees, – ⏑ – ⏑, are undesirably preceded by another trochee).* He shares with Cicero a preference for the last three types in the above table, but is not nearly so keen on the ditrochee (not having been reared on the Asiatics), nor so averse to the heavy dispondee – – – ⏓. (I hope no one will subject my own speeches, which have less excuse, to a similar scrutiny. Avoidance of dispondees is particularly hard.)

It should be emphasized that in one respect it is not comparative but absolute frequencies that matter.[1] In writing Latin today we should beware of over-using what were really quite rare clausulae because we have learnt from scholars' analyses that they were *relatively* frequent. The *absolute* frequency of the famous 'esse videatur' type in Cicero is only 4·7 per cent.

It is surely right also to be suspicious of ancient theory, which can be palpably wrong: for it is one thing to feel, and quite another to rational-ize one's feeling, especially if one has to invent a technical vocabulary to do so, or if one takes the easier course of adopting an existing one that does not really fit.† We have already met with such a difficulty in the case of the Roman accent.

* But I see that Cicero has seven trochees at the end of a sentence (before a quotation) at – ⏑ – ⏑ – ⏑ – ⏑ – ⏑ – ⏑ – ⏑ *Orator*, 224: 'comprehensione longiore sustinentur'.

† The ancient *testimonia* are set out fully in H. Bornecque's *Les clausules métriques latines* (1907), and more briefly in A. C. Clark's *Fontes Prosae Numerosae* (1909).

(c) Feet, ictus and verse-sections

In early times verse was the natural medium of literary expression for all subjects. Prose is said to have been invented in the sixth century by Pherecydes of Syros; but in early examples, in Heraclitus and Herodotus for instance, we still find embedded the rhythms of epic.[1] Thucydides, on the other hand, has been shown by de Groot to have used a practically unrhythmical style corresponding to the natural character of the language.[2] As already stated, rhythm combined with periodic structure, perhaps with special attention to clausulae, was first made a feature of epideictic prose by Thrasymachus; he may have got the idea from the Mimes of Sophron of Syracuse, which were written in rhythmic prose or *vers libre* divided into *cola* or members.[3] It was now the iambic or trochaic metres that were influential. Plato, however, reacted against poetic rhythms for prose, which he sometimes parodies in others.* In him we see prose becoming self-consciously an art different from poetry. As Shelley said, 'He rejected the harmony of the epic, dramatic and lyrical forms, because he sought to kindle a harmony in thoughts divested of shape and action, and he forebore to invent any regular plan of rhythm which would include, under determinate forms, the varied pauses of his style'.[4] By Aristotle's time rhythm had become subordinate to the construction of periods.

Dionysius of Halicarnassus concludes his work *On Literary Composition* with two interesting chapters (25–6) on how prose can resemble verse in rhythm, and *vice versa*. First he takes a passage from Demosthenes to show that its beauty depends on the unobtrusive introduction of 'metres and rhythms of a kind' (μέτρα καὶ ῥυθμούς τινας). They are stray and irregular (πεπλανημένα, ἀτάκτους). And he proceeds to demonstrate that in the passage concerned there are sequences which, with a little alteration or extension, would be recognizable as forms of verse. He also quotes words from the opening sentence of the *De Corona*, τοῖς θεοῖς εὔχομαι πᾶσι καὶ πάσαις, and from a later passage, to illustrate Demosthenes' (alleged) predilection for cretic (– ◡ –) rhythm.

---

* The *Phaedrus* is exceptional, part of it being designedly poetic in choice of words, avoidance of hiatus, and rhythm (see esp. 237A, 267CD). In the *Symposium* Agathon's speech (194E–197E) contains parody of poetic rhythms; also Diotima's (208C ff.). (E. Norden, *Kunstprosa*, pp. 43, 110.)

Turning to lyric poetry in which the strophes are compiled of various forms of verse, he transcribes Simonides' *Danaë* not in metrical but in syntactical lines, to show how hard it then becomes to detect the metrical structure.*

It will be seen that Dionysius isolates two not co-extensive elements—feet, and verses or sections of verse. Let us take them separately. Analysis in terms of feet, though familiar, seems not very helpful after all. Most prose writers have rhythmic idiosyncrasies. These can even be used like fingerprints to distinguish between genuine and spurious works, or between earlier and later in some cases. Plato, for instance, became fonder as he grew older of successions of short syllables, preferring to write τινὰ τρόπον rather than τρόπον τινά: his dialogues were not for declamation. Demosthenes, on the other hand, rarely has more than two shorts together ('Blass's Law'). One can see how this would make for both ease and impressiveness in utterance. One can also see how it would make – ◡ – – ◡ – a quite likely sequence to turn up.† But why formulate this as a fondness for *cretics*? How do you decide where to begin counting and how to group the syllables? Dionysius himself admits, as to a passage from Plato's *Menexenus*, that there may be alternative ways of scanning it, choosing one on grounds of appropriateness to the sense.[1] Quintilian, no doubt remembering what Dionysius or his source had said about the *De Corona*, asserted that cretic rhythm was excellent to begin with, and then quoted the opening of Cicero's *Pro Murena*, 'Quod precatus a diis immortalibus sum...'. These thirteen syllables do contain three, not consecutive, cretics; but is not the total rhythm, if anything, trochaic?[2] And incidentally the *De Corona* actually *opens* with the words πρῶτον μέν, ὦ ἄνδρες Ἀθηναῖοι, before those quoted above, which some people seem to forget.

In fact, why bring in 'feet' at all? Prose rhythm is a matter of by no means wholly regular distribution of long and short (or stressed and unstressed) syllables: 'feet' are primarily components of regular verse.‡

* Of course the music would make things clearer. Cicero remarks (*Or.* 183) that in certain metres, if the music is taken away, the words seem to lack rhythm.

† Actually analysis has shown that the sequences – ◡ ◡ – ◡ ◡ and – ◡ ◡ – – ◡ ◡ – were more *sought* by Demosthenes than – ◡ – – ◡ –. De Groot, *Handbook* (1918), pp. 9, 29–31.

‡ Quintilian got as far as saying, 'the theory of feet is much harder in prose than in verse' (ix, 4, 60). Novotný is mainly sceptical about them, *Rev. Ét. Lat.* 1926, pp. 224–5).

Of course the terms can be convenient as a shorthand way of describing a sequence, or the general movement of a passage;* but as a basis for rhythmic theory as to prose they are a will-o'-the-wisp. It was natural that the pioneer critics Isocrates and Aristotle should analyse prose-rhythm in such terms, since prose had only recently developed as an alternative to poetry and no other approach would suggest itself; nor had they the convenient symbols for long and short that we have. But I believe it was unfortunate that their authority set this fashion. Their most distinguished latter-day victim was George Saintsbury, whose massive *History of English Prose Rhythm* (1912) adopts the pedal system with enthusiasm† and applies it in analyses, inevitably to some extent subjective, which can dissect anything but explain nothing. One is reminded of the laborious Nosoponus, an imaginary scholar satirized by Erasmus in his *Ciceronianus*, who had constructed an immense table of all the feet used by Cicero at the beginning and end of his periods, cola and commata, and of those used in the other parts. We have only to read chapters 191–5 of Cicero's *Orator* to see the confusion that this approach can create. Cicero himself, after struggling not very success-fully to expound Greek theory, sensibly concludes: 'My own opinion is that all feet are mingled and jumbled up in prose, because if we used the same one repeatedly it would be verse, and prose ought not to be as rhythmic as verse.' Quintilian was justly surprised that the greatest authorities should have thought that some feet should be specially selected, and some condemned, as if there were any foot that must not inevitably occur in prose.[1] Indeed when, after burrowing through forty-three niggling chapters on the use of this foot and that, he comes up at last for fresh air, he nearly bolts for freedom:

My purpose in discussing this topic at length is not to lead the orator to enfeeble his style by pedantic measurement of feet and weighing of syllables; for oratory should possess a vigorous flow, and such solicitude is worthy only of a wretched pedant, absorbed in trivial detail.... Prose-structure, of course, existed before rhythms were discovered in it, just as poetry was originally the

* As by Dionysius, *De Comp.* 18; also by 'Longinus', who attributes the sublimity of a passage in Demosthenes to its being composed in dactylic, the noblest and grandest of rhythms (hence associated with epic), *De Subl.* 39. The correct word for a unit in prose-rhythm was actually βάσις, not πούς.

† H. Blair had given good reasons for not analysing English prose in terms of feet, *Rhetoric* (1783), no. 13, p. 141.

outcome of a natural impulse and was created by the instinctive feeling of the ear for quantity and the observation of time and rhythm, while the discovery of feet came later.....Further, it is not so important for us to consider the actual feet as the general rhythmical effect of the period, just as the poet in writing a verse considers the metre as a whole, and does not concentrate on the six or five individual feet that constitute the verse.*

If prose has no regular feet, then it has no ictus. This is a most important corollary, fatal to much of modern theory, notably Zander's. Let me quote from Broadhead, who is admirably clear on the point:

This recurring, dominant note arises, however, only when there is a *regular alternation* of long and short syllables; in prose this sometimes occurs, but the very fact that it was studiously avoided by ancient writers points to the conclusion that the assumption of an ubiquitous prose-ictus is not only wholly unnecessary, but is dependent on a fundamental misconception of the real meaning and nature of an ictus.[1]

Cicero says as much: prose has no rhythmical measures like those beaten out by the piper—'tibicinii percussionum modi' (the piper who accompanied lyric verse beat time with a foot-instrument).[2] Successions of iambs and tribrachs were to be avoided precisely because they produced marked *percussiones*.[3] 'The style of oratory', says Quintilian, 'will not stoop to be measured by the beat of the foot or the fingers.'[4]

Is it possible, then, that Dionysius' other principle is nearer the truth— that when we feel prose to be rhythmic it is because there are embedded in it sections at least of what our conscious or subconscious ear recognizes as verse? The ear is very impressionable: it absorbs rhythms and prompts us to reproduce them. The translators of King James' Bible fell occasionally into a hexameter, such as

How art thou fallen from heaven, O Lucifer, son of the morning!

or

Art thou he that should come, or do we look for another?

Collects and other parts of the English Prayer Book have rhythms reminiscent of the Missal and Breviary on which they were based.[5]

---

* IX, 4, 112; 114–15, tr. H. E. Butler (Loeb). 'Verse itself is not recognized by abstract reason, but by our natural feeling; it existed before theory measured it and explained what had happened': Cic. *Or.* 183. 'I have never been able to retain the names of feet and metres, or to pay the proper respect to the accepted rules of scansion....It is only the study, not of poetry but of poems, that can train our ear': T. S. Eliot, *The Music of Poetry*, 1942, p. 9.

F. L. Lucas, after analysing a number of passages, concludes: 'English prose of a poetic kind contains, I think, far more hidden metre than, so far as I know, has ever been recognized. But this is a dangerous secret, to be breathed only with discretion.'[1]

Demetrius, claiming to be the first to write on the subject (his date is unfortunately uncertain)* also suggested that prose composition might be made attractive by working in verses, whole or partial. 'The actual measures must not, of course, obtrude themselves on the attention if the words are read connectedly; but if the sentence is divided and analysed part by part, then and only then ought the presence of measures to be detected by our own ears.'[2] (He added that even a generally rhythmical style would produce the same effect, professing to find this in Plato, the Peripatetics, Xenophon, Herodotus and Demosthenes, but not in Thucydides.)

As to *complete* verses, most ancient rhetorical critics agreed with Isocrates and Aristotle, that they should not occur in prose.[3] (Iambic trimeters, arising naturally from common speech, were not wholly avoidable nor really objectionable[4]—like blank verse in English prose, of which however an excess, such as sometimes occurs in Dickens, can be distracting.)† There must be no absolute regularity, yet the whole must, in Cicero's qualified phrase, fall 'sub aurium mensuram *aliquam*'. But how could odd fragments of different kinds of verse, strung together by neutral sequences of syllables, generate rhythm, the essence of which is recurrence? I suppose Dionysius would have to answer: 'They are reminiscent of rhythms which have been established as such by recurrence in verse.'

Quintilian seems at times to hanker after a similar theory. Having

---

* His latest editor, G. M. A. Grube (1961) inclines to think he was writing, not in the second century A.D., but at Alexandria not long after 270 B.C. (pp. 39–56).

† I notice this sequence in Mr John Sparrow's *Sense and Poetry* (1934), p. 9:

> just as a word familiar to us from
> the prayers and devotions of our youth
> will diffuse
> over the least ecclesiastical
> of contexts, faint but unmistakable,
> the fragrance of the hassock and the pew.

F. Marx found 240 iambic senarii in Celsus. Detecting inadvertent and barely appreciable verses in Isocrates or Cicero has been a favourite exercise of pedants, ancient and modern. (L. Laurand, *Études* (1907), pp. 134–7.)

said that even part of a verse can be ugly in prose if it is the second half and is used as a cadence (for example, 'quo me vertam, nescio', the second half of an iambic trimeter), he ventures the suggestion that the reverse may be pleasing—the *first* half of a verse, especially of the septenarius or octonarius, may make a pleasing clausula (for example, 'in Africa fuisse', the opening of a senarius, is the end of the first clause in Cicero, *Pro Ligario*, and his famous clausula 'esse videatur' is the beginning of an octonarius). Conversely, the end of a verse may make a good beginning in prose (for example, 'Etsi vereor, iudices' and 'Animadverti, iudices', each the second half of an iambic trimeter, are the openings of Cicero's *Pro Milone* and *Pro Cluentio* respectively).*

But this strikes one as an aberration on Quintilian's part. All his examples are taken from the openings of *works*. It was indeed common to cite the first instance in a work (if only to make things easier in an age when books were rolls); but here the suspicion arises that he may not have looked very far before jumping to conclusions. Anyway, he goes on to say, in orthodox rhetorical tradition, that care must be taken to avoid anything ἔνρυθμον, like Sallust's 'Falso queritur de natura sua' (which sounds harmless enough!); and he takes Plato himself to task for beginning the *Timaeus* with a (barely perceptible) hexameter-opening followed by an Anacreontic—

εἷς, δύο, τρεῖς, | ὁ δὲ δὴ τέταρτος ἡμῖν, | ὦ φίλε

—a sequence which was equally open to the objection that

δύο, τρεῖς, | ὁ δὲ δὴ | τέταρ|τος ἡ|μῖν, ὦ | φίλε

could be scanned (by a sufficiently determined ear, one may think) as an iambic trimeter. He also criticizes Thucydides (who was innocent of any such niceties) for letting slip 'mollissimum rhythmorum genus' —ὑπὲρ ἥμισυ Κᾶρες ἐφάνησαν (presumably because of the hexameter-ending ὑπὲρ ἥμισυ Κᾶρες, since he could hardly have objected to Κᾶρες ἐφάνησαν, the metrical equivalent of 'esse videatur').[1] In more sensible mood, however, he has already insisted that all prose can be analysed into short lines or sections of verse, but has branded as tiresome (*molesti*) critics who treat it so, as though it were lyric poetry.[2]

* IX, 4, 72–5. Modern critics who have tried to apply a similar theory include H. Bornecque, *Clausules* (1907), p. 50, and C. Zander, *Eurhythmia*, II (1913), 525 ff.

It has also been observed, by Bornecque, that Cicero and his follower, Pliny the Younger, in their more carefully composed works avoid falling into a succession of more than four identical feet (to put it in those terms), and that they make a point of breaking their rhythm as soon as possible after the beginning, a scruple which did not trouble a Sallust or a Livy.[1]

There were in fact two distinct traditions at Rome. There was the rhetorical, derived through Cicero from Hellenistic practice. This avoided verse-rhythms to such an extent that Bornecque could state it as a ruling principle that 'any metre in any way connected with poetry is avoided' and that the preferred clausulae were precisely those that could *not* be associated with any verse-metre.[*] And there was the historical, exemplified by Sallust and Livy, which by contrast affected rhythms, and often phraseology, reminiscent of poetry.[2] We shall discuss these two in turn. But first something must be said about the development of clausulae, and about rhythm in the rest of the sentence.

(d) Clausulae

How can 'clausula' be defined? Schmid insists that it was not a technical term to Cicero, who used it simply to mean 'the close of a sentence'. He is pointing out how little Cicero has to say on the subject, in support of his view that a rhythmical close was only a small part of rhythm, and in criticism of the vast over-emphasis laid upon it by modern theory.[3] Be that as it may, Cicero does discuss the rhythm of the end of sentences.[†] He says that when he names the feet in clausulae he is not speaking of the last only, but of the last two at least, and often the last three;[4] and the entity he is discussing here has been conveniently named 'clausula' by modern researchers. Speakers came to realize that it was the end of the sentence that mattered most rhythmically, that rang in the ears of the audience. It was here that numbers 'apparent et

---

* *La prose métrique dans la correspondance de Cicéron* (1898), p. 198, etc. This is not wholly true: there were 'positive' as well as 'negative' clausulae (A. W. de Groot, *Handbook*, 1918, pp. 64–6). F. Marx (edn. of Celsus, p. xcviii) and F. Novotný (*Eurhythmie*, p. 209) believed on the contrary that poetic cadences *gave rise* to prose clausulae: for example, $- \cup - \breve{}$ is the close of a phalaecian hendecasyllable, $- \cup - - \breve{}$ of a choliambic. This seems to me much more dubious. Cicero said that prose rhythm should be as unlike that of poetry as possible (*Or.* 227).

† Cf. Seneca (*Ep.* 114, 16) on Cicero's *compositio*: 'in exitu lenta...devexa et molliter desinens nec aliter quam solet, ad morem suum pedemque respondens' (*desinens*, Laurand: MSS. *detinens*).

intelleguntur', here that any boring recurrence was remarked. 'Haec est sedes orationis, hoc auditor expectat, hic laus omnis declamantium.'[1] But how far did the clausula in fact extend? De Groot, more scientific than others, remarks that the further you get from the end of a sentence, the more indifferent you find the quantity of the syllable to be: a clausula begins where the quantity of the syllable ceases to be indifferent.[2] (A sentence may be deemed to end where a modern editor would print a full stop, exclamation mark or question mark.) But we must not be too mechanical. In odd instances at least interpunctuation or natural grouping of words may have modified the effect.

When artistic prose first developed, individual authors tended to prefer certain clausulae, but they did not agree with one another. The highest common factor was the ditrochee (= 'dichoreus'), $- \cup - \overline{\cup}$, the only clausula that Demosthenes went out of his way to favour.* Its normal incidence in unartistic Greek prose is 14·2 per cent: in Demosthenes the figure is 18·9 per cent. But Plato came to avoid it (*Republic* 13·9 per cent, *Laws* 5·7 per cent). Again the hexameter-ending $- \cup \cup - \overline{\cup}$ occurs in the *Republic* in its normal, natural frequency of 6·5 per cent, but in the *Laws* it has dropped to 1·3 per cent. This is in line with Plato's reaction against poetic rhythm. More and more he came to favour the paeonic ending $\cup \cup \cup -$ which was less associated with poetry. Demosthenes tended to avoid this, perhaps because it involved three successive shorts (see above); but in Plato it attains the high frequency of 18 per cent in his latest work, the *Laws*.[3]

In Hellenistic times an important figure is Hegesias of Magnesia (fl. *c.* 250 B.C.), of the Asiatic school of rhetoric. His few fragments show him as favouring particular clausulae, which were, as we shall see, largely those which Cicero was to favour: the 'Asiatic ditrochee' (often preceded by $- \cup -$), $- \cup \cup \cup - \overline{\cup}$ (= *esse videatur*), and to a less extent $- \cup - - \overline{\cup}$. Unlike Cicero, but in Platonic tradition, he also favoured $\cup \cup \cup -$.[4] Already a limited number of clausulae are becoming 'canonized' to an extent unknown in the fifth and fourth centuries.†

---

* *Absolutely* he used most, according to Norden (*Kunstprosa*, p. 923[3]) $- \overline{\cup} - - \overline{\cup}, - \overline{\cup} - - \overline{\cup} \cup$, $- \cup \cup - - \overline{\cup}, - \cup \cup - - \cup \overline{\cup}, - \overline{\cup} - \overline{\cup}$. The weakness, however, of an analysis that allows $- - - -$ as a variety of $- \cup - \cup$ is apparent.

† For modern theories of clausulae see Appendix II (*a*).

(e) Beginnings and middles

Already in antiquity it was debated whether only the end of the sentence should be rhythmical or the whole.[1] Aristotle, as we have seen, recommended a particular paeon ($-\cup\cup\cup$) as suitable for beginning. The story of Plato's trying out the opening words of the *Republic* in different orders is well known.[2] (Boris Tomashevsky has shown that in Pushkin's prose the beginnings as well as ends of sentences tend towards greater rhythmical regularity than the rest.)[3] Cicero, writing under Aristotle's influence in the *De Oratore*, says that '*et primi* et postremi pedes' must have their rhythm attended to; yet analysis has not revealed any special tendencies in his own openings.[4]

What about the middle part of the sentence? A remark of Quintilian's is sometimes quoted with approval: 'Rhythm (*numerus*) pervades the whole body of prose throughout its extent. For we cannot speak without employing the long and short syllables of which feet are composed.'[5] But the second of these sentences shows how little importance we need attach to the first: not every series of longs and shorts constitutes what we should recognize as rhythm. Cicero is more explicit. In the *De Oratore* he makes Crassus say: 'Nor need you worry about the paeons and dactyls we were talking about: they will turn up in prose of their own account—yes, they will fall in and report themselves as present without being summoned.'[6] This might mean no more than Quintilian said—that any piece of writing can be arbitrarily divided into feet. Or it might mean, don't *worry* about rhythm: you will find you have created it by trained instinct. This seems more plausible, in view of what follows:

Only let your habitual practice in writing and speaking be to make the thoughts end up with the words,* and the combination of the words themselves spring from good long free *numeri*, specially the dactylic (*heroö*) or the first paeon or the cretic, though with a clearly marked close of varied forms (for similarity is particularly noticed at the close); and if the first and last feet of the sentences are regulated on this principle, the metrical shapes of the parts in between can pass unnoticed—only provided that the actual period is not shorter than the ear expected or longer than the strength and breath can last out.

* That is, not to have to pad: padding may seem more applicable to 'periodic' than 'metric'.

On this we may note: (1) That in general the rhythm should, in Cicero's opinion, be free (*numeri liberi*), but the clausula more marked. (2) That *medii possunt latere*. Here the nuance may be: either that in the middle the rhythm need not be so strict as to be noticeable; or that its art can be concealed (λανθάνειν), which was always considered a virtue.[1] I incline to the former interpretation, which is clearly supported by Quintilian.[2] (3) That once again Cicero blurs a sentence about 'metric', both at the beginning and the end, with a remark that concerns 'periodic'.

And now the corresponding passage in the *Orator* again:

Therefore, since the ear is always awaiting the end and takes pleasure in it, this should not be without rhythm, but the period ought even from the beginning to move towards such a conclusion, and to flow from the start in such a way that at the end it will come naturally to rest.... The outline of the thought is no sooner formed in the mind than the words begin to muster; and these the mind, the swiftest thing there is, immediately distributes so that each one falls into its proper place in the ranks, and the orderly line of words is brought to a close now with one, now with another rhythmical figure. And all the words both at the beginning and in the middle should look to the end.* For in oratory sometimes the speed is swift, sometimes there is a slow and steady progress, so that at the very beginning you must consider how you wish to end the sentence.[3]

Most of this seems meant to refer to 'metric' (though some might be more plausible if it referred to 'periodic'). It is not surprising, therefore, that some researchers have tried to detect careful rhythm throughout the sentence. If anyone protests that this implies more than even Ciceronian skill could compass, they can answer that Cicero himself adduced as an encouragement the virtuosity of Antipater of Sidon, who could improvise verses of all kinds.[4] Indeed, he says paradoxically elsewhere, rhythmic prose is harder to write than verse, because in verse the rules are fixed, whereas prose has no rhythm such as the piper beats out with his foot: all is judged by the instinctive pleasure of the ear.[5] Again and again Cicero emphasizes, after Aristotle, that this rhythm is something only *akin* to verse and approximate. A remark of his that 'the thunderbolts of Demosthenes would not have such force but for the rhythm (*numeri*) with which they are whirled and sped on their way'

---

* At 203 he says explicitly that *numerus* is in place throughout the whole period, 'in tota continuatione verborum'. Cf. Quint. IX, 4, 61.

was criticized by some as implying that prose rhythm could be reduced to rules. Quintilian comments that, if he had really meant that, he could not agree with him; but that Cicero had made it abundantly clear elsewhere that he did not think prose rhythm could be measured.*

Is there any evidence that Cicero took particular care over the rhythm of his internal cola? He may imply that he does so when he says that clausulae must be attended to *even* more carefully than the rest of the sentence.[1] It would be natural if, at least where there is a strong pause, he instinctively favoured the same endings for cola as for sentences. Laurand examines a passage from the Sixth Philippic and shows that most of the cola end with canonical types.[2] Zieliński in his later work sought to establish a grandiose theory on this basis. He came to the not surprising conclusion that the longer a pause was, the more likely it was to be preceded by one of the canonical clausulae; or as he puts it, periods have the rhythmic cream, cola the milk, commata the skimmed milk.† But both his method and its application were vulnerable.[3] Genuine tendencies can only be established by laborious analyses like Novotný's and Broadhead's which take into account what the natural incidence would be (and there is still the problem of deciding in each case how the *membra* or cola are constituted).

De Groot is perhaps near the mark when he says:

What counts in the rhythm of Ciceronian periods is not primarily the ends of the cola and commata themselves. One observes a tendency to 'isochrony', but not to metrical equality. It seems in fact that the rhythm of ancient prose is based above all on the length of these parts of the sentence; the different clausulae have only a small rhythmic value of their own, and often constitute only, so to speak, the acoustic means of expressing the 'punctuation' of the period.‡

Laurand's conclusion is that 'it is impossible to find the application of definite rules, or even of very distinct preferences, in the beginning or the middle of sentences';[4] and that is as far as I think we can safely go for the present.

---

* *Or.* 234. Quint. IX, 4, 53–6. For some modern theories see Appendix II (*b*).

† H. D. Broadhead independently reaches a similar conclusion, *Rhythm* (1922), ch. VI.

‡ *La prose métrique* (1926), p. 18. This does not prevent him from assiduously marking the rhythms at the end of cola in the examples he gives from Cicero (pp. 48–9) and all other writers in this same work, and in his *Prosarhythmus* (whose tables were presumably drawn up on this basis), and generalizing accordingly.

II. DEVELOPMENT OF PROSE RHYTHM AT ROME

(a) Early prose

In early times, before the middle of the second century B.C., Latin prose was unaffected by Greek art. In so far as it showed rhythmic tendencies, these were due to the proportionally smaller number of short syllables in the language, and to the fact that the majority of grammatical terminations were long (or capable of becoming so 'by position') and monosyllabic: sequences occurred which could be described as spondaic, or less frequently, iambic. The natural language of Rome was solemn and instinct with *gravitas*. In the following passage from the *Tabulae Censoriae*,[1] chosen at random, there are 27 short syllables and 73 long: roughly 1:3, whereas in Greek the normal proportion is about 3:4.

Praec(o) in templo primum vocat, postea de moeris item vocat. Ubi lucet, censores scribae magistratus murr(a) unguentisqu(e) unguentur. Ubi praetores tribunique plebei quiqu(e) inlicium vocati sunt venerunt, censores inter se sortiuntur, uter lustrum faciat. Ubi templum fact(um) est, post tum convention(em) habet qui lustrum conditurus est.

The first Latin prose work that has come down to us complete is a handbook, not literature—Cato's *De Agri Cultura*. But it has a short literary preface, whose clausulae are as follows:*

(1)	si t(am) honestum sit	– ∪ – – ∪
(2)	feneratorem quadrupli	– – – ∪ ∪ –
(3)	existimare	– ∪ – ∪
(4)	bonumque colonum	– ∪ ∪ – ∪
(5)	laudabantur	– – – ∪
(6)	et calamitosum	– ∪ ∪ ∪ – ∪
(7)	occupati sunt.	– ∪ – – –

Since (1), (3), (6) and (7) were common Hellenistic forms, we might suppose that Cato was paying uncharacteristic attention to the Graeculi.

* From study of clausulae it emerges (1) that synaloepha generally operates, but less automatically than in verse; (2) that vowels are not generally lengthened in the 'positio debilis', but otherwise are before two consonants or impure *s*; (3) that the final syllable is of indeterminate length (*anceps*), as Cicero said, though a long may be preferable, as in poetry. (Novotný, *État actuel* (1929), pp. 81–2, 79, 59; Laurand, *Études* (1907), p. 159.)

But (2) was not common, and (4) and (5) were positively avoided by them. So the rhythms here are probably haphazard, as in the rest of the treatise.

What about his speeches? The fragments we have indicate that he used short, pithy sentences, as we should expect of him. Gellius quotes a dozen lines from one.[1] Its clausulae (if such they can be called) are:

cibaria curat(a) esse	∪ ∪ — — — ∪
atque flagro caedi	— ∪ — — — —
videre multi mortales	∪ — — — — —
servitutem ferre potest	— — — ∪ ∪ —
boni consulitis	∪ — — ∪ ∪ ∪
ubi fides maiorum	∪ ∪ — — — ∪
te facer(e) aus(um) esse	— ∪ ∪ — — ∪
fletum fact(um) audivi	— — — —
nimis aegre ferunt	∪ ∪ — — ∪ —
habituros dum viverent.	— — — ∪ —

What is surprising here is that Cato has not, in ten cases, fallen even by chance into any of the clausulae favoured by the Asiatics; and only the last can be called Ciceronian.

Yet by all accounts the Romans were remarkably sensitive to the element of quantity in their language. Words which had the same spelling but different quantity were felt to be different words.[2] Cicero could say without fear of derision that even the 'vulgus imperitorum', though its normal speech was 'extra numerum',[3] felt good or bad rhythm by instinct ('tacito quodam sensu'); and that without having any technical knowledge the whole theatre audience protested if a verse was delivered with a false quantity. In the case of an orator they did not protest if his rhythm was defective, but they felt it nevertheless. 'I have often seen assemblies', he says again, 'burst into applause at a happy cadence.'* He recalls how he was standing in the crowd when Gaius Carbo uttered a stirring period ending 'temeritas fili comprobavit':
'It was marvellous what a shout arose from the crowd at this ditrochee.'[4]
One might suspect that the budding orator, aged sixteen at the time,

---

* Or. 168, 174; De Or. III, 195–8; Parad. III, 26. Cf. Quint. IX, 4, 116. The Greek ἄμουσος ὄχλος was apparently no less sensitive, being indignant at any fault in music or rhythm (Dion. Hal. De Comp. 11). We hear of audiences which foresee, and shout or stamp out, the clausulae in advance when a speaker falls into monotonous regularity (Dem. De Eloc. 15; 'Longin.' De Subl. 41).

was mistaken in the reason, lending his own ears to the mob; but Augustine too speaks of 'numerositas clausularum' which 'arouses such acclamations'.[1] To the Romans periodic oratory was as much an art as poetry.[2]

The ditrochee indeed deserves a paragraph to itself. It was something of a touchstone. Alone in being positively sought, as we have seen, by Demosthenes, but progressively avoided by Plato, it was canonized by the Asiatics. Cicero said in the *Orator* that it was in itself a splendid cadence, but for this very reason a danger to due variety. Its natural frequency in Latin is about 17·0 per cent: in Vitruvius it reaches 39·2 per cent, which shows the necessity for Cicero's warning. He himself in his early *De Inventione* used it to the extent of 35·6 per cent. But the *Orator* is a work in which he is at pains to defend himself to Brutus and the Atticists from the charge of being too Asiatic. In fact its use diminishes to 25·3 per cent in his latest work. We find it avoided, as we might expect, by Brutus in his letters, and by post-Ciceronian writers such as Mela (1·0 per cent), Petronius and the Senecas, but restored to some favour in the reaction associated with Quintilian.[3] Both in theory and in practice it was rarely preceded by another trochee, or by the equivalent tribrach (Cicero often had a cretic here). Presumably this was to avoid a too poetic rhythm.

A generation after Cato, Gaius Gracchus made a name for oratory. His teacher was an Asiatic, Menelaus of Marathus. His fragments show some tendency to rhythm and canonical clausulae, especially the ditrochee, but it is still rather casual.[4] Cicero, in fact, uses him as an example of a speaker who is *inconditus* (unorganized): in his speech before the censors (124 B.C.) he had a sentence, 'Abesse non potest quin eiusdem hominis sit probos improbare qui improbos probet'; by an easy change he could have ended more neatly with 'quin eiusdem sit hominis qui improbos probet probos improbare—in fact with Cicero's own favoured clausula, cretic + ditrochee. This bears out Cicero's statement that the importance of rhythm in oratory had only recently been recognized at Rome.[5]

There is no reservation when we come to Quintus Metellus Numidicus (consul 109 B.C.), from whose speeches Gellius quotes three appreciable passages.[6] These have together ten sentences, and their clausulae include three examples of each of the future favourites of Cicero, $-\cup- \stackrel{\cup}{-}$ and $-\cup-- \stackrel{\cup}{-}$, and two of an Asiatic favourite he was to use slightly more than the normal average of times, $-\cup-\cup\cup \stackrel{\cup}{-}$. The author of the *Rhetorica ad Herennium* recommends that word-order be manipulated in the interests of rhythm ('verba sicuti ad poeticum quendam exstruere numerum'), provided that the sense is not thereby obscured. He gives as an instance a sentence made to end 'virtūte prō vestrā', presumably because, though this order was slightly unusual, it produced the favourite clausula $-\cup---$, as against the unfavoured $----- \cup$ of 'prō vestrā virtūte'.* He himself favours what were becoming the canonical forms, the only Ciceronian ones he avoids being $-\cup--\cup \stackrel{\cup}{-}$ and $----\cup \stackrel{\cup}{-}$. (But a later date for this treatise than the orthodox 86–82 B.C. has recently been proposed, partly as a result of clausula-study itself.)[1]

(b) Cicero and the rhetorical tradition

Cicero's early work *De Inventione* already shows marked preferences in clausulae. Investigation reveals that in this matter he is in the tradition of Hegesias, a man of whose style he otherwise speaks most contemptuously, but he may well have been indoctrinated by some later authority, such as his teacher in rhetoric, the Rhodian Apollonius Molo. The following table shows the chief types he uses, with the percentage of their occurrence in his speeches and of their normal frequency in the language.[2]

		Cicero	Normal
$-\cup-- \stackrel{\cup}{-}$	omne debetur	16·2	7·4
$----\cup \stackrel{\cup}{-}$	omni debebitur	9·7	5·4
$-\cup--\cup \stackrel{\cup}{-}$	omne debebitur	8·3	2·9
$----\cup- \stackrel{\cup}{-}$	ex omni debiturus	7·7	3·5
$-\cup--\cup- \stackrel{\cup}{-}$	omnibus debiturus	5·0	2·4
$-\cup-\cup \stackrel{\cup}{-}$	omne debuit	4·9	4·4
$-\cup\cup\cup- \stackrel{\cup}{-}$	debuerat omne	4·7	2·4
		56·5	28·4

---

* IV, 44. Quintilian (VIII, 6, 62) quotes the opening of Cicero's *Pro Cluentio* for hyperbaton, 'Animadverti, iudices, omnem accusatoris orationem in duas divisam esse partes': correct order would be 'in duas partes divisam esse', but this would be 'durum et incomptum'. Is the implication that Cicero sought the favourite clausula $---\mid-\cup--$, as against $------\cup$?

It will be seen that seven types out of a much larger total of possibles account for well over half of Cicero's clausulae; and that in the case of six at least he uses them about twice as often as an unindoctrinated writer would do. But what he avoids is equally interesting. Like Hegesias, he dislikes the heavy spondaic ending $---\smile$ for oratory, using it only in 6·2 per cent of cases as against a natural frequency of 23·5; and, as is well known, he avoids above all the hexameter-ending, $-\smile\smile-\smile$, using it only in 1·9 per cent as against the natural 8·5. But unlike Hegesias, he avoids also the fourth paeon $\smile\smile\smile-$, recommended by Aristotle and favoured by Plato and many Greeks, and the dactylic $-\smile\smile-\smile$.

Cicero shows care over his clausulae not only in his public and forensic speeches—though he was aware that in these an obtrusive attention to rhythm might tell against an orator[1]—but in all his serious prose works, and even in most of the letters *Ad Familiares*, though not in those to his intimate Atticus.[2] He consciously took more trouble over them in brilliantly worked-up speeches, and in exordia, perorations and emotional passages, but less in informal narratives or legal discussions.[3] He was also aware that different kinds of speech or writing called for different styles and rhythmic qualities.[4] Sometimes he will waive the normal rule that the verb should come at the end in the interest of rhythm, writing 'in gratia potest esse' for 'esse potest', or 'asperiora videntur esse' to avoid a hexameter-ending.[5] Occasionally word-order seems to have been strained in aid of the clausula, or otiose words added for the benefit of rhythm (a habit he himself derided in the Asiatics).[6] The famous *esse videatur*, which sometimes seems to mean no more than *sit*, occurs 83 times (not every other time, as Tacitus' Aper pretended). Its use diminishes with time, perhaps through contemporary criticism (did his audiences begin to stamp it out?), though Quintilian still speaks of apes who think that no more than this is needed to reproduce the style of the master.[7]

It is however important to realize that by no means all the clausulae found in Cicero's serious writings can be called canonical. He did not, he insisted himself, work strictly to rule.[8] Nor did his practice conform wholly to the theory he enunciated at *Orator*, 212–18. There he recommends most of the clausulae he uses, but is embarrassed, as we saw in the case of elision (p. 21), when he finds Greek theory clearly belied by Roman experience. Aristotle, you will remember, recommended the fourth paeon ∪∪∪– as the best clausula. Cicero accepts this without comment at *De Oratore*, III, 193; and at 183 he tries to justify it by saying that a paeon is more or less equal to a cretic (both are equivalent to five shorts). At *Orator*, 196, he again gives the paeon general primacy simply on Aristotle's authority—'quoniam optimus auctor ita censet'. But in 214 a specific instance brings him up against reality. He has praised Carbo's 'temeritas fili comprobavit' (see p. 154), and to reinforce his point that the merit lay in the ditrochee he adds: 'Change the words to *comprobavit fili temeritas* and the effect is gone, although *temeritas* is a fourth paeon, the foot which Aristotle considers best (not that I agree).'[1] Yet in the next paragraph he is hedging again. He includes the paeon, as metrically equivalent to the cretic, among pleasing clausulae: 'the ancients consider it the best cadence: I do not absolutely reject it, but I prefer others'. In practice he used it rarely in his earlier speeches, and later abandoned it entirely; but when theorizing he always found it hard to shake himself free from the authority of the great Greek critics, and he speaks impatiently of those who would dare to do so: 'quis ergo istos ferat qui hos auctores non probent?'[2] Actually, while ostensibly following Aristotle, he seems to be relying more on some Hellenistic source (the same is true of the *Topica*), and even so misinterpreting sometimes. In one place Bornecque and Laurand can only save him by gratuitous assumption of a lacuna from condoning the hexameter ending –∪∪–⏑.[3] Yet not only do statistics show that he went out of his way to avoid this form: we can see him specially choosing words (for example *volitantem* for *volantem* after *remisque*), determining word-order, and even straining syntax, to the same end.[4]

Cicero always emphasized the importance of variety,[5] and although he showed marked preferences he was by no means hide-bound in his practice. But his own authority, paramount in rhetorical prose as Virgil's became in hexameter verse, defeated his good intention. His imitators fixed upon his favourite forms (apart from the ditrochee, as already explained), and established a narrow canon. From now onwards attention was paid to these by nearly all prose writers, even composers of handbooks like Vitruvius and Celsus.[6] Even Seneca the

Younger, who was a leading example of the contemporary reaction against the periodic style of Cicero, tends to fall into his favourite clausulae, using $-\cup--\underset{\smile}{-}$, for instance, in 28·5 per cent of cases (Cicero speeches 16·2, normal 7·4).[1]

But we must not leave the rhetorical tradition without discussing the powerful opposition that developed in Cicero's own day. There were plain-style orators who shared the feeling of the Stoics (and Dean Swift) that all this artistry was suspect and meretricious.* An orator should persuade by convincing the understanding, not playing on the emotions. They professed to go back to Lysias, and called themselves 'Atticists'. Some of them were by no means inconsiderable. There was Calvus, the inseparable poet-friend of Catullus. One recalls how Vatinius, prosecuted by him, protested 'Am I to be condemned because he is eloquent?', and how at the same trial someone near Catullus in the crowd threw up his hands and exclaimed, 'Ye gods, how that little titch can talk!'[2] We learn from the *Dialogus* of Tacitus that Calvus and Brutus criticized Cicero for diffuseness and lack of sinew, and from Quintilian of contemporaries who classed him with the turgid Asiatics.[3] He wrote the *Orator*, it would seem, partly to make the defence that (as in philosophy) he was an eclectic, fitting his style to the subject in hand, and partly to try and make the cultured Brutus feel he should not let himself be classed with these so-called 'Atticists', who imagined that ruggedness was in itself a virtue.[4] 'No one', he says, 'has ever not wanted to speak in this rhythmic way, nor has anyone who *could* do so ever refrained. Those who have adopted a different style have done so because they could not attain to this; and so they suddenly turned into "Atticists".'[5] Examination of the extant letters of Brutus indicates that he had some preference for the Ciceronian clausula $-\underset{\smile}{-}--\cup\underset{\smile}{-}$, but that he avoided the forms Cicero most favoured, $-\cup-\underset{\smile}{-}$ and $-\cup--\underset{\smile}{-}$, and did not avoid Cicero's *bêtes noires*, $-\cup\cup-\underset{\smile}{-}$ and $---\underset{\smile}{-}$.[6] This suggests that the Atticists were not so much indifferent to rhythm as reacting against the tradition represented by Cicero.

---

* 'Dean Swift despised musical arrangement altogether' (H. Blair, *Rhetoric*, no. 13, 1783). There is documentary evidence that St Jerome, though familiar with the conventional clausulae, disregarded them for his translation of the Bible through respect for the order of words in the sacred text before him. (Augustine, *De Doct. Christ.* IV, 40–1; cited by W. H. Shewring, *C.Q.* 1933, pp. 47–8.)

The case of Caesar is not so simple. In some respects he shares the tendencies of the historians: but he favours $-\cup--\smile$ even more than Cicero himself, and in his speeches he uses the rhythms of the Ciceronian tradition.[1] It was Pollio who seemed to Seneca the complete contrast to Cicero, bumpy and jerky and liable to leave off where you least expected: in Cicero all sentences come to an end (*desinunt*), in Pollio they break off (*cadunt*). Likewise to Quintilian Pollio seemed so untouched by Ciceronian polish and charm of style that you would think him a generation older.[2] Yet to Tacitus he seemed 'numerosior';[3] and in so far as the passage quoted by the elder Seneca enables us to judge, in speeches at least his favourite clausulae were Cicero's.*

(c) Sallust and the historical tradition

When Cicero said that history was of all branches of writing the most oratorical ('opus unum hoc oratorium maxime'), he probably meant that it was a subject that lent itself to treatment in a distinguished style— the subject for a Gibbon.[4] But Quintilian spoke more precisely for the Roman tradition when he said that it was the nearest to poetry—in a sense poetry without metre ('carmen solutum').[5] Just as in Herodotus we find traces of epic rhythm, so we find them in the Roman historians. Caelius Antipater (late second century B.C.) opened a book of his work on the Punic Wars with the words, 'In priore libro *has res ad te scriptas Luci misimus Aeli*...'. The words italicized are a crude hexameter with no proper caesura—an accident, one might think, but for the tortured word-order, which was criticized by the Auctor ad Herennium as typical of him.[6] In fact Cicero puts Caelius' intention beyond doubt when he laughs at him for being so naive as to promise in his preface that he will not transpose words obtrusively in the interests of rhythm.[7] Livy, as is well known, begins his preface in epic rhythm, 'Facturusn(e) operae pretium sim...', perhaps thinking of a line of Ennius which begins 'Audirest operae pretium'.† Ennius stands to him as Homer to

---

* *Suas.* 6, 24. He avoids, however, the Ciceronian type $-\cup--\cup\smile$.

† Enn. fr. 465 V.[8] The earliest editors of Livy, from whom our MSS. descend, being nurtured in the oratorical tradition, got rid of this rhythm by emendation; but Quintilian rebuked them (IX, 4, 74).

Herodotus, who incidentally (if Aristotle's text and not our manuscripts' is correct) began his history with an epic rhythm,

$$\text{—} \cup \cup \text{—} \quad \text{—} \quad \text{—} \quad \cup \cup \text{—} \quad \cup \cup \text{—}$$

Ἡροδότου Θουρίου ἥδ᾽ ἱστορίης ἀπόδειξις.[1]

When Tacitus began his *Annals* with a hexameter (albeit one such as 'det motus incompositos'),

Urbem Romam a principio reges habuere,

he was with clear intent putting himself in the great Roman historical tradition, with a possible reminiscence of Sallust if not also of some lost line of Ennius.*

With Sallust, who began to publish just about the time of Cicero's death, this historical tradition comes out as not merely partial to poetic rhythm,† but in reaction against the established rhythms of the Hellenistic-oratorical tradition. Two simple tables will make this fact leap to the eye.‡ Here are Sallust's commonest clausulae compared with (*a*) the normal for the language, (*b*) Livy, (*c*) Cicero:

Type	Normal	Sallust	Livy	Cicero
$\text{—}\,\text{—}\,\text{—}\,\cup$	23·5	25·3	31·8	6·2
$\text{—}\,\cup\,\cup\,\text{—}\,\cup$	8·3	10·6	11·0	1·9

(It will be seen that hexameter-endings are affected by the historians a little beyond the normal for the language.)

And here are Cicero's commonest clausulae compared with (*a*) the normal, (*b*) Sallust, (*c*) Livy:

Type	Normal	Cicero	Sallust	Livy
$\text{—}\,\cup\,\text{—}\,\cup$	17·2	25·3	6·3	11·0
$\text{—}\,\cup\,\text{—}\,\text{—}\,\cup$	7·4	16·2	4·1	5·0

Cicero says at *Orator*, 216, dealing with clausulae: 'Not even the spondee is to be entirely repudiated. Since it consists of two long syllables,

---

* De Groot, *Prosarhythmus* (1921), pp. 22–6. He cites an article by V. Lundström, 'Nya Enniusfragment', *Eranos* (1915), pp. 1 ff., which shows that it it was quite common in antiquity to begin a work with a verbal reminiscence of the opening of a previous work, by way of acknowledging indebtedness or admiration.

† The first two chapters of the *Catiline* show four hexameter endings, as Laurand demonstrates (*Études*, 1936, p. 175).

‡ The figures must be regarded as approximate. They are based on de Groot's as reproduced by W. H. Shewring (*C.Q.* 1931, pp. 13, 15, 16), and an amplification of de Groot's work by R. Ullman (*Symb. Osl.* 1925, pp. 65–75).

it seems rather heavy (*hebetus*) and slow; yet it has a steady movement which is not without dignity.' But though damned by him with this faint praise, it is (to acquiesce for the moment in the language of feet) the historians' favourite; if we allow the cretic to be the chief basis of Cicero's clausulae (see p. 237), then we must allow the spondee to be the chief basis of theirs. But I would rather simply say that they preferred types with more long syllables.

Sallust, with his famous *brevitas* and his emulation of Thucydides, was leader of a general revolt against Ciceronianism.[1] Livy in most respects thought of himself as a Ciceronian, and not as a Sallustian;[2] but in this matter of clausulae he is, consciously or unconsciously, loyal to the historical tradition.

Tacitus in his history was the reverse of a 'periodic' writer: he did everything he could to break loose. An appreciable avoidance of the clausula – – – ⌣ (normal 23·5 per cent, Tacitus 17·7) and of – ∪ ∪ ∪ – ⌣ (= *esse videatur*) suggests that he may not have been quite indifferent to rhythmical considerations; on the other hand his use of – ∪ – ⌣ (18·8) is strikingly near to the normal 17·2, contrasting with 6·3 in Sallust and 11·0 in Livy and with the general desertion of this old Asiatic favourite even in the rhetorical tradition after Cicero. It looks as though he were determined in this, as in other respects, to go his own way.* It is significant that there is (so far as I can find) no reference to rhythm in the 856 pages of Syme's great work on Tacitus: he shunned all semblance of the periodic style.[3]

III. CONCLUSION

Cicero's followers pedantically cultivated his commonest clausulae till they choked out others. The types were

(1) clausulas esse   or esse credebant

(2) clausulas fecimus   or esse credemini

(3) clausulas feceramus   or esse concluderamus.†

---

* The *Dialogus de Oratoribus* was a different matter. Here he complied with the style appropriate to the genus, the Ciceronian tradition.

† – ∪ – ∪ ∪ ⌣ also retained some popularity.

In the early empire accent began again to assert itself over quantity in Latin. Foreigners found that it came to them more naturally. Thus the Syrian Commodianus (*c.* A.D. 238) begins his *Instructiones* with what he meant to be a hexameter,

> Prima praefatio nostra viam erranti demonstrat.[1]

Before A.D. 300 we find the grammarian Sacerdos *describing* the clausulae in metrical terms, but *selecting* them by accentual prejudice: he only recommends those which gave rise to the medieval accentual clausula, the so-called 'cursus'.[2] The cursus, as Norden observed,[3] was an accentual abstraction from the above three types:

´ ´ o o o o o	(*planus*)
´ ´ o o o o o o	(*tardus*)
´ ´ o o o o o o o	(*velox*).

After St Gregory the Great (end of sixth century) rhythm was generally neglected for four centuries, save in isolated pockets, to be revived in the eleventh century and adopted by the Roman Curia. The rules for the cursus were published by Gregory VIII, and we find them observed in the Latin of Dante and Petrarch; but Renaissance scholarship banished them as barbarous.

Cicero was very sharp about people who denied the reality of prose rhythm because it defied analysis: 'I do not know what sort of ears they have,' he said, 'nor indeed whether they are human at all.'[4] In Greek and Latin, including medieval Latin, there was at least the clausula to take hold of. But in modern languages its nature is remarkably elusive, especially in one like English, in which sentence-accent is so much a matter of discretion. A research student once called on E. M. Forster and asked if he would read aloud a passage from his works so that he could mark where the stresses fell. Forster obliged, but somewhat disconcerted his visitor by reading it with different stresses when asked to do it again. Yet we keep getting on to some sort of trail. What is it that makes us, as we write, instinctively choose on each occasion between alternative forms of words—*though* or *although*, *till* or *until*, *round* or *around*, *rise* or *arise*, *special* or *especial*? Largely, I think, a sense of rhythm. Quintilian seems to have thought the same when he said that you can choose whatever form 'compositio' prefers as between *vitavisse* and *vitasse, deprehendere* and *deprendere*: and again when he asked himself why Cicero, in the opening sentence of the *Verrines*, wrote *hosce* for *hos*, and could only reply, 'perhaps I cannot account for it, but only feel it is better'.[1] Rhythm forces itself on our attention when we compare unsophisticated prose with sophisticated, or Thucydides with Demosthenes; and analysis confirms the verdict of the ear by revealing definite tendencies in the latter, not in the former. Or conversely, we feel it when rhythm is dislocated, as by conscientious parsons who bring the Litany up to date, amending 'all that travel by land or by water' to 'all that travel by land, water or air'.

It may be that rhythm is more apparent at the end of sentences. I have always been struck by the conclusion of the Collect for the Second Sunday after Easter. Its petition begins with no regular rhythm —a high proportion of unstressed syllables interrupted by a stumbling-block of adjacent stresses: 'Give us grace that we may always most thankfully receive that His inestimable benefit'; but it continues, 'and also

> daily endeavour ourselves to follow
> the blessed steps of His most holy life'

—an Alcaic decasyllable rounded off by a blank verse. But I do not believe there is any cursus or clausula in English that can be identified as a type.[2]

Saintsbury concluded his long investigation with the dictum that the essence of prose rhythm lies in variety and divergence.[3] Variety is no doubt important: the ancient critics would have agreed there. But it is hard to see how it can be the *essence* of rhythm, which is a matter of measure and proportion. Wellek and Warren seem at least to be somewhere on the target: rhythmic prose 'differs from ordinary prose by the greater regularity of stress-distribution, which, however, must not reach isochronism (that is, regularity of time between rhythmical accents)'.[4] Not a very clear basis for a keen aesthetic pleasure! But that is where we have got back to after more than two thousand years of practice, theory and criticism.

PART III

STRUCTURE

6

PERIODIC PROSE

I. NATURE OF THE PERIOD

(a) The legacy of Aristotle

Structural artistry in mature Latin literature was largely a development of the virtues of the rhetorical 'period'. It was Thrasymachus who introduced period and 'colon', as well as rhythm, while Gorgias was responsible for the figures of rhetoric—assonance, balance, antithesis; that is, they consciously exploited features which had cropped up spontaneously in speech or literature.[1] Isocrates consummated their combined arts; but elegant though his periods may be, he was not so good at using periodic art to reinforce meaning as Demosthenes.[2] Isocratean art was suitable for 'epideictic' oratory, which the audience regarded as analogous to poetry, but not for serious business, when it might give councillors or jurors the impression that they were being beguiled against their better judgement.[3] As to the nature of the period, ancient critics were by no means clear or consistent. In what sense was such a sentence a περίοδος, a way round or circuit?

Let us begin, as before, with the fountain-head, the chapter in Aristotle's *Rhetoric*, III, 9, which follows that on rhythm.[4] Here are the essential passages, again in Jebb's translation:

The style must be either *running* (εἰρομένη—strung together) and unbroken in its chain, like the preludes of dithyrambs, or compact (κατεστραμμένη), like the 'strophe' and 'antistrophe' of the old poets....By a 'running' style I mean one which has no end in itself, until the sense comes to an end. It is unpleasing on account of this indefiniteness (ἄπειρον—see on rhythm, p. 136 above); for everyone wishes to descry the end. This is the reason why men gasp and become exhausted only at the goal;* they do not grow weary before, because they have the end in view. This then is the *running* species of style.

---

* ἐπὶ τοῖς καμπτῆρσιν ἐκπνέουσι καὶ ἐκλύονται. The turning-points could mark the end in the στάδιον or one-lap foot-race (see Cope and Sandys *ad loc.*). For Schmid's differing interpretation of this analogy see p. 169.

The *compact* style is that which is in periods; and by a period I mean a sentence which has a beginning and an end in itself, and is of a size to be taken in at one view (εὐσύνοπτον). Such a style is pleasing and easy to follow; pleasing, because it is the reverse of indefinite, and because the hearer always fancies that he has grasped something, and has something defined; whereas it is unpleasant to foresee nothing and to get nothing done. The style is easy to follow, because it is easy to remember; and this because periodic composition has number, the easiest of all things to remember. Hence all men remember verse more easily than unfettered prose; for verse has a number which is its measure. The period must also contain a complete sense. . . .

A period is either composed of members (κῶλα)* or simple. The period of members is a sentence complete in itself, with distinct parts, and such that it can be comfortably delivered (εὐανάπνευστος). . . . A member is one of the two parts of this period; by a simple period I mean that which consists of one member. 'Members', as well as periods, must be neither curt nor long. Brevity often trips up the hearer; for when he is still straining forward to that measure of which he carries a definition (i.e. preconceived notion) in his own mind, and then is violently checked by the cessation of the sentence, it necessarily happens that he stumbles, as it were, from the convulsion. Long sentences, on the other hand, leave the hearer behind; just as people who turn beyond the ordinary limit leave behind the companions of their walk.† In the same way the period which is too long becomes a speech in itself, or something like the prelude of a dithyramb. . . .

On this we may make the following observations.

(1) Ancient critics, in speaking of prose periods, often seem to have the strophe (σύστημα) of lyric poetry in mind.

(2) Aristotle envisages periods only of two or one members ('dicola' and 'monocola'), though far more complicated yet highly artistic sentences were to be found in Isocrates, for instance. Was this because he thought that anything more than a dicolon was too long to be uttered in one breath?‡ Or was he under the influence of current metrical theory?[1] Whatever the reason, the analogy from running he has just used and the phrase 'a member is one of the two parts of this

---

* Jebb gratuitously adds 'several' to ἐν κώλοις, and conceals the fact that by using ἕτερον Aristotle shows that he has only two-limbed periods in mind, as Demetrius observed (*De Eloc.* 34).

† The image is of a portico with a natural, though exceedable, turning-place for peripatetics.

‡ εὐανάπνευστος. Cf. Dion. Hal. *De Comp.* 23; Cic. *De Or.* III, 182. Demosthenes was said to have developed such good breath-control by exercises that he could raise and lower his voice twice within a sentence (Cic. *De Or.* I, 261).

period' inevitably suggest the hairpin racecourse, and the metaphor from it at Aeschylus, *Agamemnon*, 344,

κάμψαι διαύλου θάτερον κῶλον πάλιν

to turn round and complete the other limb of the course.

Schmid therefore wishes to take περίοδος as a metaphor from such a racecourse.[1] It is certainly apt—more apt than on any other interpretation; for the speaker, like the runner, can take in the whole course at the start, and plan his tactics and breath-control accordingly (εὐσύνοπτος, εὐανάπνευστος). It provides a good sense for the term κατεστραμμένος —turned back on itself. But unfortunately it involves taking καμπτῆρες to be the turning-point, not the end, of the race; and to say that only there do the runners gasp and relax, not getting tired previously because they can see the end ahead,* does not make good sense. Nor can the image of the hairpin racecourse be easily applied to what Aristotle calls περίοδοι of one member.†

(3) Aristotle commends periods for qualities consistent with his general aesthetic theory. These enable us to ascribe a certain aptitude to the word περίοδος, though a much vaguer one. To Aristotle beauty depended chiefly on order, symmetry and limit.‡ As he said in the previous chapter, 'the unlimited is vague and unsatisfactory'.[2] In the *Poetics* he laid it down that tragedy was 'a representation of an action that is whole and complete and of a certain magnitude'.§ Again in epic the story must be constructed, as in tragedy, round a single piece of action 'whole and complete in itself, with a beginning, middle and end, so that, like a living organism, it may produce its own peculiar form of pleasure'. We begin to recognize what he was looking for in the period ('of a certain magnitude' is relevant as well as wholeness and completeness). Now the figure which *par excellence* was whole and perfect (ὅλη καὶ τέλειος) was the circle—balanced, neat and free from straggling superfluity. So the word περίοδος or circuit seems to have

---

* 'Erst an den καμπτῆρες atmen daher (die Läufer) aus und entspannen sich; denn das End voraus sehend ermüden sie nicht vorher' (p. 121). I hope I have not misinterpreted.

† Schmid's explanation (*Prosarhythmus* (1960), p. 123) is hard to accept.

‡ τοῦ δὲ καλοῦ μέγιστα εἴδη τάξις καὶ συμμετρία καὶ τὸ ὡρισμένον, *Met.* M 3, p. 1078 a 36 (Zehetmeier, *Philologus*, 1930, p. 200).

§ VII, 1450 b 8: κεῖται δ' ἡμῖν, τὴν τραγῳδίαν τελείας καὶ ὅλης πράξεως εἶναι μίμησιν ἐχούσης τι μέγεθος (Zehetmeier, *ibid.* p. 203).

been applied to sentences which had analogous qualities to this—as we say, 'a well-rounded period'—without being more than vaguely applicable.*

(4) Aristotle makes things much more difficult by saying that a period can be one-membered. Zehetmeier, taking limitation to be the chief desideratum, suggests that it is the rhythm at the beginning and end that marks off a sentence as a period.[1] Aristotle did indeed express an opinion at the end of his previous chapter (not very well supported, see p. 137), that the first and fourth paeons were suitable feet for beginning and ending a period respectively, and that rhythm could make the reader aware that the close had come. But can one really say that the rhythms at the beginning and end of monocola in the Attic orators are so marked? The rhetorician Hermogenes (c. A.D. 170), who based himself on 'the ancients', alleges that a monocolon qualifies as a period if the word-order is so arranged by hyperbaton that the reader's mind is in suspense as to the meaning until the end (an experience only too familiar to readers of German).[2] This seems at least as plausible an explanation, and incidentally it seems to link up with what Demetrius says about the καμπή or συστροφή at the end.† But the monocolon remains an Aristotelian mystery. For Cicero no such thing existed.[3]

(5) Aristotle mentions only in passing that 'a period must contain a complete sense'. The instance he gives shows that he means something quite obvious—that the structure of the sentence must be such that it does not seem to finish before the sense is complete. Of the subtler relationship between meaning and artistry he does not speak.

So much for what Aristotle said. It is important to set it out because, although later writers constantly refer to this chapter, they were often talking about a different conception of period and trying to make his words apply to it. Later Peripatetic views on periods are best represented by the first thirty-five chapters of Demetrius' De Elocutione, of unknown date.

---

* This is how Donysius seems to have conceived it: for example, περιόδῳ τε καὶ κύκλῳ περιλαμβάνειν τὰ νοήματαί (Isoc. 2, 538); εἰς περιόδου κύκλος, ὁμοειδὴς σχημάτων τάξις (De Comp. 19).

† 10, 17; see p. 171 n.

170

(b) Views of Demetrius and 'Longinus'

Demetrius begins by comparing a member in prose with a verse in poetry—not quite aptly, since a member is a unit of thought, not rhythm, as he promptly admits. Such members should not be too short, except when the context makes shortness expressive and appropriate, nor too long except in elevated passages (where presumably the speaker is 'carried away'). A period of such members he first defines (10) as 'an organization of members or phrases deftly fitted to the subject in hand'. Notice that he stresses this quality of expressive logical power much more than Aristotle. But he proceeds to praise Aristotle's definition, 'a period is a portion of speech having a beginning and end', since 'the use of the word περίοδος implies that there has been a beginning at one point and will be an ending at another, and that one is hastening to a goal like runners at the start. For they see the beginning and end of the course at the same time. Hence the name περίοδος, from the similarity to paths that go round in a circle and come back again (κυκλοειδέσι καὶ περιωδευμένοις)'.* Here Demetrius seems to be thinking of the hairpin racecourse which fits Aristotle's two-limbed period only. Yet elsewhere (16) he speaks of periods as normally consisting of from two to four members, and he gives an admirable simile (13) for what Greco-Roman writers in general as well as ourselves conceive a period to be: 'the members in the periodic style may be compared with stones which support and hold together a vaulted roof'.†

* For περίοδος as 'a coming round to a starting-point' cf. Plutarch, *Sol.* 4.

† Demetrius does however allow (deferential to Aristotle as ever) that there can be a simple, single-member period (17). He says it must qualify by length, and by the καμπή at the end. What is this καμπή? He quotes as illustration 'Ἡροδότου Ἀλικαρνησσέος ἱστορίης ἀπόδεξις ἥδε' and 'ἡ γὰρ σαφὴς φράσις πολὺ φῶς παρέχεται ταῖς τῶν ἀκουόντων διανοίαις'. Elsewhere (10) he quotes from Demosthenes, 'μάλιστα μὲν εἵνεκα τοῦ νομίζειν συμφέρειν τῇ πόλει λελῦσθαι τὸν νόμον, εἶτα καὶ τοῦ παιδὸς εἵνεκα τοῦ Χαβρίου, ὡμολόγησα τούτοις, ὡς ἂν οἷός τ' ὦ, συνερεῖν', and comments that it has a kind of καμπή or συστροφή at the end. Καμπή should mean a 'turn' (cf. καμπτήρ), or possibly 'goal'. Volkmann rendered it as 'Abründung' (*Rhetorik*, pp. 508–9). If it can mean a 'twist', a sharp rounding-off of *sense*, it fits in well enough with the first and third examples, and with Demetrius' demonstration, by recasting the third (11), that periodic merit can be dissipated by rearrangement. But the second example seems quite featureless (cf. Zehetmeier, *Philologus*, 1930, pp. 426–7). Schmid claims that καμπή is the point in the middle of a period when the rhythm turns back on itself (*Prosarhythmus*, 1959, p. 130). This fits in with Demetrius' phrases κατὰ τὸ τέλος (10), περὶ τὸ τέλος (17), since turning-posts are sometimes so called. But do Greek rhythms in fact behave according to his theory? For further discussion of the underlying confusion see Grube's notes on 12 and 17. He translates καμπή as 'turn', but does not discuss it in his appendix on technical terms.

To this we may add the testimony of the author *On the Sublime*, no trifler with art for art's sake:

Nothing is of greater service in giving grandeur to such passages than the way in which the various members are put together. It is the same with the human body. None of the members has any value by itself apart from the others, yet one with another they all constitute a perfect organism (σύστημα). Similarly if these effects of grandeur are separated, the sublimity is scattered with them to the winds: but if they are united into a single system and embraced moreover by the bonds of rhythm, then by being merely rounded into a period (αὐτῷ τῷ κύκλῳ) they gain a living voice. In such a period, one might say, the grandeur comes from a multitude of contributors.[1]

In sum, to Aristotle a period was a sentence consisting of one or two members, complete in rhythm and thought, of such a size that the speaker could compass it in one breath; to Demetrius it was one of two to four members, compact and well proportioned, with the subordinate parts of the thought put first and the operative word at the end.

(c) Views of Cicero and Quintilian

A passage from Cicero's *Orator* (37–8) may serve to introduce the art as practised at Rome:[2]

There are several kinds of speeches differing one from other and impossible to reduce to one type; so I shall not include at this time that class to which the Greeks gave the name of epideictic (Lat. *demonstrativum*), because they were produced as show-pieces, as it were, for the pleasure they will give, a class comprising eulogies, descriptions, histories and exhortations...and all other speeches unconnected with the battle of public life (*forensis contentio*). Not that their style is negligible, for it may be called the nurse of that orator whom we wish to delineate and about whom we design to speak more particularly. This style increases one's vocabulary, and allows the use of a somewhat greater freedom in rhythm and sentence-structure. It likewise indulges in a neatness and symmetry of sentences, and is allowed to use well-defined and rounded periods; and the ornamentation is done of set purpose, with no attempt at concealment, but openly and avowedly, so that words correspond to words as if measured off in equal phrases, frequently opposites are put side by side, and things contrasted are paired; clauses are made to end in the same way and with similar sound. But in actual legal practice we do this less frequently and certainly less obviously.

Any study of artistry in prose must take the epideictic as a starting-point, since here the features often disguised in forensic speeches may be most easily observed. Cicero himself is liable to do so, though he insists that the *Orator* is directed to speaking as a force in public life,[1] and that the epideictic is only partially relevant to it. He claims, no doubt justly, to give a fuller account than any predecessor of periodic structure, at *De Oratore*, III, 173–98, and more importantly at *Orator*, 164–78, 204–11 and 221–6.* What Quintilian says at IX, 4, 22–44, and 122–30, is almost wholly based on the *Orator*.[2]

A certain doubt concerning the essence of the period is suggested by the variety of words used for it by Roman critics.[3] The earliest, the Auctor ad Herennium, uses *continuatio*, explaining it more vaguely than Aristotle as 'a compact and continuous group of words in which the expression of thoughts is complete (*absoluta*)'.[4] Cicero and Quintilian likewise include *continuatio* in their list of words for 'period'.[5] But elsewhere these critics sometimes use it in the wider sense of a verbal continuum or sentence (= *complexio, perpetuitas verborum*);[6] and in one place Cicero actually says 'numerus in continuatione nullus est', explaining it as a series of words *not* organized artistically into *articuli* (κόμματα) and *membra*,[7] so that *continuatio* is here the opposite of 'period'!

Aristotle's notion of it as bounded (πεπερασμένος) is represented by the terms *circumscriptio* or *conclusio*; but *conclusio* introduces further confusion, since it may seem in some contexts, most misleadingly, to refer to the 'conclusion' of a sentence in our sense of the word, and so to a rhythmic clausula,† quite apart from the fact that it is also a normal word for 'peroration'. In one passage it is coupled with '*certos cursus*', which is glossed by Sandys as περιόδους.[8] Can this be a reminiscence of the race-track metaphor? As being easy to grasp, εὐσύνοπτος, it is called *comprehensio*. Another word is *conversio*, which might seem an attempt to render καμπή, but Cicero definitely equates it with *ambitus*,[9]

---

* The discontinuity here is a symptom of the fact, already noted, that he does not extricate this subject from that of rhythm.

† Thus in the Loeb editions G. L. Hendrickson probably mistranslates at *Brutus*, 33 and H. M. Hubbell at *Orator*, 169, 170; whereas H. Rackham avoids the pitfall at *De Oratore*, II, 34; III, 174. Cicero uses the phrase 'verba versu includere', *De Or.* III, 184. Cf. 'verba finientur', *Or.* 164; 'concluse apteque', 177.

which is the commonest rendering of περίοδος. *Ambitus*, with *circuitus*, *circumductum* (or *circumductio*) and *orbis verborum*, represents the Greek idea that a period somehow goes round and returns to its starting-point, or at least is 'well-rounded' like a circle.* Quintilian, however, generally avoids the problem of definition by using the naturalized word *periodus*.

(d) Features of the period

'Quod carmen artificiosa verborum conclusione aptius?' exclaims Antonius in the *De Oratore*:[1] 'Is any poem better turned than an artistic piece of periodic prose?' Cicero speaks of the skilled orator organizing a period as soon as he knows what he wants to say, his mind disposing the words with lightning rapidity in appropriate order and rhythm relative to a foreseen ending.[2] It is a matter of ear and trained instinct, not of regular measure. Indeed, if he finds it has turned out too regular, he modifies it:† 'when he has bound it in rhythm and form, he looses it and frees it again by changing the order'.[3] But he must not be caught doing so.[4] If a period goes on too long, or ends too soon, this is detected by the ear. (The ear, you notice; but the thought must be completed simultaneously.)[5] Cicero criticized the Asiatics for introducing 'inania quaedam verba' to fill up the 'numeric' form.[6] But surely this is just what one associates with Cicero himself. And is it necessarily a vice? Quintilian asks, 'Why can it happen that in a period we feel that, even when the sense is complete, there is something missing?' He proceeds to quote the opening of the *Verrines*: 'Neminem vestrum ignorare arbitror, iudices, hunc per hosce dies sermonem vulgi atque hanc opinionem populi Romani fuisse', and comments, 'Why was it not enough to say "sermonem vulgi fuisse" (for that would have been tolerable artistically)?‡ I cannot tell, but my ear tells me that without the redundancy (of the addition "atque hanc opinionem

---

* This is clearly Cicero's conception when he says, 'placet omnia dici...illa circumscriptione ambituque, ut *tanquam in orbe inclusa* currat oratio quoad insistat in singulis perfectis absolutisque sententiis' (*Or.* 207). Cf. ἡ περίοδος σύνθεσίς τίς ἐστι περιηγμένη (Dem. *De Eloc.* 30).

† In his earlier speeches Cicero himself tended to an excess of isocolic antithesis (Laurand, *Études*, 1907, pp. 130 f.).

‡ 'Compositio enim patiebatur': presumably he means that the sentence would not have been intolerable, its second colon being no shorter than the first; or possibly that the clausula would have had the same rhythm.

populi Romani") the period would not have been complete.'* The Book of Common Prayer is full of cases in which a synonym appears to have been added to prevent a period from being *curtum*; for example,

> the Scripture moveth us in sundry places
> to acknowledge and confess our manifold sins *and wickednesses*.†

In order to be easily grasped and uttered a period was supposed to be limited in length to what could be managed in one breath. Demetrius gives four cola as a *maximum*, Cicero is less rigid, mindful perhaps of his own tendencies (he has one of thirteen cola at *In Pisonem*, 96). He too prescribes as a 'full period' four cola of a length approximate to a hexameter; but he qualifies this by saying that he has in mind a mean (*mediocritatem*), since often a longer or shorter sentence will be appropriate.‡ Indeed it is important to intersperse periods with shorter sentences to avoid satiety if for no other reason. The shortest of these, the 'incisa', he compares with little daggers (*pugiunculi*). In forensic speeches, indeed, they may predominate.[1]

One general principle of organization is that the last member should be longer than the rest, 'as though containing and embracing all', as Demetrius says; 'otherwise the period will seem mutilated and lame'.[2] Cicero's Crassus lays down that the later members must be either equal to the preceding, or 'quod etiam est melius et iucundius', longer.[3] This has been dubbed in modern times the 'Law of Increasing Members'.§ It is a law of universal literary, and indeed musical, application. It is found in the earliest stratum of the *Iliad*, the Catalogue in book II. Here the order of names may well have been determined by natural artistic ear, and the common caesuras of the hexameter lent themselves to the effect; for example, 502:

Κώπας | Εὔτρησίν τε | πολυτρήρωνά τε Θίσβην.

* IX, 4, 119. Cf. Cic. *Or.* 168: 'meae quidem (aures) et perfecto completoque verborum ambitu gaudent, et curta sentiunt nec amant redundantia'.

† When Wilde read from his proofs, 'The world has become sad because a puppet was once melancholy', Yeats asked, 'Why do you change "sad" to "melancholy"?' Wilde replied that he wanted a full sound at the close of his sentence.

‡ Dem. *De Eloc.* 16; Cic. *Or.* 221-2. Quintilian (IX, 4, 125) understands 'hexametri' here to mean 'senarii'; but this is probably a mistake, for in colometry and stichometry the unit of measure was the *dactylic* hexameter ('μέχρι τοῦ ἡρωϊκοῦ': Hermogenes, 243, 28). Cf. H. Diels, *Hermes* (1882), p. 379.

§ O. Behaghel, *Indogerm. Forsch.* XXV (1909), 139. He studies it in Greek and Latin, and in old and modern German. A fuller study of its operation in Latin may be found in E. Lindholm, *Stilistische Studien u.s.w.* (1931). Cf. E. Fraenkel, *Horace* (1957), p. 351 n.

It is a feature of early religious formulae, such as ὗε, κύε, ὑπέρχευε. Its operation is clearest when least dictated by the sense, as in the carol refrain

> Ding dong ding,
> Ding-a-dong-a ding,
> Ding dong ding dong ding-a-dong ding.

It can be felt even on the smallest scale:

> Friends, Romans, countrymen...
> Dubo...Dubon...Dubonnet.

On the grand scale it may be illustrated from the speech of Abraham Lincoln, a very Gorgianic orator, at Gettysburg:[1]

> But in a larger sense
>> we cannot dedicate,
>> we cannot consecrate,
>> we cannot hallow this ground.

And in ampler members:

> We here highly resolve that these dead shall not have died in vain;
> that this nation, under God, shall have a new birth of freedom;
> and that government of the people, by the people, for the people,
> shall not perish from the earth.

Denniston instances a period at Demosthenes, VIII, 21–2, which has six οὔτε clauses, the first four short, the next two much longer and sub-divided, the last very elaborately so.[2]

There are naturally exceptions to the law. An apodosis, we are told, should be shorter than a protasis.[3] Certainly this can have a trenchant effect. Look at some verses of I Corinthians xiii, for example,

κἂν ἔχω προφητείαν καὶ εἴδω τὰ μυστήρια πάντα καὶ πᾶσαν τὴν γνῶσιν,
κἂν ἔχω πᾶσαν τὴν πίστιν ὥστε ὄρη μεθιστάναι, ἀγάπην δὲ μὴ ἔχω,
οὐθέν εἰμι. *

---

* I give this instance to draw attention to the remarkable 'periodic' of this chapter, sometimes quite Gorgianic.

Verse 7. οὐ χαίρει ἐπὶ τῇ ἀδικίᾳ, συγχαίρει δὲ τῇ ἀληθείᾳ, πάντα στέργει, πάντα πιστεύει, πάντα ἐλπίζει, πάντα ὑπομένει. Here we have two balanced, antithetical, assonant cola, followed by a tetracolon with anaphora and gradual increase of members.

Verse 11. Another tetracolon with repetition and gradual increase: ὅτε ἤμην νήπιος, ἐλάλουν ὡς νήπιος, ἐφρόνουν ὡς νήπιος, ἐλογιζόμην ὡς νήπιος.

C. Antonius devised an effective deflation:

> Sed neque accusatorem eum metuo, quod sum innocens,
> neque competitorem vereor, quod sum Antonius,
> neque consulem spero, quod est Cicero.[1]

Or again, considerations of precedence may prevail over purely artistic canons. More important things and persons come first—

> Aeneas Anchisiades | et fidus Achates:

Achates knows his place. On the other hand Quintilian remarks that one would expect a lesser marvel to be made to lead up to a greater, but that Cicero reverses this order in the interests of structural grace ('vicit compositionis decor'), so that the longer member comes second:

> Saxa atque solitudines voci respondent;
> bestiae saepe immanes cantu flectuntur atque consistunt.[2]

We may question his major, but what matters is his artistic feeling.

Tetracolon in its simplest form is exemplified in Cicero's famous denunciation of Catiline: 'abiit, excessit, evasit, erupit'.[3] A short example with increasing members is 'non metus, non religio, non deorum vis, non hominum existimatio'.[4] Such structure may be felt even when it is not coterminous with the sentence, or again, when it is split into *pugiunculi*, as in a passage Cicero quotes from himself:

> domus tibi deerat? at habebas: pecunia superabat? at egebas.[5]

In a famous example (criticized by Demetrius for artificiality) Demosthenes contrasted his early life with that of Aeschines:

ἐτέλεις, ἐγὼ δ᾽ ἐτελούμην· ἐδίδασκες, ἐγὼ δ᾽ ἐφοίτων· ἐτριταγωνίστεις, ἐγὼ δ᾽ ἐθεώμην· ἐξέπιπτες, ἐγὼ δ᾽ ἐσύριττον. *

Verse 12. An ampler tetracolon, with repetition and parallelism:

> βλέπομεν γὰρ ἄρτι δι᾽ ἐσόπτρου ἐν αἰνίγματι,
> τότε δὲ πρόσωπον πρὸς πρόσωπον·
> ἄρτι γινώσκω ἐκ μέρους,
> τότε δὲ ἐπιγνώσομαι καθὼς καὶ ἐπεγνώσθην.

And finally the triad πίστις, ἐλπίς, ἀγάπη.

* 'You were initiating, I was initiated; you taught, I attended; you acted minor parts, I was a spectator; you failed in them, I hissed.' (*De Cor.* 265; Dem. *De Eloc.* 250, and Rhys Roberts's note for Milton, *Apology for Smectymnuus.*)

Milton adapted this, but spoilt the effect not only by verbosity but *by adding a fifth member*. Naturally there is a certain tendency for a tetra-colon to fall into balanced and often antithetical halves.

A much greater part is played by tricolon, which the Auctor ad Herennium describes as 'commodissima et absolutissima exornatio',[1] and the elder Seneca called 'this latest (? or novices') craze' (*novicium hunc morbum*) in the declamation schools of his day.[2] Triads had magic properties. They occur naturally in such primitive formulae as the hymn of the Arval Brothers. And indeed tricolon crescendo is a feature of Christian liturgy:

> Te Deum laudamus;
> Te Dominum confitemur;
> Te aeternum Patrem omnis terra veneratur;
>
> Tibi omnes angeli,
> Tibi caeli et universae potestates,
> Tibi Cherubim et Seraphin incessabili voce proclamant.

The Litany provides good illustrations, since its petitions are organized, it would seem, largely on artistic principles. Of the first eight, no fewer than six are of this form, for example

> From all blindness of heart,
> From pride, vain-glory and hypocrisy;
> From envy, hatred, malice and all uncharitableness....

The simplest possible tricolon is Caesar's 'veni, vidi, vici'. But some of the most effective examples have increasing members (or embracing third member), and are thrown into relief, as above, by anaphora, another feature of archaic religious formulae.

Symmetry goes with antithesis, and assonance with symmetry. Temper these with rhythm, and subject them to a larger proportion, and you have the ideal rhetorical period. If it proves to be less com-monly found in practice than one might expect from the lip-service of criticism, it nevertheless provided a notion which exercised a consider-able and generally beneficent influence on literary art. Since most of Cicero's speeches are political or forensic, we must not expect it to be characteristic of anything but his exordia, perorations and set-pieces, at any rate in his mature period.

II. ARTISTIC STRUCTURE IN LATIN PROSE

(a) Oratory

The best way to appreciate the impact of Greek rhetorical art on Latin prose in the latter part of the second century is to observe what immediately preceded it. We are fortunate in possessing a sufficiently long excerpt from a speech made in the Senate by the elder Cato on behalf of the Rhodians in 168 B.C.—and Cato was renowned as an effective orator.

Scio solere plerisque hominibus rebus secundis atque prolixis atque prosperis animum excellere atque superbiam atque ferociam augescere atque crescere. Quo mihi nunc magnae curae est, quod haec res tam secunde processit, ne quid in consulendo adversi eveniat, quod nostras secundas res confutet, neve haec laetitia nimis luxuriose eveniat. Advorsae res edomant et edocent, quid opus siet facto; secundae res laetitia transvorsum trudere solent a recte consulendo atque intellegendo. Quo maiore opere dico suadeoque, uti haec res aliquot dies proferatur, dum ex tanto gaudio in potestatem nostram redeamus.

Atque ego quidem arbitror, Rhodienses noluisse nos ita depugnare uti depugnatum est, neque regem Persen vinci. Sed non Rhodienses modo id noluere, sed multos populos atque multas nationes idem noluisse arbitror. Atque haud scio an partim eorum fuerint qui non nostrae contumeliae causa id noluerint evenire: sed enim id metuere ne, si nemo esset homo quem vereremur, quidquid luberet faceremus. Ne sub imperio nostro in servitute nostra essent, libertatis suae causa in ea sententia fuisse arbitror. Atque Rhodienses tamen Persen publice numquam adiuvere. Cogitate, quanto nos inter nos privatim cautius facimus. Nam unusquisque nostrum, si quis adversus rem suam quid fieri arbitratur, summa vi contra nititur ne advorsus eam fiat; quod illi tamen perpessi.[1]

'All that', comments Gellius, 'could perhaps have been expressed more elegantly and rhythmically (*distinctius numerosiusque*), but I do not think it could have been expressed more forcefully or vividly.' Inelegant it certainly is. The first, short sentence has *atque* five times, the third being an odd-man-out since it connects clauses instead of words. 'Augescer(e) atque crescere' is ugly in sound and too lilting in rhythm. 'Secundis atque prolixis atque prosperis' is too pleonastic. The second sentence is falsely balanced, because the *quod* clauses are not syntactically parallel; and 'luxurios(e) eveniat' is again too tripping a clausula. In the next *res* is unnecessarily repeated; and the fourth has a hexameter-ending, 'nostram redeamus'. In the succeeding paragraph every other sentence begins with *atque*. The second has *sed* with two different forces and *multas* repeated too conscientiously. (Such repetition is harmless, but dulls the effect for more significant use.) Again there is a hexameter-ending 'luberet faceremus', and again a valueless repetition, *nostra*, and a clumsy one, *advorsus eam*; and there are two dispondaic clausulae, 'adiuvere' and 'tamen perpessi'.

Cicero was surprised that early writers, who are sometimes found accidentally constructing good periods, did not observe their effectiveness and consciously cultivate them.[1] What was needed was the elimination of syntactical inconsistencies—sense constructions, anacolutha, *nominativi pendentes*, etc.—organization which should allow the subject to remain unchanged throughout, and 'hypotaxis', the logical subordination of clauses, to replace 'parataxis', or simple juxtaposition. In Cicero's opinion it was M. Aemilius Lepidus Porcina, consul in 137, who first introduced to Rome the Greek smoothness, the periodic form and 'the artistic pen' (*artifex stilus*).[2] The fragments of the speeches of the younger Scipio and Laelius, and of Gaius Gracchus, show them groping at least after artistic form; and in the next generation those of L. Licinius Crassus (140–91), hero of the *De Oratore*, are sufficient to allow us to see why Cicero looked back upon him as one of his masters. Crassus was steeped in Greek; and it was from the study of Isocrates and Ephorus that Cicero developed his periodic art.[*]

We have seen that he was alive to the danger that any parade of such art in political and forensic speeches might prejudice the hearers against an orator's case. No one likes to feel he is being 'got at' against his better judgement. At the most it might be used to heighten the effect of exordium or peroration. It belonged however chiefly to 'epideictic' oratory, where the audience was content to be carried away, or to occasions on which the decision was practically foregone.[†] Where, then,

---

[*] *Or*. 207. Cf. H. Nettleship, *J.P.* 1886, pp. 40–4. Cicero was greatly helped by the new syntactical device of ablative absolute with present participle (L. R. Palmer, *The Latin Language*, 1954, p. 130).

[†] *Or*. 37, 170, 209–10. Cf. Ar. *Rhet*. 1, 3, 2; Quint. IX, 4, 128–9. Demetrius says (*De Eloc*. 252), of the style he calls δεινόν, that it requires a succession of short periods (of two members or so), since periods formed of many members produce κάλλος rather than δεινότης.

in the extant speeches of Cicero shall we look for this style? I will plump for the *Pro Archia* and the *Ninth Philippic*.* The former, a specimen of his earlier style, was delivered in 62, six years or so before the *Orator* was composed. There was little case to answer, so five-sixths is devoted to a eulogy of literature (Archias being a poet). And indeed Cicero begins by warning the jury that, despite the solemn surroundings, he proposes to expatiate on this topic in a style 'remote from what is customary in court and even from forensic language' (3). The *Ninth Philippic* belongs to the last year of the orator's life; and since it was made for the purpose of proposing public honours for his dead friend Servius Sulpicius Rufus (writer of the famous letter of consolation on Tullia's death), it is in the nature of funeral panegyric, a branch of the epideictic.

The exordium (1–$4a$) and the peroration (31–2) of the *Pro Archia* contain ten sentences in all. Their lengths are noteworthy. If we take as our measure the maximum hexameter, seventeen syllables, these sentences contain the following totals of hexameter-equivalents: 8, $4\frac{1}{2}$, $4\frac{1}{2}$, 3, $2\frac{1}{2}$, 16, 4, 7, 10, 5. So much for lip-service to the Greek prescription of 4 as the measure of a 'full period'. Of the ten clausulae no fewer than six display the Asiatic ditrochee.

The opening period was famous in antiquity:[1]

> Si quis est in me ingeni, iudices,
>   quod sentio quam sit exiguum,
> aut si quae exercitatio dicendi,
>   in qua me non infitior mediocriter esse versatum,
> aut si huiusce rei ratio aliqua ab optimarum
>   artium studiis ac disciplina profecta,
>   a qua ego nullum confiteor aetatis meae tempus abhorruisse,
> earum rerum omnium vel in primis hic Aulus Licinius
>   fructum a me repetere prope suo iure debet.

Notice how both the three protases and the three relative clauses respectively increase, and how the ample apodosis seems to embrace them all.

In the body of the speech the sentences are naturally shorter in

---

* Cicero himself instances the praises of Sicily in his *Verrines*, Actio Secunda, II, 2.

general, but the structure is still largely periodic. Here is another famous passage, the praise of liberal studies (16):

> Quodsi non hic tantus fructus ostenderetur,
> et si ex his studiis delectatio sola peteretur,
> tamen ut opinor hanc animi remissionem humanissimam
> ac liberalissimam iudicaretis.

(Tricolon crescendo with assonance.) Then

> Nam ceterae neque temporum sunt, neque aetatum omnium, neque locorum;

('neque locorum' is lighter than the two preceding cola, since it is not a climax artistically, but a lead into the fuller period that follows):

> at haec studia
>> adulescentiam alunt,
>> senectutem oblectant,
>> secundas res ornant,
>> adversis perfugium ac solacium praebent,
>> delectant domi,
>> non impediunt foris,
>> pernoctant nobiscum,
>> peregrinantur,
>> rusticantur.

You will remember how Cicero said that the trained orator would modify a period which would otherwise be too regular. Here we may feel we can see him doing so: without the intrusive 'ac solacium' and 'pernoctant nobiscum', the regularity would be intolerable.

The *Pro Archia* is 'exquisitely composed' (Lord Brougham), but still rather elaborate (witness the above passage), perhaps a little Asiatic. The style of the *Ninth Philippic* is different and more mature. I reckon that it contains approximately 69 sentences, and that of these only eleven exceed the length of four full hexameters; nor does any exceed it by more than a few words.* (By contrast the vote proposed at the end is a huge rigmarole strung together with 'cum...' as similar documents today are strung together with 'whereas...'.)

---

* *Distinctio* must be to some extent subjective. The second sentence is the longest, but some might divide it at 'futurus'.

Here is a typical passage (10–11):

Reddite igitur, patres conscripti, ei vitam c(ui) ademistis.

Vita enim mortuorum in memoria est posita vivorum.

Perficite, ut is quem vos inscii ad mortem misistis immortalitatem habeat a vobis.

Cui si statuam in rostris decreto vestro statueritis, nulla eius legationem posteritatis obscurabit oblivio.

Nam reliqua Servi Sulpici vita multis erit praeclarisque monumentis ad omnem memoriam commendata.

Semper illius gravitatem, constantiam, fidem, praestantem in re publica tuenda curam atque prudentiam omnium mortalium fama celebravit.

Nec vero silebitur admirabilis quaedam et incredibilis ac paene divina eius in legibus interpretandis aequitate explicanda scientia.

Omnes ex omni aetate qui in hac civitate intellegentiam iuris habuerunt, si unum in locum conferantur, cum Servio Sulpicio non sint comparandi.

Nec enim ille magis iuris consultus quam iustitiae fuit.

Ita ea quae proficiscebantur e legibus et ab iure civili semper ad facilitatem aequitatemque referebat, neque instituere litium actiones malebat quam controversias tollere.

Ergo hoc statuae monimento non eget, habet alia maiora.

Haec enim statua mortis honestae testis erit, illa memoria vitae gloriosae, ut hoc magis monimentum grati senatus quam clari viri futurum sit.

These twelve sentences display eight different clausulae, six of them from among Cicero's favourites (see p. 156). The Asiatic ditrochee occurs in only one. Of the elaborate balance and structure of the Isocratean period there is scarcely a trace until the last sentence, with its graceful antitheses. Rhetoric has been absorbed and disciplined in a style both varied and simple, despite every temptation from the occasion to be fulsome.

(b) History

So much for oratory. Meanwhile, history had emerged from the chronicle stage with the *Commentaries* of Julius Caesar. Here we should not expect to find the periodic style. Any detectable artistry would have defeated his purpose of giving the impression that the facts were speaking for themselves. The style is good because it is both clear and appropriate—'pura et inlustris brevitas' was Cicero's appreciation.[1] It is noteworthy that speeches are rarely given in *oratio recta*: there was to be no temptation to rhetorical embellishment.[2]

But there were also orators at this time who cultivated a rugged style and called themselves Thucydideans;[3] and soon there emerged a Thucydidean historian, who was however a highly self-conscious and mannered artist, Sallust.[4] He was reacting against the oratorical style which had dominated Greek historical writing since Ephorus and Theopompus, the pupils of Isocrates. It is true that he retains a few characteristics of the traditional style. We find the tricolon crescendo on a small scale in his description of the Numidian race as 'infidum, ingenio mobili, novarum rerum avidum'. On a larger scale we find it fairly often.[5] Here is an example in which all the cola are bipartite:*

> dominari illi volunt, vos liberi esse;
> facere illi iniurias, vos prohibere;
> postremo sociis nostris veluti hostibus, hostibus pro sociis utuntur.

And here is a tetracolon crescendo, from the character-sketch of Sempronia:[6]

> sed ea saepe antehac
> fidem prodiderat,
> creditum abiuraverat,
> caedis conscia fuerat,
> luxuria atque inopia praeceps abierat.

Sallust has also a way of coupling words which are practically synonyms, and sometimes he may have done this to improve the weighting of a final colon—'famam atque gloriam', 'maerore et luctu', 'varius incertusque', 'gaudium atque laetitiam', 'facie voltuque'.[7] But all this

---

* *Jug.* 31, 23. This comes from a speech inserted to illustrate Memmius' eloquence, but 'huiuscemodi' (30, 4) shows it is not reported verbatim but worked up by Sallust, as even extant speeches generally were by historians (for example, Cato's and Caesar's in the *Catiline*).

amounts to little. We have seen (p. 161) that he eschewed the rhythms of the oratorical tradition. Even the younger Seneca found his sentences 'amputated and apt to end before one expects'.[1] That would seem to mean that he had no care to satisfy architectonic expectations, arresting attention by abruptness.[2] But reading through his extant works I have been at a loss for an illustration. This may simply be due to insensitivity in my ear; but I cannot help wondering whether Sallust ever did raise such expectations, for he is not a periodic writer in the sense we have been considering. Abrupt his sentences certainly are, and generally short, with hurried asyndeton. He is full of archaisms and Grecisms. He eschews normal word-order, saying, for instance, 'designati consules' (hence, perhaps, his passion for chiasmus). The close of the *Jugurtha* seems wilfully unstudied, with its double change of subject and its simple conclusion:

Sed postquam bellum in Numidia confectum et Iugurtham Romam vinctum adduci nuntiatum est, Marius consul absens factus est *et ei* decreta provincia Gallia *isque* Calendis Januariis magna gloria consul triumphavit, *et* ea tempestate spes et opes civitatis in illo sitae.

One of his mannerisms is to clinch a long sentence with a short epigrammatic one, as here:

Ea tempestate in exercitu nostro fuere conplures novi atque nobiles, quibus divitiae bono honestoque potiores erant, factiosi domi, potentes apud socios, clari magis quam honesti, qui Iugurthae non mediocrem animum pollicitando accendebant, si Micipsa rex occidisset, fore ut solus imperi Numidiae potiretur: *in ipso maximam virtutem, Romae omnia venalia esse.* Sed postquam Numantia deleta P. Scipio dimittere auxilia et ipse revorti domum decrevit, donatum atque laudatum magnifice pro contione Iugurtham in praetorium abduxit ibique secreto monuit, ut potius publice quam privatim amicitiam populi Romani coleret neu quibus largiri insuesceret: *periculose a paucis emi quod multorum esset.*[3]

Or again he will sum up with an exclamatory ἐπιφώνημα: 'tanta vis gratiae atque pecuniae regis erat', or 'tanta lubido in partibus erat', or 'tanta mobilitate Numidae se gerunt'.[4] He will prolong a sentence with a string of adjectives and appositions: 'Sed ubi in Africam venit, exercitus ei traditur a Sp. Albino proconsule iners imbellis, neque periculi neque laboris patiens, lingua quam manu promptior, praedator ex sociis et ipse praeda hostium, sine imperio et modestia habitus.'[1] Or he will append a participial phrase, for example 'existimans...', a very Thucydidean trait.[2]

All this is foreign to the oratorical tradition. But he was not intent on producing beautiful prose. He did not want to charm his reader to sleep, but continually to jolt him awake. His narrative must be expressive. The confusion of a battle is vividly conveyed by confusion of syntax:

dispersi a suis pars cedere alii insequi, neque signa neque ordines observare, ubi quemque periculum ceperat ibi resistere ac propulsare, arma tela equi viri hostes atque cives permixti, nihil consilio nihil imperio agi, fors omnia regere.

Jugurtha ranges the battle in a frenzy of historic infinitives: 'circumire, hortari, renovare proelium et ipse cum delectis temptare omnia, subvenire suis, hostibus dubiis instare, quos firmos cognoverat eminus pugnando retinere.'[3] With his keen, restless intelligence and his hatred of the hackneyed—qualities which determine his style—Sallust is the forerunner of Tacitus.

To Cicero however history was a branch of epideictic oratory which had as yet had no worthy exponent at Rome.[4] He laid down the rules for it through the mouth of Antonius in the *De Oratore*.[5] It requires *exaedificatio* and *exornatio, in verbis* as well as *in rebus*. It must be smoothly flowing, equable and extensive, that is, 'periodic'. He found an avowed supporter in Livy.* Yet Livy's 'periods' are not generally like Cicero's. Indeed it is doubtful whether we should speak of him as a periodic writer at all, in the sense in which we have seen the term defined. His sentences are not rounded.† The difference was well brought out by Nettleship:[6]

Cicero aims simply at such a balance of clauses as will raise the expectation and satisfy the demands of the ear: Livy wishes to do this and a great deal more. Cicero's grammatical construction is perfectly simple, and not modified by the exigencies of his theory of composition. Livy, on the contrary, in order to build a harmonious clause, tempers and varies his grammatical constructions so as to produce a welded mass of writing over which the reader must pause before he can grasp it as what it is, a carefully articulated whole....

* A. H. McDonald gives a helpful account of Livy's style in general in *J.R.S.* (1957), 155–72.
† I cannot recognize 'regular periodic structure', properly so-called, in the specimen v, 47, 1–6, quoted as exemplifying this by P. G. Walsh, *Livy* (1961), p. 250.

Cicero aims always at being understood at first hearing or first reading: his style is that of an orator. Livy's style is that of a scholar, not of a statesman. He speaks not to be heard but to be read, and aims mainly at satisfying the taste of literary men and winning admiration for his art. His method consists in ingenious condensation of thoughts and combination of clauses. In the first he probably wishes to rival Sallust, in the last to comply with the precepts of Cicero.

One literary man whose taste Livy satisfied was Housman, to whom he was the greatest of Roman stylists.

It is in the speeches attributed to characters that we should expect Livy to come nearest to Cicero. Then let us take an example from his best-known book (the speaker is Quintus Fabius Maximus):[1]

Si aut collegam, id quod mallem, tui similem, L. Aemili, aut tu collegae tui esses similis, supervacanea esset oratio mea; nam et duo boni consules, etiam me indicente, omnia e re publica fide vestra faceretis, et mali nec mea verba auribus vestris nec consilia animis acciperetis. Nunc et collegam tuum et te talem virum intuenti mihi tecum omnis oratio est, quem video nequiquam et virum bonum et civem fore, si altera parte claudente re publica malis consiliis idem ac bonis iuris et potestatis erit.

So far, except for the clausulae, this is in the Ciceronian tradition. The opening sentence has a neat antithesis in the first part and a more elaborate one, with assonance, in the second. The next is progressive rather than balanced, but hypotactic, economical and fairly straight-forward. The rest of the speech, however, consists almost entirely of short sentences, sometimes pointed by antithesis, leading up to this peroration (19–22):

Veritatem laborare nimis saepe aiunt, exstingui nunquam. Gloriam qui spreverit, veram habebit. Sine timidum pro cauto, tardum pro considerato, imbellem pro perito belli vocent. Malo te sapiens hostis metuat quam stulti cives laudent. Omnia audentem contemnet Hannibal, nihil agentem metuet. Nec ego ut nihil agatur hortor, sed ut agentem te ratio ducat, non fortuna. Tuae potestatis semper tu tuaque omnia sint. Armatus intentusque sis. Neque occasioni tuae desis neque suam occasionem hosti des. Omnia non properanti clara certaque erunt. Festinatio improvida est et caeca.

What is this but *Sallustiana brevitas*? Indeed Livy's style in general, whatever his professed allegiance, seems to me to be at least as much a refinement of Sallust's as a development of Cicero's.

187

In the narrative portions, except where he is consciously developing the annalistic style, Livy seems above all bent on variety; as well he might be, in view of the length of his work and the proportion of it devoted to descriptions of military operations. The studied periods of rhetoric would have made action seem like play-acting. Sometimes he seems even to go out of his way to dislocate periodic structure, by the use of parenthesis for instance.[1] He is apt to tack on participles, letting one incident develop out of another as in real life; or to let a muddled sentence represent a confused scene. For it is propriety of movement that makes his prose at its best so vivid. Here is the rout at Trasimene:[2]

Magnae partis fuga inde primum coepit; et iam nec lacus nec montes pavori obstabant; per omnia arta praeruptaque velut caeci evadunt, armaque et viri super alium alii praecipitantur. Pars magna, ubi locus fugae deest, per prima vada paludis in aquam progressi, quoad capitibus exstare possunt, sese immergunt; fuere quos inconsultus pavor nando etiam capessere fugam impulerit; quae ubi immensa et sine spe erat, aut deficientibus animis hauriebantur gurgitibus aut nequiquam fessi vada retro aegerrime repetebant atque ibi ab ingressis aquam hostium equitibus passim trucidabantur.

How expressive this is! First the panic of short sentences—*chacun pour soi*. No time for connecting participles. And how the rhythm makes them fall over one another—'super ali(um) alii praecipitantur'! And then the long, ineluctable sentence about those who exhausted themselves by swimming with no hope of reaching safety. This is not the sort of artistry we have been considering before. There is no elegance of rhythm. The clausulae are nearly all dispondaic, with a hexameter-ending thrown in. This is the art, not of τὸ καλόν, but of τὸ πρέπον.

7

ARCHITECTONICS OF VERSE

I. GENERAL

Early Latin verse, as represented by Ennius, seems innocent of architectonic structure, whether in the management of long sentences or in the disposition of short ones (though few of the fragments are long enough to enable us to judge). The poet gives the impression of versifying what he has to say just as it occurs to him; and indeed the same is generally true of the originally improvised Homeric poems he was emulating. This is λέξις εἰρομένη. In his admirer Lucretius we still find many sentences that straggle as he tacks on clause after clause in the impetuosity of his thought. Subordinate clauses depend even to the sixth degree, whereas in the whole *Aeneid* there are only five sentences that have them to so much as the third degree.[1] Wave after wave sweeps on. There is a cumulative effect, but the mind and ear of the reader are apt to get tired.

The utterance of Catullus too, in his shorter poems at least, is that of natural speech. But here we feel that the artlessness is conscious and highly effective art: the very naturalness keeps the emotion bare of any trappings of insincerity, as often in Donne or in modern poetry. He writes as one speaking directly from the heart, often talking to himself. Take no. 83:

> Lesbia mi praesente viro mala plurima dicit.
>   haec illi fatuo maxima laetitia est.
> mule, nihil sentis. si nostri oblita taceret,
>   sana esset: nunc, quod gannit et obloquitur,
> non solum meminit, sed, quae multo acrior est res,
>   irata est; hoc est, uritur et loquitur.

Lesbia says many nasty things to me in the presence of her husband. This gives the greatest pleasure to that dolt. Mule, you are unaware. If she forgot me and said nothing, she would be cured. As it is her snarling and abusing me shows that she not only remembers, but what is a much keener thing, she is angry: that is, she is burning and so she speaks.

But he was capable, when it was appropriate, of a wholly different style. Consoling his dearest friend for the loss of his beloved by a delicate reference (so we may take it) to the elegy he has written on her,[1] he composes as carefully as Cicero would in a letter written on such an occasion, and casts his thought in a finely moulded period (no. 96):

> Si quicquam mutis gratum acceptumve sepulcris
> accidere a nostro, Calve, dolore potest,
> quo desiderio veteres renovamus amores
> atque olim missas flemus amicitias,
> certe non tanto mors immatura dolori est
> Quintiliae quantum gaudet amore tuo.

If anything to please and cheer the silent grave can come from our grief, Calvus, from the longing with which we recall bygone loves and weep for long-lost friendships, surely Quintilia does not grieve so much for her untimely death as she rejoices in your love.

But it was, so far as we know, the Augustans, and Virgil in particular, who first regularly applied to Latin poetry the experience of oratorical prose. Once the effect was seen, it was sought by most good writers, all the more so as the practice of declaiming poetry developed.[2] The *ear* had to be satisfied, and the sense immediately grasped. But it was not the art of Isocrates, with his long sentences so perfectly balanced and signposted that you never got lost, nor that of Cicero's early speeches written when he was still under the influence of the Asiatics. It corresponded rather to Cicero's mature style (see p. 182), in which sentences rarely exceeded the equivalent of four hexameters. Like Cicero, Virgil is so grand that he may give the impression of having normally composed in long, rolling periods. But this is not so. His style is δεινός[3] (forceful) and *concitatus* (energetic). It relies, not on elaborate subordination of clauses (hypotaxis), but rather on the juxtaposition of short sentences (parataxis) often without explicit connection, *pugiunculi* enlivened by all the rhetorical figures*—antithesis, anaphora, question, exclamation, symmetry, chiasmus, homoeoteleuton and the rest—and proportioned to each other in length or weight as demanded either by the sense or by aesthetic principles. Michael Grant, quoting the opening sentence of *Paradise Lost*, says that it 'proclaims in all its com-

---

* Quintilian, Macrobius and others regularly quote Virgil to illustrate these figures.

plex fabric that the *Aeneid* is its model'.[1] This is true only if we take it to mean that the *first sentence* of the *Aeneid* is its model: for in general there is a difference. Milton did indeed learn an immense amount from study of Virgilian verse, but his poetry was meant to be read, not heard. It therefore tends to longer, hypotactic sentences. Thus the description of Satan at I, 192–220 consists of one 29-line paragraph made up of three highly complex sentences, the middle one of which is parenthetical. Virgil, on the contrary, is not complex.

We must not however suppose that the Roman rhetoric of the age was entirely responsible for this trend in style. Here too there had been interaction between it and the Alexandrian poetry introduced by the Neoteroi, itself the first non-dramatic poetry of any note to be composed after Gorgias and Thrasymachus had made writers conscious of figures of speech and artistic structure. Take anaphora. We are so used to it as the favourite ornament of the Alexandrians and the piston-rod or driving-force of Augustan poetry, that it is astonishing to look back and find that it hardly occurs in Homer (see p. 66).

Nor was it individual sentences only that had to be artistically constructed, but paragraphs which might consist of more than one sentence. It is pertinent to observe the treatment of the openings of long poems (or books within them), since here we may be sure the poet was particularly anxious about proportion. In general these should be long enough to launch the poem and give it impetus, but not so long as to be hard to grasp. The *Iliad* begins with a paragraph of seven lines, Μῆνιν ἄειδε...δῖος Ἀχιλλεύς (which surely belongs to a literary rather than extempore stage of the composition). This we may feel to be about right, and indeed it looks as if ancient poets felt the same. At all events, the *Aeneid* followed suit (in λέξις εἰρομένη):

> Arma virumque cano Troiae qui primus ob oris
> Italiam fato profugus Lavinaque venit
> litora, multum ille et terris iactatus et alto
> vi superum, saevae memorem Iunonis ob iram,
> multa quoque et bello passus, dum conderet urbem,
> inferretque deos Latio, genus unde Latinum
> Albanique patres atque altae moenia Romae.*

---

* Note how both Homer and Virgil begin with a keyword and end with the name of the 'hero'.

Further examples are the proems of Lucan's *Pharsalia* and Statius' *Achilleid* (perhaps in conscious imitation), of the *Peleus and Thetis*, *Georgics IV* and *Paradise Regained*. Some other passages which linger in the memory for their architectonic rightness will be found on examination to consist likewise of seven lines—the opening of Aeschylus' *Agamemnon* (Θεοὺς μὲν αἰτῶ...ἀντολάς τε τῶν), where the ear resents any attempt to bracket the seventh line, and Clytemnestra's ironic flourish of metaphors that trumpet her husband's entry into the palace (ῥίзης γὰρ οὔσης...δῶμ' ἐπιστρωφωμένου); or the splendours of nature that are the first adornment of Achilles' shield at *Iliad*, XVIII, 483–9 ('Εν μὲν γαῖαν ἔθηκε...λοέτρων 'Ωκεανοῖο); or the climax of Anchises' speech in Hades ('Excudent alii...debellare superbos'). Sometimes the effect is like that of the *tricolon abundans*, as in the two opening sections of the prophecy in the *Pollio*:

> { Ultima Cumaei venit iam carminis aetas:
> { magnus ab integro saeclorum nascitur ordo.
> { iam redit et Virgo, redeunt Saturnia regna,
> { iam nova progenies caelo demittitur alto.
> { tu modo nascenti puero, quo ferrea primum
> ⎨ desinet et toto surget gens aurea mundo
> { casta fave Lucina: tuus iam regnat Apollo.
>
> { teque adeo decus hoc aevi, te consule, inibit,
> { Pollio, et incipient magni procedere menses;
> { te duce, siqua manent sceleris vestigia nostri,
> { irrita perpetua solvent formidine terras.
> { ille deum vitam accipiet, divisque videbit
> ⎨ permixtos heroas, et ipse videbitur illis,
> { pacatumque reget patriis virtutibus orbem.

(Those who take 'te duce' with the previous line destroy the artistic form.)

But the exordium of the *Georgics* is an interesting exception. Lucretius had begun his poem *effusis habenis* with a nine-line, rather breathless, invocation in the form associated with cletic hymns, '*Venus*... (*quae*)...*quae*...*quae*...*te*...*te*...*te*...*tibi*...*tibi*...'. Virgil, after a brief prospectus of contents, plunges at line 5 into two 19-line sentences of a sweep unparalleled in the rest of his works, the first corresponding to the invocation of the twelve deities of agriculture at the beginning of Varro's *De Re Rustica* (though with variations of his own choosing), the second a baroque invocation to Caesar as a new god. The movement is highly Lucretian, and is clearly meant to give the impression of one carried away by an enthusiasm that breaks all bounds of normal classic art. Similarly Horace begins his epinician ode, IV, 4 ('Qualem ministrum...'), with a quite exceptional (and wilfully complicated) sentence of 28 lines, because that seemed characteristic of his model:

> monte decurrens velut amnis imbres
> quem super notas aluere ripas
> fervet immensusque ruit profundo
> Pindarus ore

like a torrent running down from a mountain which rainstorms have swollen above its familiar banks Pindar boils over and rushes on unbounded with deep voice (IV, 2, 5–8).

Another feature of the new art was interplay between sentences and metrical lines or stanzas—'the sense variously drawn out from one verse into another', as Milton put it in the preface to *Paradise Lost*. This not only banished monotony, but gave scope for effects of exquisite subtlety.

We know how carefully Virgil worked, licking his lines into shape (he said) as a she-bear licks its cubs.[1] The *felicitas* of Horace was proverbially *curiosa*. There will always be, as there were in Quintilian's day, those who prefer the apparent spontaneity of Lucretius and Catullus. But to some extent periodic writing must have become instinctive to the Augustans; and in any case there is no reason why the styles of these consummate writers should be put into competition. Why not enjoy them all for what they are? So much said, let us examine more closely the artistry of periodic verse in Golden Latin—hexameter, elegiac and lyric.

II. HEXAMETERS

> Nam primum astrorum volucris te consule motus
> concursusque gravis stellarum ardore micantis
> tu quoque, cum tumulos Albano in monte nivalis
> lustrasti et laeto mactasti lacte Latinas,
> vidisti et claro tremulos ardore cometas

> multaque misceri nocturna strage putasti,
> quod ferme dirum in tempus cecidere Latinae,
> cum claram speciem concreto lumine luna
> abdidit et subito stellanti nocte perempta est.

To illustrate the straggling, undisciplined form that a sentence might take in pre-Virgilian hexameters I have printed above one not from Lucretius, whose indifference to some of the refinements of contemporary verse is as notorious as it is understandable, but from a passage of 78 lines which is quoted by Cicero from his own *De Consulatu Suo*.[1] Even the master of the prose period did not feel, it seems, that the same aesthetic principles should apply to verse. The speaker here is the Muse Urania, who ought to have known better.

Catullus, in his epyllion *Peleus and Thetis* (64), offends in a different way. His individual lines are melodious; but out of 408 only about 40 have any appreciable pause within, while 284 have (in Mynors's edition) a stop at the end. This is not a symptom of *naïveté* (for Ennius and Lucretius had been as free in this respect as the old Greek epic), but of deference to *late* Alexandrian poetic practice, which restricted pauses to the end or the caesura.[2] And it was unfortunate, aggravating the monotony caused by the rhythmic tendencies we have already noted (p. 129): the sense is not 'variously drawn out from line to line'.

Virgil was certainly impressed by the *Peleus and Thetis*: he echoes it a number of times, and his *Pollio* is largely a response to it. But the influence which was to mould his style came directly from Theocritus, whose cadences he studied to reproduce in the *Eclogues*. In him he found the varied pauses, the anaphora and other figures of the 'pathetic' style. (Only asyndeton was more Latin than Greek.)

> πῇ ποκ' ἄρ' ἦσθ' ὅκα Δάφνις ἐτάκετο, πῇ ποκα Νύμφαι;
> ἦ κατὰ Πηνειῶ καλὰ τέμπεα; ἦ κατὰ Πίνδω;
> οὐ γὰρ δὴ ποταμοῖο μέγαν ῥόον εἴχετ' Ἀνάπω,
> οὐδ' Αἴτνας σκοπιάν, οὐδ' Ἄκιδος ἱερὸν ὕδωρ.

> quae nemora aut qui vos saltus habuere, puellae
> Naides, indigno cum Gallus amore peribat?
> nam neque Parnasi vobis iuga, nam neque Pindi
> ulla moram fecere, neque Aonie Aganippe.

There too he found the tricolon with anaphora:

τῆνον μὰν θῶες, | τῆνον λύκοι ὠρύσαντο, |
τῆνον χὠκ δρυμοῖο λέων ἔκλαυσε θανόντα.

πολλαί οἱ πὰρ ποσσὶ βόες, | πολλοὶ δέ τε ταῦροι, |
πολλαὶ δ' αὖ δαμάλαι καὶ πόρτιες ὠδύραντο.

illum etiam lauri, etiam flevere myricae,
pinifer illum etiam sola sub rupe iacentem
Maenalus....

venit et upilio, tardi venere bubulci,
uvidus hiberna venit de glande Menalcas.[1]

But notice how Virgil evades the expected by making 'Maenalus' over-
step the line-end. Notice too how the rhythm of

πῆ ποκ' ἄρ' ἦσθ' ὅκα Δάφνις ἐτάκετο, πῆ ποκα Νύμφαι;

is echoed, but *not in the corresponding line of the sense*:

nam neque Parnasi vobis iuga, nam neque Pindi.

Virgil was in fact 'filling his mind with the finest cadences he could
discover' *in the abstract* (see p. 36). As for variety of pauses, one need
only repeat a few lines from *Eclogue* v (60–6):

nec lupus insidias pecori nec retia cervis
ulla dolum meditantur; | amat bonus otia Daphnis. |
ipsi laetitia voces ad sidera iactant
intonsi montes; | ipsae iam carmina rupes,
ipsa sonant arbusta: | deus, deus ille, Menalca! |
sis bonus o felixque tuis! | en quattuor aras; |
ecce duas tibi, Daphni, duas altaria Phoebo.

As usual, Virgil represents in this respect a reaction to a mean position
between ancient looseness and neoteric purism.

The style thus assimilated served in due course for the *Georgics*, with
refinements and variations and with overall influence from the Ciceronian period.* Thus in the *Eclogues* we find tetracolon in primitive
simplicity (III, 80–3):

Damoetas: triste lupus stabulis, maturis frugibus imbres,
arboribus venti, nobis Amaryllidis irae.
Menalcas: dulce satis umor, depulsis arbutus herbis,
lenta salix feto pecori, mihi solus Amyntas.

---

* There are periods already in the *Eclogues*; for example, III, 35–9; VI, 31–40, 74–81: E. Fraenkel,
Vergil und Cicero, Atti Mantova (1926), p. 225.

13-2

In the *Georgics* such complete symmetry is avoided; for example (I, 341–2):

> tum pingues agni, et tum mollissima vina,
> tum somni dulces, densaeque in montibus herbae;

or (II, 435–6):

> aut illae pecori frondem, aut pastoribus umbram
> sufficiunt, saepemque satis, et pabula melli.

There are few sentences in the *Georgics* of more than four lines, and everything is done to maintain variety, energy, appropriateness and grace in a subject that could not please without their aid. Here is the death of the ox (III, 511–30):

> ecce autem duro fumans sub vomere taurus
> concidit, et mixtum spumis vomit ore cruorem
> extremosque ciet gemitus. it tristis arator
> maerentem abiungens fraterna morte iuvencum,
> atque opere in medio defixa relinquit aratra.
> non umbrae altorum nemorum, non mollia possunt
> prata movere animum, non qui per saxa volutus
> purior electro campum petit amnis; at ima
> solvuntur latera, atque oculos stupor urget inertis,
> ad terramque fluit devexo pondere cervix.
> quid labor aut benefacta iuvant? quid vomere terras
> invertisse gravis? atqui non Massica Bacchi
> munera, non illis epulae nocuere repostae:
> frondibus et victu pascuntur simplicis herbae,
> pocula sunt fontes liquidi atque exercita cursu
> flumina, nec somnos abrumpit cura salubris.

But lo, the bull, steaming under the ploughshare's weight, falls, and vomits mingled blood and foam, and utters dying groans. Sad the ploughman goes and unyokes the steer that grieves at his brother's death, and leaves the plough stuck in mid-work. No shades of deep woods, no soft meadows can rouse the beast's spirit, no stream that rolls clearer than amber over the pebbles to seek the plain; but his flanks give way, dizziness oppresses his lifeless eyes and his neck sinks with drooping weight to earth. What good do his toil and services do him? What good his having turned the heavy soil with the share? And yet no Massic gifts of Bacchus, no feasts of many courses have ruined his kind: they feed on leaves and a diet of simple grass; their drinks are clear springs and racing brooks, nor does care break their healthful slumbers.

In this passage 'concidit' is made more dramatic by position (see p. 66). The monosyllabic *it*, coming first in its sentence, focuses the eye on the desolate ploughman. Next we have tricolon with anaphora and increasing members (*non...non...non...*); and instead of the sense being completed with the line, it breaks off at $4\frac{3}{4}$,* as though to shut out the poignant memory of pleasing scenes—'at ima solvuntur latera'; which in turn is the first member of another tricolon crescendo, this time without anaphora. Then two bitterly brief ironical questions; a restless '*non...non...*' movement to suggest the hectic life of pleasure-seeking; and finally, by contrast, three lines of simple and dignified rhythm to convey the sober innocence of animal life in the country.

The *Aeneid* too, in this as in other respects, is a blend of the Homeric and the Alexandrian. To maintain the simplicity of parataxis Virgil uses parenthesis and other devices freely.[1] Generally the style is dictated by the context. In his normal narrative the lines tend to be more end-stopped than elsewhere, and the sentences a little longer. At the other extreme is a speech like this, in which Juturna raves hysterically in prescience of her brother Turnus' death (XII, 872–84):

> quid nunc te tua, Turne, potest germana iuvare?
> aut quid iam durae superat mihi? qua tibi lucem
> arte morer? talin possum me opponere monstro?
> iam iam linquo acies. ne me terrete timentem,
> obscenae volucres: alarum verbera nosco
> letalemque sonum, nec fallunt iussa superba
> magnanimi Iovis. haec pro virginitate reponit?
> quo vitam dedit aeternam? cur mortis adempta est
> condicio? possem tantos finire dolores
> nunc certe, et misero fratri comes ire per umbras!
> immortalis ego? aut quicquam mihi dulce meorum
> te sine, frater, erit? o quae satis ima dehiscat
> terra mihi, manisque deam demittat ad imos?

The tricolon structure is ubiquitous: I need only quote one famous example with both crescendo and anaphora (XII, 826–7):

> sit Latium, sint Albani per saecula reges,
> sit Romana potens Itala virtute propago.

---

* In the whole *Aeneid* only 24 lines are punctuated here: see Norden's admirable Appendix II, 'Periodik', to his edition of *Aeneid* VI, p. 389 n. 6^3.

On the other hand Virgil has a way of crystallizing in a short phrase something he has just said more diffusely, as (I, 278–9):

> his ego nec metas rerum nec tempora pono:
> *imperium sine fine dedi.*

> *for these I have set no limits of space or time: I have given them dominion without end.*

He uses isocolia and parallelism at every turn. He also likes to repeat the same idea in different terms, in the manner of antiphonal poetry.[1] Thus at IX, 773–4 we hear of Amycus,

> quo non felicior alter
> unguere tela manu *ferrumque armare veneno*

> *than whom none could more successfully smear weapons by hand and 'arm iron with poison';*

and the story goes that in mid-recitation, from a beginning exactly comparable to this, Virgil completed extempore an unfinished line, and called at once for his tablets to inscribe the addition (VI, 164–5):

> quo non praestantior alter
> aere ciere viros *Martemque accendere cantu*

> *whom no one excelled at rousing men with the bronze 'and kindling Mars with music'.*[2]

A very effective way of clinching a paragraph was what the rhetoricians called an ἐπιφώνημα, a flourish which in verse consisted usually of a single line.* Examples beginning with *tantus* crowd into mind (the first from Lucretius):

> tantum religio potuit suadere malorum.

> tantus amor laudum, tantae est victoria curae.

> tantus amor florum et generandi gloria mellis.

> tantae molis erat Romanam condere gentem.†

---

* Quint. VIII, 5, 11: 'extrema quasi insultatio...rei narratae vel probatae summa acclamatio.' Cf. Dem. *De Eloc.* 106–8.

† *So much evil could come of religious persuasion* (Lucr. I, 101). *Such is their love of praises, their desire for victory* (Virg. G. III, 112). *Such is their love of flowers, and glory in generating honey* (G. IV, 205). *Such a massive task it was to found the Roman nation* (A. I, 33). For examples from Sallust see p. 185.

Sometimes they are a gnomic or epigrammatic summing-up:

> omnia vincit Amor: et nos cedamus amori.
>
> una salus victis nullam sperare salutem.
>
> coniugium vocat: hoc praetexit nomine culpam.
>
> quod spiro et placeo, si placeo, tuum est.*

A single line could also seal a narrative passage; for example,

> mens immota manet, lacrimae volvuntur inanes.†

In particular it could convey an order or exhortation at the end of a speech:

> durate, et vosmet rebus servate secundis.
>
> vade age, et ingentem factis fer ad aethera Troiam.
>
> naviget! haec summa est, hic nostri nuntius esto.‡

Mackail, discussing possibly unfinished passages in the *Aeneid*, remarks that 'it is a feature of the matured Virgilian style to continue the period a line further than where in the hands of a less potent master of rhythm it would conclude.§ This is also characteristic of Milton; in both poets it is this overarching superflux of rhythm which gives their period its unique richness.'[1] This may depend (to give examples different from Mackail's) on a participle or adjective, as in

> pascentem niveos herboso flumine cycnos.
>
> vipereum crinem vittis innexa cruentis.
>
> attollens umero famamque et fata nepotum.¶

---

* *Love conquers all: let us too yield to love* (Virg. E. x, 69). *The only safety for the losers is in hoping for no safety* (A. II, 354). *She calls it marriage, with that name disguises her sin* (A. IV, 172). *That I am alive and please, if please I do, is thy gift* (Hor. Odes, IV, 3, 24).

† *His mind remains unmoved, tears fall to no effect* (A. IV, 449). There are five examples in book VIII alone—101, 125, 305, 369, 423. Cf. VII, 722; x, 768; XI, 867, 915; XII, 553, 696.

‡ *Endure, and keep yourselves for happier times* (A. I, 207). *Go now, and by your deeds exalt Troy to the skies in greatness* (III, 462). *Let him sail! That is the sum; this be the message from me* (IV, 237). Cf. I, 401; v, 71; VII, 340; XI, 335.

§ We may compare Quintilian's asking, 'Why can it happen that in a period we feel that, even when the sense is complete, there is something missing?' (IX, 4, 119). Cf. Cic. Or. 168 (see p. 175 n.).

¶ *Feeding snow-white swans on her reedy river* (G. II, 199). *Her snaky locks entwined with gory fillets* (A. VI, 281). *Raising on his shoulders the fame and destiny of his progeny* (A. VIII, 731). Cf. VI, 702; VII, 669; x, 832; XII, 611.

It may be tacked on with 'and', as in

> ...tibi res antiquae laudis et artis
> ingredior, sanctos ausus recludere fontis,
> *Ascraeumque cano Romana per oppida carmen,**

or in the exordium of *Paradise Lost,*

> ...That to the height of this great argument
> I may assert Eternal Providence,
> *And justify the ways of God to men.*

Or it may be asyndetic, as in

> parcere subiectis et debellare superbos.†

Yet such expectation, once established, can be broken for effect, as Virgil does occasionally in his later work (and Milton in *Paradise Regained*). Similarly he sometimes varies the monotony of the established $2\frac{1}{2} + 3\frac{1}{2}$ hexameter by letting the sense run over the strong caesura with a pyrrhic word, and so dividing the line exactly in half, as in

> aut Ararim Parthus bibet | aut Germania Tigrim.[1]

Horace in his *Satires* was not concerned to write in periodic style. Artistically they derive their piquancy from the contrast of a heroic metre being broken up and made the vehicle of casual-sounding conversation: for example,

> ne te morer, audi
> quo rem deducam. si quis deus 'en ego' dicat
> 'iam faciam quod vultis: eris tu, qui modo miles,
> mercator; tu, consultus modo, rusticus: hinc vos,
> vos hinc mutatis discedite partibus. heia!
> quid statis?'—nolint. atqui licet esse beatis.

> *To be brief, listen how I will put the matter to the test. If some god were to say, 'Look, I will now do as you wish: you, hitherto a soldier, shall be a merchant; you, hitherto a lawyer, a farmer: change your parts and cross the floor: Go! Why are you standing still?'—They would refuse. Yet their wish is in their hands.*[2]

Unlike the epic poets, he often has a strong break even in the last two feet of the line.[3]

The *Epistles* are for the most part still *sermo,* but no. 13 for instance,

---

* *For thee I essay a theme of ancient praise and art, daring to unseal sacred fountains, and sing the song of Ascra through the townships of Rome* (G. II, 174–6).

† *To spare the conquered and beat down the proud* (A. VI, 853).

an indirect consignment to Augustus of a book (presumably the *Odes*), is elegantly composed, with anaphoric tricola—

> si validus, si laetus erit, si denique poscet,

and

> ut rusticus agnum,
> ut vinosa glomus furtivae Pyrria lanae,
> ut cum pilleolo soleas conviva tribulis—

and with a single-line exhortation to round it off:

> vade, vale, cave ne titubes mandataque frangas.

No. 6 (*Nil admirari*) is a diatribe in verse presaging Juvenal. The first half is rhetorical, *concitatus*, full of antithesis and balanced phrases; only in the second does the old conversational style get the upper hand. Horace was of course capable of writing in the epic manner also, if need be. He uses it for burlesque purposes at the end of the story of the town and country mice (*S.* II, 6, 100 ff.), and ironically to Augustus when disclaiming ability to write epic (*Ep.* II, 1, 250–6):

> nec sermones ego mallem
> repentes per humum *quam res componere gestas,*
> *terrarumque situs et flumina dicere et arces*
> *montibus impositas et barbara regna tuisque*
> *auspiciis totum confecta duella per orbem*
> *claustraque custodem pacis cohibentia Ianum*
> *et formidatam Parthis te principe Romam,*
> *si, quantum cuperem, possem quoque.*

(note the strong alliterative effect of *c*, *p* and *t* in the last two lines). The treatises that form the Second Book of the *Epistles* are in general more smoothly written, the verse of the Epistle to the Pisones (*Ars Poetica*) being quite largely end-stopped.

As for Ovid in the *Metamorphoses*, we have only to read the first paragraph (after the brief proem) to see how elaborate, indeed how excessively exact, his symmetry can be. First we have two balanced sentences of $2\frac{1}{2}$ lines each:

> Ante mare et terras et quod tegit omnia caelum
> unus erat toto naturae vultus in orbe
> quem dixere Chaos: rudis indigestaque moles
> nec quicquam nisi pondus iners congestaque eodem
> non bene iunctarum discordia semina rerum.

Then a tetracolon with anaphora (1 + 1 + 1½ + 1½ lines), each member constructed round a long verb after strong caesura:

> nullus adhuc mundo *praebebat* lumina Titan,
> nec nova crescendo *reparabat* cornua Phoebe
> nec circumfuso *pendebat* in aëre tellus
> ponderibus librata suis, nec bracchia longo
> margine terrarum *porrexerat* Amphitrite.

Then triadic structure with formal enlargement:

> utque erat et tellus illic et pontus et aër
> sic erat instabilis tellus, innabilis unda,
> lucis egens aër:

and finally a chiastic passage leading to an antithetic tetracolon:

> nulli sua forma manebat
> obstabatque aliis aliud, quia corpore in uno
> frigida pugnabant calidis, umentia siccis,
> mollia cum duris, sine pondere habentia pondus.

Seldom can Chaos have been described with such meticulous orderliness. In fact, as already observed, Ovid was not primarily interested in appropriateness or expressiveness of style. For the rest, he had learnt from Virgil the advantage of short sentences, of clarity and simplicity; but in structure, as in rhythm, he sacrificed Virgilian variety to smoothness and rapidity. His medium is a comfortable, well-sprung, well-oiled vehicle for his story. Everything depends on whether the story itself can retain the reader's attention.

III. ELEGIACS

In his longer elegiac poems 65–8 and 76 Catullus sometimes uses periodic structure, sometimes not. No. 65 is chaotic, a letter whose 24 lines consist of a single sentence enclosing a 10-line parenthesis. But the first part of 68 is another letter beginning with a 12-line period which might be a straight versification of one of Cicero's:

> *quod* mihi fortuna casuque oppressus acerbo
> conscriptum hoc lacrimis mittis epistolium,
> naufragum ut eiectum spumantibus aequoris undis
> sublevem et a mortis limine restituam,

> quem neque sancta Venus molli requiescere somno
>   desertum in lecto caelibe perpetitur,
> nec veterum dulci scriptorum carmine Musae
>   oblectant, cum mens anxia pervigilat,
>   *id gratum est mihi*, me quoniam tibi dicis amicum
>   muneraque et Musarum hinc petis et Veneris.

In the Allius elegy (68, 41–148), though there is an elaborate chiastic arrangement of *themes*, the management of the sentences is positively clumsy; thus 107–16 is a single sentence with three relative clauses in a dependent chain and an *ut* clause tacked on after that. No. 76, on the other hand, begins with a six-line period, *Siqua recordanti*....

Elegiac verse could never develop into anything comparable in structure to Virgilian hexameters. It did indeed come under the influence of rhetoric, and reflect its development after the death of Cicero towards short, epigrammatic sentences. But the variety and the appropriateness essential to the Virgilian style were precluded by the fixed caesura and latter-half rhythm of the pentameter and by the growing tendency to close the couplets (see p. 134). Tibullus composed in blocks of couplets whose themes led subtly into each other. In his cult of simplicity he inclined to the paratactic and the asyndetic. Propertius also composed in blocks, which some have tried to make into regular stanzas;[1] but his are apt to be starkly juxtaposed, sometimes as theme and mythological parallel, sometimes with an implicit psychological connection which the reader is left to divine. He is capable of hypotactic periods, yet it would be hard to determine on grounds of periodic art that a couplet was either spurious or missing in Propertius—and indeed many re-arrangements have been proposed without thought of such art; whereas in Virgil we might sometimes suspect for aesthetic reasons that a line had dropped out, even if the remainder made good enough sense.

Within these limits, however, it was possible to use not only the rhetorical figures, but also some features of periodic art. Thus in Ovid's elegy on the death of Tibullus (*Am.* III, 9) we find tricolon crescendo with anaphora (21–2):

> quid pater Ismario,
> quid mater, profuit Orpheo?
> carmine quid victas obstupuisse feras?

And later a double form of tricolon crescendo extending over two couplets (37–40):

> vive pius—
>> moriere;
> pius cole sacra—
>> colentem | mors gravis a templis in cava busta trahet;
> carminibus confide bonis—
>> iacet, ecce, Tibullus; | vix manet e toto
>>> parva quod urna capit.

And parallelism, especially between hexameter and pentameter, is a regular feature in Ovid.

IV. LYRICS: HORACE

(a) Meineke's Law

The impact of the rhetorical period on lyric poetry is much more interesting. But first we must consider the effect of stanza-form, which practically concerns Horace only.

In the *Epodes* Horace kept his couplets closed to an extraordinary degree. Hardly ever does an epithet in one qualify a substantive in another,* never a genitive. The effect is one of extreme simplicity, and indeed of monotony if carried on for too long, as in no. 5, which extends to over a hundred lines. The exception is 13 (*Horrida tempestas*), the nearest to the Odes, and in the opinion of many the best: this has, despite an invariable break after the eighth syllable of each even line— for example,

> nivesque deducunt Iovem; | nunc mare nunc siluae—

a remarkably varied movement.

Only one of the Odes has so free a movement, I, 7 (*Laudabunt alii*), and it is also similar in theme and treatment, with its heroic speech of Teucer at the end corresponding to that of Chiron. Its metre is that of *Epode* 12, and altogether there is good reason for dating it among the earliest of the Odes. But meanwhile Horace was learning to compose in the Aeolic four-line stanzas—Alcaics, Sapphics, Fourth and Fifth Asclepiads. Of his 104 lyric poems all but 25 are in one of these forms.

---

* *Iucundior* at II, 55 is predicative, and quite exceptional. Less striking examples occur at XI, 16-7; XII, 10-11; XIII, 8-9. XVII is in a monostichic metre, so falls outside our scope.

And we now come to the remarkable fact known as Meineke's Law: although half of the Epodes comprise lines whose total is not divisible by four, there is no such Ode.*

Meineke in his 1834 edition printed all the Odes in quatrains, though he did not apparently attach great significance to his discovery. English editors have generally not so divided those 25 non-stanzaic poems. Heinze did so where he thought the organization of the sense justified it, but he wavered sometimes as between his edition with commentary and his Insel edition. He did not live to expound his reasons, and the first systematic study of the phenomenon was made in 1939 by Karl Büchner.[1]

Büchner begins by rejecting Elter's idea that the law was connected with singing. The only Horatian poem which we know to have been sung, the *Carmen Saeculare*, is differentiated from nearly all the others by the fact that its stanzas are all made self-contained. This is also true of the Ode which is most like a hymn, I, 21 (*Dianam tenerae*), and of that which is most like a song, III, 9 (*Donec gratus eram tibi*), even though the latter is not in a metre of fixed four-line stanzas. The exceptions prove the rule. Nor is there any reason why music for monostichic metres such as the First Asclepiad should have conformed to a four-line pattern. And finally, we have seen that scholarly opinion inclines against the supposition that the Odes in general were for singing.

But even in Sappho and Alcaeus, whose poems were sung, though there is generally some pause in the sense at the end of a stanza, there is also quite frequently enjambment between stanzas. In Horace the majority of quatrains are end-stopped. Asyndeton is common: the reader is left to make the connection, as in Tibullus and Propertius, though more than thirty times anaphora provides an invisible bridge. Büchner analyses the cases of enjambment in these four-line metres, Alcaics, Sapphics, etc. He finds that there are a few main types. The leading idea encroaches on the beginning of the succeeding stanza by

* III, 12 (*Miserarum est*) is peculiar: it can be considered to consist of four enormous lines of ten ionic feet ($\cup\cup--$) each, well marked off by the sense. IV, 8 (*Donarem pateras*) totals 34 lines in the MSS., but should total probably 32, for two are intrusive: l. 17, 'non incendia Karthaginis impiae', which has no proper caesura and seems to refer to the wrong Scipio, may have been introduced by someone who wanted a referent for 'eius' and did not realize it comes two lines later in 'laudes'; l. 33, 'ornatus viridi tempora pampino', is borrowed from III, 25, 20, where it is more appropriate. Lenchantin de Gubernatis (*Athenaeum*, 1944–5, pp. 72–90) belittles the significance of Meineke's Law, of which Prudentius showed no consciousness.

the agency of the verb with or without accompaniment, or by a proper name. The second stanza is sometimes a supplement to the first; or the structure may be such that one stanza comprises the principal and the other a subordinate clause. In general the bridge begins in the last line, or else at the beginning, of one stanza, and ends in the first line of the next; but in Book IV there is a tendency to much longer movements, which may plausibly be attributed to the influence of Pindar, so strong in that Book.[1]

The crux is in the 25 Odes which are composed in distichs or monostichs. Are their totals of lines divisible by four because Horace was consciously or unconsciously adapting these metres to the artistic form of the quatrain, in which he was now composing as he had not been at the time of the Epodes? An abstract form latent in a poet's mind can have such influence. Let me give an odd illustration. In Shakespeare's *Two Gentlemen of Verona* Lucetta tries to moderate Julia's passion, but she replies,

> The more thou damm'st it up, the more it burns.

She then launches into a set speech, beginning with a theme from Ovid's *Metamorphoses*,

> The current that with gentle murmur glides....

This speech strikes one as a lyrical poem in its own right; and on inspection it proves to consist of 14 lines, of which the first eight are simile, the last six application, with the lines falling neatly into couplets. Put in rhymes, and it would be a Shakespearian sonnet of the strictest form.[2]

Büchner investigates these 25 Odes to see whether, as regards the sense, they show the imprint of the four-line stanza form, bearing in mind the types of enjambment found in the quatrain metres. Some fit perfectly, with no enjambment. Nearly everyone prints III, 9 (*Donec gratus eram*) as six quatrains. I, 13 (*Cum tu, Lydia*) and I, 19 (*Mater saeva Cupidinum*) are almost as regular. III, 19 (*Quantum distet ab Inacho*) can be printed as seven quatrains with only one enjambment. These are in Third Asclepiads. But in others the effect is more blurred, especially those in the monostichic and the dactylic metres. Büchner (and Klingner, whose Teubner text follows him) have to admit that four will not comply (I, I; II; 18; 28). If that were all, one could say that it is mere chance that these have each a total of lines divisible by four. But there are others which will not seem to every reader to square with Büchner's interpretation; some or all of those which, in addition to these four, Heinze decided not to print in quatrains*—I, 7; 8; 36; II, 18; III, 15; 24; 25; 30; IV, 11. I confess that I find it particularly difficult to perceive any trace of stanza-form in III, 25 (*Quo me, Bacche, rapis*), a poem in which enthusiasm is conveyed by the very avoidance of formal orderliness, not to mention others. If anything up to a dozen poems refuse to give evidence, then Meineke's Law remains a mystery—for Horace can hardly be suspected of introducing a mathematical rule for no aesthetic reason.†

It should however be noted that, although I, 1 and III, 30 are generally assumed to have been written last as Prologue and Epilogue to the whole collection I–III, several of these nonconformist odes have been thought on other grounds to be early—I, 7; 18; 28; II, 18; III, 15; 24. It would take some time for the experience of composing in Aeolic quatrains to have its effect on Horace's composition in distich and monostich metres, so this supposition would be consonant with Büchner's theory, which without being perhaps a convincing explanation of Meineke's Law may yet contribute to our understanding of Horace's artistic development.

(b) Periodic structure

Periodic structure can be seen at its simplest in the first stanza of the Hymn I, 21—*tricolon abundans*:

> Dianam tenerae dicite virgines,
> intonsum pueri dicite Cynthium,
> Latonamque supremo
> dilectam penitus Iovi.

* He did not live to explain his reasons, nor to see Büchner's interpretations; but he seems to have been guided by considerations of sense.

† J. P. Postgate suggested that a taste for pairing might be at work, but in general he was sceptical about the whole affair. He did however show that Asclepiad distichs at least tend to group themselves in quatrains to the extent that at the end of even lines hiatus is much commoner (10 to 3) after the multiples of four lines, indicating a bigger break there (*C.R.* 1918, pp. 23–8). N. E. Collinge insists that only metrical criteria are relevant in the first instance (*hiatus, synaphea, syllaba anceps*). Testing by thought-features, for example transitions, antitheses, verbal anaphora, can only be secondary (*The Structure of Horace's Odes*, 1961, p. 60 n.).

This tripartite structure is amplified with stanzas as the unit in III, 28.

> Festo quid potius die
>   Neptuni faciam? prome reconditum,
> Lyde, strenua Caecubum
>   munitaeque adhibe vim sapientiae.
>
> inclinare meridiem
>   sentis, et, veluti stet volucris dies,
> parcis deripere horreo
>   cessantem Bibuli consulis amphoram?
>
> nos cantabimus invicem
>   Neptunum et viridis Nereidum comas;
> tum curva recines lyra
>   Latonam et celeris spicula Cynthiae;
>
> summo carmine, quae Cnidon
>   fulgentisque tenet Cycladas et Paphon
> iunctis visit oloribus
>   dicetur, merita Nox quoque nenia.

The tripartite 1 + 1 + 2 structure is here repeated on a smaller scale in the final section. But the form is not mechanical; for whether we put a comma at 'oloribus' or 'dicetur', there is an unexpected variation at the end, an addition which produces an exquisite dying close.

Such variation is a common feature of the Odes: Horace is apt to begin with self-contained stanzas* and then pass to ones which are continuous or enjambed or broken up into short sentences, sometimes only in the last two. A simple case is III, 20 (*Non vides, quanto*), which has only four stanzas, though the fact that the first has a stop in the middle and the second is a subordinate clause to it makes this imperfect as an example. The effect is seen more clearly in II, 2 (*Nullus argento*) and II, 16 (*Otium divos*): after four and seven self-contained stanzas respectively the ode is rounded off with two that are enjambed, apparently for purely aesthetic reasons. In a long poem it is unlikely that all the previous stanzas should be self-contained: that would be monotonous and at times inappropriate to the sense. Thus III, 4 (*Descende caelo*) ends with two enjambed stanzas broken into three sentences, whereas of the previous eighteen no fewer than fifteen end with a pause, generally a full

---

* Or at least stanzas with a natural pause at the end.

stop; but the three which portray the battle of the gods and giants are continuous, enjambed and anaphoric as the excitement demands ('Sed quid Typhoeus...Patareus Apollo'). And in III, 29 (*Tyrrhena regum*) the last two stanzas are again enjambed, whereas of the previous fourteen nine have a marked pause at the end; but in the middle there are five, including the picture of the river in spate, which are headlong and enjambed ('prudens futuri...hora vexit').* This ode begins with two stanzas which are continuous before the stanza-unit asserts itself: III, 2 (*Angustam amice*) begins with three; but four end-stops have established it before the last two stanzas, which are a good example of breaking up and enjambment in finale:

> est et fideli tuta silentio
> merces: vetabo qui Cereris sacrum
>   vulgarit arcanae, sub isdem
>   sit trabibus, fragilemque mecum
>
> solvat phaselon: saepe Diespiter
> neglectus incesto addidit integrum;
>   raro antecedentem scelestum
>   deseruit pede Poena claudo.

Loyal silence also has its sure reward. I will forbid the man who has divulged the secrets of Ceres' mysteries to be under the same roof or launch a fragile barque with me: often Jupiter neglected has taken the sinless with the sinner: rarely has Retribution, though lame, left the tracks of the culprit.

The broken movement here serves more than the pure aesthetic purpose we have been considering: it is expressive, of anxiety. In I, 17 (*Velox amoenum*) five stanzas (two of them united by anaphora) establish the stanza-unit, and thus convey the restful atmosphere of the Sabine valley; then the last two, enjambed and restless in movement, are a reminder by contrast of rowdy parties in the city. Such a final movement can also express excitement: in I, 9 (*Vides ut alta*), after three end-stopped stanzas, it helps to suggest, over another three, the pleasures that youth must seize while it can; in II, 7 (*O saepe mecum*), after five end-stopped stanzas, there follow two that suggest the excitement of

---

* V. Pöschl conceives this Ode as a triptych of 4 + 8 + 4 stanzas; and further, as a system of four groups of four stanzas which reproduces on a large scale the movement of the four lines of the Alcaic stanza (*Maecenasode*, 1961, pp. 36, 40).

the party that is to welcome Pompeius back—enjambed and divided into six sentences:

> oblivioso levia Massico
> ciboria exple. funde capacibus
>   unguenta de conchis. quis udo
>   deproperare apio coronas
> curatve myrto? quem Venus arbitrum
> dicet bibendi? non ego sanius
>   bacchabor Edonis: recepto
>   dulce mihi furere est amico.

Fill the bumpers of Massic for forgetfulness. Pour unguents from capacious shells. Who is busying himself with running up wreaths of moist parsley or myrtle? Whom will Venus appoint master of the revels? I am going to be madly tipsy as a Thracian: I want roaring fun when my friend has come back again.

In several odes such a final movement after regular stanza-units is associated with urgent appeal: in I, 24 (*Quis desiderio*), in I, 35 (*O diva gratum*), in II, 9 (*Non semper imbres*), in III, 10 (*Extremum Tanain*).

It is noteworthy that none of the dozen examples I have given comes from Book IV.* As already said, this runs to ampler movements. These are rare in the first collection; but I, 37, the Cleopatra ode, is an exception: as Heinze says, the whole poem (32 lines) is one great period: pent up anxiety bursts out in a flood of relief, triumph and admiration. Similarly in I, 36 (*Et ture et fidibus*), joy at Numida's return finds expression in an ode consisting of three headlong sentences of nine, seven and four lines. On the other hand joy at Murena's election as augur is expressed in III, 19 (*Quantum distat ab Inacho*), after two four-line sentences, in a rapid fire of short ones—twelve in twenty lines—with enthusiastic anaphora.

These last two examples are from poems in Third Asclepiads, a couplet-metre liable, as we saw, to become quatrain in Horace. In I, 3 (*Sic te diva*), also in this metre, an expectation of four-line (or at least eight-line) division is well established, so that we can be startled when it is overstepped by Death at l. 33:

> post ignem aetheria domo
> subductum Macies et nova Febrium

---

* IV, 11 (*Est mihi nonum*) is however an example: the last three stanzas have a broken movement after the regularity of the first six.

terris incubuit cohors
semotique prius tarda necessitas
Leti corripuit gradum.

After fire had been brought down from its heavenly home Leanness and a new
troop of Fevers brooded over the earth, and what had before been the distant,
tardy necessity of Death gathered pace.

The metre, like Death, has reached forward, caught up a line—'corripuit gradum'. In I, 4 (*Solvitur acris hiems*) the first 12 lines fall into three
well-marked quatrains. We are thus lulled into expecting a regular,
pretty spring-song, the more to be shocked by the sudden knocking of
'pallida Mors', with the broken, anxious movement of the last eight
lines.

Some of the shorter odes in excited mood are broken throughout
into short sentences which prevent any orderly system of stanza-units
from making itself felt—I, 14 (*O navis*), I, 26 (*Musis amicus*), I, 34
(*Parcus deorum*), III, 25 (*Quo me, Bacche*), IV, 13 (*Audivere, Lyce*). I, 27 is
not quite in this class. It is indeed in short sentences throughout,
realistically representing conversation at a rowdy party; yet the first
two stanzas are not only self-contained but insistently parallel; they call
for order:

Natis in usum laetitiae scyphis
pugnare Thracum est: *tollite barbarum*
morem verecundumque Bacchum
sanguineis prohibete rixis.

vino et lucernis Medus acinaces
immane quantum discrepat: *impium*
lenite clamorem, sodales,
et cubito remanete presso.

To fight with goblets made for purposes of joy is Thracian: away with such
barbarous habits and keep bloody quarrels far from temperate Bacchus. Wine
and lamplight should be worlds apart from Median dirks: allay your impious
clamour and stay leaning on your elbow.

W. Christ suggested that a tendency of I, 12 (*Quem virum aut heroa*)
to fall into five triads of stanzas may reflect the five triads of strophe–
antistrophe–epode in the Second Olympian of Pindar, the model of the
poem.[1] Some of the odes seem carefully designed as symmetrical
groups of stanzas. Indeed we may sometimes suspect padding for this

purpose, as with the somewhat otiose third stanza which expands II, 4 (*Ne sit ancillae*) into 3 + 3 form.[1] We have seen (p. 174) how orators sometimes introduced 'inania quaedam verba' in the interests of periodic form: I cannot help feeling that this is sometimes the case in Horace. Take the opening of III, 3:

> Iustum et tenacem propositi virum
> non civium ardor prava iubentium,
>   non voltus instantis tyranni
>   mente quatit solida, neque Auster
>
> dux inquieti turbidus Hadriae,
> nec fulminantis magna manus Iovis;
>   si fractus illabatur orbis,
>   impavidum ferient ruinae.

The man who is just and tenacious of his purpose neither the zeal of citizens urging to evil courses, nor the face of the threatening tyrant can shake from his firm resolve, nor the South Wind, boisterous master of the restless Adriatic, nor the mighty hand of fulminating Jove: if the world collapses upon him, he will take the crash unafraid.

How much ingenuity has been expended in trying to extract significance from the four several dangers this man has to face! He can hardly be Augustus, still less Horace. No, he is surely hypothetical. What was needed was two stanzas to balance the pair beginning *hac* that follows, and they had to be filled up. In the days when people knew the Odes by heart Walter Headlam used to say that you could detect where Horace was padding: it was where one's memory faltered.

8

WORD-PATTERNS

I. HYPERBATON IN GENERAL

One of the stylistic devices introduced by the Greek Sophists into prose was *hyperbaton*, leap-frog instead of natural word-order. It came to be used to avoid hiatus or to achieve a desired rhythm, deftly by some, clumsily by others. Dionysius of Halicarnassus wrote a whole treatise on it. In early Latin prose it was unknown. We begin to find examples of it at the turn of the first century B.C., when Greek influence had made itself strongly felt; and a warning against making the leaps too wide was given by the Auctor ad Herennium.[1] Yet Sallust used it little, and Cicero less perhaps in his earlier than his later works.[2] In poetry however it was to become a ubiquitous feature. What may have begun as a licence to help out metre ended as an ornament of style. It was affected by the Alexandrians and Neoteroi. Virgil discarded it progressively;* yet even he was criticized for 'peior mixtura verborum' in the line

saxa vocant Itali mediis quae in fluctibus Aras
rocks rising in mid-ocean the Italians call 'The Altars'.[3]

But Ovid went further; for example,

molle, Cupidineis nec inexpugnabile telis,
cor mihi, quodque levis causa moveret, erat,

where plain prose would say 'molle mihi cor erat nec inexpugnabile Cupidineis telis, quodque levis causa moveret'.[4] And it is undeniable that the mind does enjoy being exercised in this way. We may feel it is too much when he writes

si quis qui quid agam forte requirat erit

---

* E. Fraenkel remarks that even arrangements like *Eclogue* II, 3,

tantum inter densas, umbrosa cacumina, fagos,

are practically unknown in the *Georgics* and *Aeneid* (*Vergil und Cicero*, p. 226). See further his *Iktus und Akzent* (1928), pp. 333–5.

(for 'si quis forte erit qui requirat quid agam');[1] but that such artifices do please* may be illustrated from a similar one which has had two thousand years of history. When Shakespeare's Enobarbus says, in a somewhat burlesque tone,

> 'Ho! hearts, tongues, figures, scribes, bards, poets, cannot
> Think, speak, cast, write, sing, number—ho!—
> His love to Antony',

or Milton,

> Aire, Water, Earth
> By Fowl, Fish, Beast, was flown, was swum, was walkt,

they are using a figure of 'correlative distribution' which can be traced from Hellenistic poets onwards through European literature,† and is apparently found in oriental literature as well. Its commonest form is the amorous conceit which emerges in Sidney as

> Vertue, beautie, and speeche, did strike, wound, charme
> My heart, eyes, ears, with wonder, love, delight.[2]

The mind must have been found to enjoy executing the necessary shuttle-service of connections for this scheme to have had such a vogue.

One artifice tried by Gorgias was interplay between two substantives and their epithets, as in τοὺς πρώτους τῶν πρώτων Ἕλληνας Ἑλλήνων.[3] This does not seem to have caught on much in Greek poetry. There are some examples in Callimachus, Theocritus, and Apollonius;[4] but Norden could find only a few even in the elegant epigrams of the early Hellenistic period: rarely anything like

> Νύμφαις δὲ σκιερῆς εὐποίκιλον ἄνθος ὀπώρης
> φύλλα τε πεπταμένων αἱματόεντα ῥόδων.‡

---

* J. B. Leishman, in a good discussion of this topic, suggests that 'in addition to the reinforced antithesis two kinds of pleasure were communicated: that of sheer pattern, and that of a certain overcome difficulty in relating the adjectives to their separated nouns, although for Roman readers this purely grammatical difficulty must surely, within the limits of a single line, have been only just perceptible' (*Translating Horace*, 1956, p. 82).

† An extreme example from Hildebert de Lavardin (d. 1133), *On his Exile*:

> larga Ceres, deus Arcadiae Bacchusque replebant
> horrea, saepta, penum, farre, bidente, mero;
> hortus, apes, famulae, pulmento, melle, tapetis,
> ditabant large prandia, vasa, domum.

F. J. E. Raby, *The Oxford Book of Medieval Latin Verse*, no. 157, ll. 3–6.

‡ *A.P.* VI, 154, 5–6. See his admirable Appendix III, 'Einiges über Wortstellung', to his edition of *Aeneid* VI.

Even in the intricate word-tapestry of Pindar such patterns, as in

ὕπατον εὐρυτίμου ποτὶ δῶμα Διὸς μεταβᾶσαι, *

had rarely emerged and had not been specially sought. In Latin the phenomenon is a symptom of the divorce of poetry from everyday speech. The freer word-order of the language facilitated it.

II. HEXAMETERS: VIRGIL

In Latin, as prose grew more artistic, epithets became features of aesthetic symmetry: there was a tendency to introduce them otiosely, for the sake of balance or antithesis.† Thus Cicero, at the beginning of the *Catilinarians*, has 'cum illum ex *occultis* insidiis in apertum latrocinium coniecimus'. We also occasionally find in him and in other prose writers interplay between substantives and epithets such as Gorgias had tried: 'permagnum optimi pondus argenti', or 'multi eiusdem aemuli rationis'.[1] But it was in poetry that this became almost an obsession (and here again we may see evidence of interaction between the orators and the Neoteroi). It was something new: in the remains of Ennius' *Annals* there are instances of separation of epithet from noun;[2] but there is no instance of schematic arrangement of two nouns and their epithets over a line, and there are not many in Lucretius. But in Catullus' *Peleus and Thetis* this amounts to an excessive mannerism‡ which cloys in itself besides emphasizing the verse too much as a unit. Yet if used with discrimination it could be very effective, as the Augustans discovered, though Virgil found it less suitable to the epic style of the *Aeneid* than to that of the *Eclogues* and *Georgics*.

The most striking of these patterns is 'that verse which they call Golden, of two substantives and two adjectives with a verb betwixt to keep the peace'.§ Let us restrict the term, as is generally done, to lines in which the epithets and nouns appear in the corresponding order, that is, a b C A B: as in

grandia per multos tenuantur flumina rivos.

---

* *Ol.* I, 43. In the rest of the *Olympians* I can find only half-a-dozen instances of any kind of interplay between two substantives and two epithets (II, 77–8; III, 5, 35 (?); IV, 20; VI, 1; IX, 97).

† It reached such a pitch in Virgil that Servius noted on *Aen.* III, 126: 'For the sake of variety he has *not* added an epithet.'

‡ 1 to every 7 lines (Norden, *Aeneid VI*, p. 394[3]).

§ Dryden, preface to *Sylvae*. Conjunctions, prepositions, etc., can be ignored.

Young[1] gives the figures for number of lines to each example as

Catullus 64	16
Eclogues	39
Georgics (1500 lines)	47
Aeneid (2000 lines)	66

Horace reserved its monumental quality for special purposes. A fine specimen lifts the thirteenth Epode from the present to the heroic world:

> nobilis ut grandi cecinit Centaurus alumno
>
> *as the famous Centaur sang to his pupil grown to manhood.*

Two in succession enhance the grandiosity of the town mouse's scene of operations (*S.* II, 6, 102–4),

> rubro ubi cocco
> tincta super lectos canderet vestis eburnos,
> multaque de magna superessent fercula cena.

where crimson-dyed draperies blazed on ivory couches, and many courses remained from a great banquet.

Another makes a brave conclusion to *Satires*, II, 2,

> fortiaque adversis opponite pectora rebus
> *and show a bold front to adversity.*

Virgil also used it finely to round off periods. Here are two splendid examples from the great finale to *Georgics*, I, which also constitute that 'overarching superflux of rhythm' at the end of a period:[2]

> solem quis dicere falsum
> audeat? ille etiam caecos instare tumultus
> saepe monet fraudemque et operta tumescere bella;
> ille etiam exstincto miseratus Caesare Romam,
> cum caput obscura nitidum ferrugine texit,
> *impiaque aeternam timuerunt saecula noctem.*
>
> scilicet et tempus veniet cum finibus illis
> agricola incurvo terram molitus aratro
> exesa inveniet scabra robigine pila,
> aut gravibus rastris galeas pulsabit inanis,
> *grandiaque effossis mirabitur ossa sepulcris.*

The chiastic form a b C B A (shall we call it the 'Silver Line', since it is not quite so absolute?) can also be used in this way, as at the end of *Georgic* II (540):

> impositos duris crepitare incudibus ensis.

This too is common in the *Peleus and Thetis* (though not half so common as the Golden), and almost equally so in the *Eclogues*; but again Virgil was sparing of its use in his more mature work.[1]

In elegiac poetry such schemes also came to be favoured, especially by Ovid. The pentameter, more compact than the hexameter, was even more susceptible of them:

> callidus in falsa lusit adulter ave.
>
> roscida purpurea supprime lora manu.
>
> frigidaque arboreas mulceat aura comas.[2]

One feels, however, that in elegy they are features of the general elegance rather than trump cards reserved for special use.

Another form of hexameter (shall we call it the 'Bronze Line'?) is that framed by epithet and noun, as in (*Aen.* VI, 137)

> aureus et foliis et lento vimine ramus.

This may seem to us, accustomed to Augustan poetry, to be a scheme likely to occur spontaneously in Latin: yet it is almost unknown in Ennius and Lucretius.[3] Or a line can be framed by two verbs,

> flebant et cineri ingrato suprema ferebant,

or two participles,

> vescentes laetumque choro paeana canentes.

Naturally the symmetry was often enhanced, as here, by assonance.

These are schemes in which the line is unit. But there are also similar figures of rhetoric, independent of lines, such as the κύκλος or circle:[4]

> *cessas* in vota precesque,
> Tros, ait, Aenea, *cessas*?

or

> *socer* arma Latinus habeto,
> imperium sollemne *socer*.

This is analogous to *chiasmus*, another feature which (apart from cases in which it distributes emphasis appropriately) seems to give a pleasure beyond that of mere variety. As regards whole sentences it appears to be a quite natural and popular phenomenon, and is found in early verse, for example Ennius, *Annals*, 269:

> spernitur orator bonus, horridu' miles amatur.

217

Where pairs of words or word-groups are involved it seems more self-conscious, especially when enhanced by repetition. Thus Sophocles'

ὦ παῖ, γένοιο πατρὸς εὐτυχέστερος,
τὰ δ' ἄλλ' ὅμοιος

becomes in Accius

virtuti sis par, dispar fortunis patris
Your father's virtues match, match not his fortune.[1]

It is noteworthy that Cicero uses chiasmus much more in his carefully composed letters than in those which give the impression of being dashed off. How elaborately he writes to Brutus,

Consules duos bonos quidem sed dumtaxat bonos consules amisimus !²
We have lost two consuls loyal indeed but no more than loyal consuls.

In Horace chiasmus may be playfully elaborate, as in

rusticus urbanum murem mus paupere fertur
accepisse cavo, *veterem vetus hospes amicum*;

or expressive, as (of changing wind) in

Romae Tibur amem ventosus *Tibure Romam*;

or decorative as well as emphatic, as in

vos exemplaria Graeca
nocturna versate manu, *versate diurna*.³

Ovid uses it freely as an adornment, with characteristic neatness:

Memnona si mater, mater ploravit Achillem.
Romulus Iliades Iliadesque Remus.
sive tuas, Perseu, Daedale, sive tuas.⁴

III. LYRICS: HORACE

The lyric 'nugae' of Catullus generally sought to make their effect, however carefully contrived, by giving the impression of spontaneous and natural expression. There is hardly any artistic word-patterning.

Significantly it is in the more formal poems in stanzas that we begin to find it—in the Hymn to Diana (34):

> tu *Lucina dolentibus*
> *Iuno dicta puerperis*,
> tu potens Trivia et *notho es*
>   *dicta lumine luna;*
>
> tu cursu, dea, menstruo
> metiens iter annuum
> *rustica agricolae bonis*
>   *tecta frugibus exples*;

and in the first wedding poem (61):

> huc veni *niveo gerens*
>   *luteum pede soccum*

and

> nuptialia concinens
> voce carmina tinnula,

and

> bona cum bona
>   nubet alite virgo.

From these we pass to the elaborate art of the Epodes and Odes of Horace, something new to Latin poetry, in which schematic arrangement plays a major part.* We find the Golden type—

> et superiecto pavidae natarunt | aequore dammae—

or the Silver type—

> niveum doloso | credidit tauro latus—

more than forty times, and there are many variations.[1] In the Pyrrha ode (1, 5), in which many have found the quintessence of the Horatian art, we have

> Quis multa gracilis te puer in rosa
> perfusus liquidis urget odoribus
>   grato, Pyrrha, sub antro?

---

* The facts are most usefully analysed in the Prolegomena to H. Darnley Naylor's *Horace, Odes and Epodes: A Study in Word-order* (1922); but he seems to go too far in his contention that when Horace departs from normal word-order he wishes to draw our attention to the abnormality and so to emphasize for us the point that he desires to make. It would in any case have been extremely hard to write in such stanzas, in which almost every syllabic position is determined as to quantity, without sometimes departing from normal word-order simply *metri gratia*; but otherwise aesthetic pattern seems to be the motive at least as often as semantic emphasis.

for what in prose might be 'quis puer gracilis liquidis odoribus perfusus te, Pyrrha, in multa rosa sub grato antro urget?' We have the alternations 'aspera nigris aequora ventis' and 'qui nunc te fruitur credulus aurea'; and a closing sentence remarkably involved,

$$\overset{1}{\text{me}} \quad \overset{2}{\text{tabula sacer}}$$

$$\overset{1}{\text{votiva}} \quad \overset{2}{\text{paries}} \quad \overset{3}{\text{indicat uvida}}$$

$$\overset{4}{\text{suspendisse potenti}}$$

$$\overset{3}{\text{vestimenta}} \quad \text{maris} \quad \overset{4}{\text{deo.*}}$$

Elsewhere we have such complications as

$$\overset{1}{\text{latentis}} \quad \overset{2}{\text{proditor}} \quad \overset{3}{\text{intimo}}$$

$$\overset{2}{\text{gratus}} \quad \overset{1}{\text{puellae}} \quad \overset{2}{\text{risus}} \quad \overset{3}{\text{ab angulo.}^{1}}$$

This is not a matter in which Horace developed progressively. In the Epodes the proportion of instances of separation of noun and epithet to adjacence is about three to two, and so it is in *Odes*, I.[2]

* There is a further involution beyond what I have indicated by the figures; for 'potenti'(*pace* Milton) almost certainly governs 'maris'—'powerful over the sea', Greek ποντομέδων.

RIVAL THEORIES TO THE PULSE-ACCENT THEORY OF LATIN DACTYLIC VERSE

A. VARIOUS EXPLANATIONS

(1) *Hexameter caesuras*

Lucian Müller opined that the 'strong' ($2\frac{1}{2}$) caesura, as in

Bella per Emathios ‖ plus quam civilia campos,

was preferred by the Romans because it came as nearly as possible in the middle of the line (yet the $2\frac{3}{4}$ caesura is still nearer, and was preferred by many of the Greeks; and 3, which would be exactly in the middle, is avoided by all); also because the first member (if dactylic) would, if repeated, make a pentameter, 'second only among the pure jewels that compose the crown of Greek metres'; for example,

Bella per Emathios bella per Emathios;

and thirdly, because the second resultant member was in itself a metrical line, the paroemiac, 'which shines with an elegance of its own'; for example,

plus quam civilia campos.[1]

He might just as well have said that he did not know the reason.

On the $4\frac{1}{2}$ type, for example

temperat alter et alterius ‖ vires necat aër,

he remarks that the first portion is a verse in itself, a dactylic tetrameter catalectic (but again, this is no recommendation: we have seen that ancient poets tried to *avoid* suggesting one metre within another). Many Greeks did not like this type much, preferring the trochaic ($2\frac{3}{4}$) caesura. The Romans used it mainly in combination with $1\frac{1}{2}$, as in

despiciens ‖ mare velivolum ‖ terrasque iacentes;

Müller presumes this was because otherwise the first portion would be too long. He does not suggest why the Romans should have felt differently from the Greeks over this. And he also notes, without explanation, that Virgil generally avoids lines with 4½ unsupported by 1½ unless he wishes to express agitation or speed or roughness, as in

una Eurusque Notusque ruunt ‖ creberque procellis Africus.

together rush Eurus and Notus, and Africus dense with storms.

Next he observes that lines with a trochaic caesura unsupported, like

spargens umida mella ‖ soporiferumque papaver,

which were always liked by the Greeks, as in

ἄνδρα μοι ἔννεπε, Μοῦσα, ‖ πολύτροπον, ὃς μάλα πολλά,

and became the favourite form with Nonnus and his contemporaries in the fifth century A.D., were practically shunned by the Romans. No explanation. The Pulse–Accent theory gives one.

Meyer did not agree with Müller. He explained many of the features of the developed Roman hexameter as used by Cicero, Catullus and Ovid, for instance, as due to imitation of the Alexandrians. But the chief feature directly contradicts this: whereas the strong (2½) caesura was slightly preferred by Homer to the trochaic (2¾), the Alexandrians preferred the latter. Ennius was therefore violently reversing the trend when he increased the proportion of strong (2½) caesuras to 80 per cent. (Otherwise one might have explained the development as a gradual process of normalizing what had been or become tendencies, such as we found in the case of Horace's lyric metres.) Meyer's own tentative explanation of this feature was, that Ennius may have felt the trochaic caesura to be too much a counterpart of the trochaic ending.[1] Is this likely? Is

infandum regina

too close a counterpart of

iubes renovare dolorem?

And why should Ennius feel this, if no Greek had? Meyer had to admit that in pentameters, owing to the caesura fixed in the middle, the second half was always a counterpart of the first (though correspondence was reduced by the preference for a spondee before the caesura).[2]

Havet sought to explain the additional caesura required by the Roman ear in a 1½ + 4½-type line as due to a change in the conditions of poetic production: Greek poetry was sung, Roman recited; without the help of music the course of the verse had to be measured out by such breaks.[1] But *Hellenistic* poetry was recited: no one supposes that Apollonius sang his *Argonautica*. And even if he had, this explanation of Roman practice would still be flimsy enough.

Nougaret suggests that the Romans avoided the trochaic caesura because the pause might tend to make the preceding short syllable seem *brevis in longo* on the analogy of the end of the line; for example,

> spargens umida mella,*

But even if this were plausible, why should the Greeks not have felt the same?

Crusius imagined Ennius as *wanting* to make pulse and accent coincide even in the earlier feet, but being frustrated by the fact that he had to get in so many words of the types 'sedens', 'pedibus', 'praeteritos'. By the nature of the Latin accent these could never satisfy the condition, so he 'put them before a caesura, or a place where a caesura was permissible' ($1\frac{1}{2}$, $2\frac{1}{2}$, $3\frac{1}{2}$): in these positions the accent would upset the tempo less badly.[2]† But where else could he have put such words? They may be commoner in Latin than Greek, but not sufficiently so to account for Ennius' remarkable preference for strong caesuras. On the contrary, Sturtevant's statistics suggest that he went out of his way to introduce them. More recently E. G. O'Neill has written of the 'localization' of word-types in the Latin hexameter, as determined by the 'inner metric'. His 'inner metric' is 'the syllabic, or quantitative, pattern of a verse-form'. This depends largely on the caesuras, and he nowhere (so far as I can see) suggests any explanation for the marked divergence of Latin from Greek practice regarding them.‡

---

* L. Nougaret, *Traité de Métrique* (1948), section 71. He uses the same argument (75, 76) against lines of the type

> hirsutumque || supercilium || promissaque barba;
> impius haec || tam culta || novalia miles habebit.

† Does he mean that Ennius fixed caesuras where such words could precede them?

‡ *T.A.P.A.* (1940), esp. pp. 349 ff. L. Nougaret has also argued from frequency of certain metrical word-types in various authors (*Rev. Ét. Lat.* 1946, pp. 261–71). He notes, as to the word-type 'potuisset', that Lucretius, Virgil and Ovid have it nearly always before a vowel though more words begin with a consonant than a vowel, and thinks this shows intention. It does, but not in his sense. Apart from the end-position, 'potuissĕt' can occur at three places in the line, 'potuissēt' at one only, and even there with some reserves.

It will be agreed, I think, that these various explanations of the Roman practice as regards caesuras neither inspire confidence individually nor suggest confidence in each other. Let us now see what has been said about verse endings by those who refuse to consider that accent can have played any part.

(2) *Verse endings*

(a) *Hexameters*

Mature Roman hexameters generally ended with one of the two types:

> sidera tollit (*or* praesentia dona)
> arma requirunt (*or* labefacta cadebant).

Since a preposition adhered to its noun,

> nocte per umbras

was equivalent to the second. There are also more occasional types involving monosyllables which can still be called permissible in Virgil:

> hos regit artus
> increpat, et vox
> haec quoque, si quis.

To say that about two-thirds of Greek hexameters end in this way only emphasizes the difference in Latin; for in Virgil the percentage is nearly 98, in Ovid nearly 99.[1] The Greek proportion is what one might expect to occur automatically from the relative frequency of disyllables and trisyllables in the language. Endings in a single non-enclitic monosyllable, like

> restituis rem,

could be ruled out in accordance with a general feeling that such words were unsuitable to end a line, or even a colon, of verse, or a sentence in verse or prose.[2] Virgil's 'procumbit humi bos' and Horace's 'audis minus et minus iam' (in Sapphics) were obviously intended to be felt as exceptional and expressive. A monosyllable not preceded by a pyrrhic word ($\smile\smile$) or another monosyllable to lighten the stress[3] was not admitted even before a strong *caesura*. That the objection was to a jolt before a major pause* is suggested by the fact that it was eased where the sense ran on, as in Virgil's (*Aen.* I, 329)

an Phoebi soror? an Nympharum sanguinis una.

Types involving a spondee in the fifth foot came generally to be avoided, though they were affected by the Neoterics in imitation of the Alexandrians. Cicero in a letter to Atticus (VII, 2, 1), having happened to write that he had had a good sea-crossing because

flavit ab Epiro lenissimus Ōnchēsmites,

adds gaily, with the words echoing in his ears, 'you can sell that σπονδειάζων to any of the νεώτεροι you choose'. The obvious reason for avoidance is the general principle that, whatever variations are allowed earlier in the line, the essential basis of the metre (in this case the dactyl) should assert itself at the end.†

But what was wrong with the types

equites trepidabant,
lucet via longo,
di genuerunt,
mentem animumque?

Weil and Benloew, in 1855, suggested that a masculine caesura in the fifth foot (4½) 'rend la chute des vers moins coulante'.[1] This is another way of putting the principle just mentioned: it made the rhythm less dactylic. There is something in this; for, as Quintilian says, 'even in the division of words there is a kind of hidden time'.[2] But why, if it is only the break at 4½ that is objectionable, do 147 of the 206 exceptions in Virgil have it preceded by a monosyllable? Meyer saw in this rule another instance of the Romans taking their cue from the Alexandrians; but if he is right, it is odd that it was precisely in the case of Greek words like *hymenaeus* that they took licence to break it.[3] Wilhelm Christ and

---

* Latin objected even more than Greek. See W. R. Hardie, *Res Metrica* (1920), pp. 52–3.

† Thus in Greek tragic iambics resolution is not allowed in the last metron, nor should a line end with a long syllable followed by an unconnected cretic word (– ◡ –), as in νώτοις οὐρανόν ('Porson's Law'). For the principle in general see L. Müller, *De re metrica* (1894), p. 198; Crusius–Rubenbauer, *Römische Metrik* (1955), section 37e. Cicero says of prose periods, 'Clausulas autem diligentius etiam servandas esse quam superiora....In oratione autem prima pauci cernunt, postuma plerique' (*De Or.* III, 192). In Russian binary metre pulse and accent must coincide in the last foot (B. O. Unbegaun, *Russian Versification*, 1956, p. 17).

others have given the simple explanation that there are not many words of the type ∪∪– ≃ in Latin. (Nougaret counted 170 in 10,000 words of Cicero.)[1] That won't do: there are 24 of them placed in other (seldom inviting) positions in the line in the first 250 verses of the *Aeneid*. And why should their use have become *progressively* rarer? Others have suggested that such endings had something soft about them, unsuited to Roman taste.[2] Un-Roman they might well come to sound, the exceptions admitted by Virgil being generally conscious imitations of Greek rhythm. But is Ennius' 'pedem stabilibat' soft or un-Roman?

What was wrong, then, with the type

terras frugiferentis?

Having put forward the explanation that words like 'genuerunt' were excluded through imitation of the Alexandrians, Meyer could not apply it to words like 'frugiferentes'. He could only suggest feebly that the prohibition was 'rather naturally' *extended* from quadrisyllables to longer words.[3] But later he thought of something better. He drew attention to certain passages in which Quintilian remarks that Cicero has been criticized for ending periods with a clausula in which one word embraces two feet, as in 'archipir|atae', and adds that even in verse this is very weak (*praemolle*), quoting Horace's 'Tyndarid|arum' (which instance one would have thought excusable as a Grecism).[4] Quintilian amplifies soon after: whereas 'criminis | causa' is strong, 'archipi|ratae' is weak, and 'facili|tatis' still weaker (though he himself practises what he here preaches against). Such words, a late grammarian says, 'seem to be in a hurry, and with uninterrupted speed of breathing to slip out'.*
Horace only twice allows an Adonic of one word to close a Sapphic stanza, and then it is a proper name: 'Mercuriusque', 'Bellerophontem'. The suggestion is that oratorical principles are here operating on verse. There may be something in this; but it cannot be held to affect words of the type ∪∪– ≃, as Norden supposed.[5] These can hardly be said to comprise two feet, any more than the –∪∪ ≃ type,[6] and it is difficult to suppose that clausulae so common as the types 'esse *videatur*' or 'esse

---

* 'Properare verba et continua spiritus celeritate labi videntur' (Diomedes, p. 469, quoted by Leo). Further support in J. Soubiran, *Pallas*, VIII (1959), 54–5.

polliceor' are included in the criticism, let alone the favourite type '$-\ \smile\ -\ \smile$' 'comprobavit'.

E. G. O'Neill states the position as follows:[1] 'A well-constructed Latin hexameter must have a short true-final in either the first or the second syllable of the dactylic thesis of the fifth foot, and should not have any sort of final in the arsis of either the fifth or the sixth foot.' This formulation is based on a theory which he has also attempted to apply to Greek, that 'final syllables had peculiar phonetic and metrical qualities which non-finals did not have, and which quasi-finals and artificial finals only approximately had'. Metrical word-types were located with reference to the values of their final syllables.[2] But, other considerations apart, the whole structure seems aesthetically implausible.*

To sum up, most of these scholars believe that ending a hexameter with a disyllable or trisyllable became the rule by a process of elimination. Single monosyllables were excluded as uncouth (there is no quarrel here). Polysyllables were excluded, some say because they were gabbled or somehow weak, some because quadrisyllables at least would be preceded by undesirable caesuras.

(b) Pentameters

Many critics, ancient and modern, have supposed that the second line of the elegiac couplet was by derivation a hexameter with each half 'catalectic', that is, having the second half of the third and sixth foot suppressed. 'There is catalexis twice; and it was this that made it appropriate for the expression of grief or other emotions. It did not roll on confidently to its close like the hexameter, but twice sank or waned or "died away in pain".'[3] This theory *might* account for its development in the dark age before Archilochus and Mimnermus (though it does not account for the name 'pentameter', which goes back at least to the fifth century).† But surely no modern composer or reader *feels* it in these

---

* For example, to say (p. 353) that the preference for type $-\ \smile\ \smile$ over type $-\ -$ at the beginning of a hexameter is explicable only in terms of their endings is absurd. There was a motive for emphasizing the metrical basis as dactylic at the beginning as well as the end of the line. A spondee with a break after it, still more with a stop after it, in this position slows up the verse considerably.

† Some metricians accounted for the term 'pentameter' by assuming that the basis was

$$-\smile\smile\mid-\smile\smile\mid--\mid\smile\smile-\mid\smile\smile-.$$

(Diomedes mentions both analyses: *Gr. Lat.* I, p. 518, 32.) When Quintilian says (IX, 4, 98) that

terms, any more than he feels the trimeter to be tripartite, and it is surely inconceivable that Tibullus, Propertius and Ovid did.* It had acquired its own, well-recognized nature as something entirely different from the hexameter. Yet some scholars have asked us to believe that, because it had become the rule that the Latin hexameter should end in a word of three or two syllables, those poets deduced mechanically that it was only logical for the pentameter to end in the same word-types minus half a foot: a monosyllable being ruled out on general and valid grounds, the disyllable alone remained eligible.[1] (In any case, if it was only a matter of pedantically applying a rule, why did it take fifty years to do it—for Cicero from the first observed the rule for hexameters?)

Meyer adduced an additional argument, as well he might. Maintaining that the Alexandrians disliked using an iambic word before a strong $(2\frac{1}{2})$ caesura in hexameters, and before the caesura in pentameters, and that Tibullus (and Ovid in his earlier work) followed them as regards pentameters, he assumed that Tibullus mechanically applied the same rule to the second half of the pentameter. But quite apart from the unlikelihood that Tibullus would adopt such a rule for pentameters and disregard it for hexameters, or that he would for no good reason restrict himself so drastically by extending it to the second half, more critical comparative statistics do not support Meyer's premises. This is a mare's nest.[2]

Axelson thinks that a different process of elimination left the disyllable in possession of the field, both in pentameters and in Senecan trimeters.[3] Monosyllables were obviously ruled out. Trisyllables would have to be preceded by a masculine break in pentameters, a feminine in trimeters; but these verse-types (and hexameters in the corresponding place) had a so-called Bridge or Zeugma,[4] which called for exactly the opposite break, a feminine in the pentameter, a masculine in the trimeter. This is arguable, but need not here be argued, for his objection to a *quadrisyllable* of type $-\cup\cup-$ seems invalid: it is, simply, that it would have seemed *praemolle*, by a surely impossible interpretation of Quintilian's

there is a 'latens tempus' between the words in the *middle spondee* of a *pentameter*, he seems to mean something like a musical rest (cf. 'inania tempora', IX, 4, 51); in which case he is surely contaminating the 'five-foot' theory with the 'catalexis' theory.

* Quintilian rightly says that poets in composing a verse consider the metre as a whole, not the component feet (IX, 4, 115).

remark (IX, 4, 64), which we have already held to apply only to longer words which could be said to comprise two feet (see p. 226).

Wilamowitz asserted that the norm of securing accent on the penultimate syllable (by ending with a disyllable) was a trait copied from contemporary Greek epigram.[1] Examination of the epigrammatists of the Augustan period suggests that this is illusory. There was, indeed, always some tendency for the final word in a Greek pentameter to be accented on the penultimate ('paroxyton'), simply because the laws of Greek accentuation made this commonest in words ending ⏑ ⏒, for example, φίλη, πόλις, ὀρέγων, οὐλομένη, not to mention less common ones like ἠιόνος. As time went on this tendency increased, partly through a growing desire to end with a definitely long syllable (which froze out endings like πόλεμος, πειθόμενος), partly through a growing aversion from having the last syllable accented.* But there are still plenty of exceptions. Let us take Crinagoras and Marcus Argentarius as specimen epigrammatists of the period. We find that the percentages for Crinagoras hardly differ from those for Tyrtaeus in the seventh century B.C., and that Argentarius actually has nearly as many proparoxyton endings as paroxyton:

Accent on:	Propenultimate	Penultimate	Ultimate
Tyrtaeus	22 (28·6 %)	45 (58·4 %)	10 (13 %)
Crinagoras	39 (28·0 %)	87 (63·0 %)	12 (9 %)
M. Argentarius	45 (44·5 %)	55 (54·5 %)	1 (1 %)

Moreover we find epigrams in both poets which have all three, or even four, pentameters accented on the propenultimate, for example Argentarius, *A.P.* VI, 248 (κύλικος, θύγατερ, ἑτοιμότατον, ἀνθέμενος).[2] It hardly looks as though they were concerned to produce an effect by ending with paroxyton words. What is true, and perhaps relevant, is that *from the second century* A.D. the Greeks began to make the accent fall on the penultimate of both hexameters and pentameters, as it does in mature Latin verse.[3] Now this is the period when Greek accent was passing from one of pitch to one of stress, and it may be that these poets

---

* F. Hanssen gave statistics which demonstrate this. In Antipater of Sidon (late second century B.C.) the proportion is 1·7%, in Philippus of Thessalonica (early first century A.D.) it is 0·9% (*Rh. Mus.* 1883, pp. 226–33).

were influenced by familiarity with stresses occurring in this position at the end of Latin verses.

K. F. Smith found an explanation in Zieliński's theory that the accentuation of classical Latin poetry and oratory was archaic, and distinct from that of contemporary speech. A word like *ferent* would be accented on the last syllable, so that coincidence of pulse and accent would be secured at the end of the pentameter also.[1] But nobody now believes in this premise. Vollmer on the contrary (and Mrs G. A. Wilkinson) have supposed that the object of the rule was to secure *contrast* in the last four syllables—one coincidence and one conflict.[2] But to what aesthetic principle would this appeal (and Axelson is right at least in insisting that 'behind metrical legislation there never stand other than purely aesthetic grounds')?[3] The opposite effect indeed is found in the hexameter, with good aesthetic justification. Wilhelm Christ simply said that this division of the dactyl allowed the line to flow more easily to its close,[4] which is true as far as it goes, while Beare can hardly be said to attempt any explanation—either as regards caesuras or ends in hexameters or pentameters.*

It will be seen that none of these various explanations of the phenomena is more cogent than in the case of the hexameter.

B. ANSWERS TO SOME CRITICISMS OF THE PULSE–ACCENT THEORY

These criticisms may best be dealt with in the form of a catechism.

Why was the type of ending 'di genuerunt' avoided?

This remains the most serious objection.

Lindsay and others have held that there was a secondary accent on polysyllables, so that here there would be a certain amount of conflict—'di genuerunt'.[5] But it is only fair to say that some do not believe there was such an accent, or alternatively (as I am inclined to agree), that it did not affect words in which a true foot was preceded by a pyrrhic ($\cup\cup$), as here.[6] And certainly no fatal conflict seems to have been felt in pentameter-endings such as 'mors adoperta caput', which contain a

---

* On pp. 173–4 he says that the Romans enforced a certain treatment of the third foot in the hexameter (that is, overwhelming preference for strong caesura) 'for some reason unknown to us'. That is all I can find in his *Latin Verse and European Song*.

word of this type. The accent on the monosyllable *mors* might weaken the accent that immediately follows it; but this would apply equally to the *di genuerunt* in the hexameter. Soubiran has pointed out that in such quadrisyllables the second short vowel was often *i* or *u* before a long vowel and so apt to become consonantal and blur the rhythm, as 'gen*w*erunt', 'fac*y*ebat', etc.;[1] but again there seems to have been no objection to words of the type 'genuere' or 'faciebat' in the second half of a pentameter.

Why were the types 'hos regit artus', 'impius ex quo' admitted?

It seems likely that a pyrrhic word or a monosyllable immediately preceded by a stressed end-syllable (which in Latin could, except in rare cases, only be a monosyllable) had its accent considerably weakened. The pyrrhics in question are often accentless 'enclitics', *quoque* being particularly common. Soubiran has shown that Virgil, unlike his predecessors or the free and easy Horace of the *Epistles*, greatly preferred that the pyrrhic here should be a purely grammatical word (*ubi, quoque,* etc.) rather than a word 'à sens plein', that there should be a stop before the preceding monosyllable, and that the sense should run on into the next line; also that the monosyllable should not be a preposition, which would bear little or no accent. All this he rightly assumes to be designed to weaken any accent on the short syllables of the fifth dactyl.[2] Similarly the final monosyllable was often enclitic, as in 'haec quoque si quis'.* Or there was a pause at the end of the fifth foot, which emphasized the first monosyllable succeeding; and in such cases the emphasis on the second was lightened also by the fact that the sense ran on swiftly to the next line,† as in

> spicea iam campis cum messis inhorruit, et cum
> frumenta in viridi stipula lactantia turgent.[3]

Why was the type 'frugiferentes' or 'concinuisse' excluded?

Because there was only a secondary accent (assuming this to have existed) to coincide with the all-important pulse of the fifth foot. And

---

* Almost always in the 155 cases in Ovid's *Metamorphoses*.

† Norden remarks, 'in general the two words are more or less closely bound together by the sentence-accent' (*Aeneid VI*, 448[3]). In the better poets punctuation at the end of the fifth foot is nearly always associated either with two monosyllables or with anaphora in the sixth (Bentley on Lucan, 1, 231) which causes the sense to run on into the next line.

in any case, as we have seen, Quintilian thought such endings 'prae-molle', 'very weak', both in prose and verse (IX, 4, 64; see p. 226). (It has been noted that 'concinuisse lyra' was a type of pentameter-ending sought by Tibullus, and to a lesser extent Ovid, but avoided by Propertius.)[1] Müller also remarked that in such words the last two syllables were often a mere termination, and as such perhaps unfitted to form the final foot of the line; but plenty of lines end satisfactorily in words with the same feature, such as *amavit*.

Why were exceptions made in the case of Greek words? *

As conscious reminiscences of Greek rhythm (and who is Havet to call this an 'error of taste' on the part of all the great Augustan poets?).[2] Also we learn from the grammarians of the empire that Greek words borrowed by a Latin author, if they retained their original form and declension, retained also their Greek accent. Servius, on G. I, 59, says that in Virgil's phrase

Eliadum palmas Epiros equarum

Epiros would be uttered with its Greek accent on the first syllable, not its Latin one on the second. Now the Greek accent in Virgil's time was apparently not yet one of stress, so it could not involve the kind of conflict we have been discussing. Quintilian tells us that Roman poets liked to give charm to their verses by introducing Greek names pronounced with a Greek accent.[3]

Why did the Augustans prefer that a spondaic fourth foot should not consist in a separate word? †

Because if Virgil had written, for example,

arma virumque cano qui Troiae primus ab oris

rather than

arma virumque cano Troiae qui primus ab oris

---

* For example, of 53 words of the type 'hymenaeus' that end lines in Virgil 50 are Greek.

† First observed by G. Cortius, editor of Lucan, 1726. See also H. A. J. Munro, Introd. to edn. of Lucretius (1864), II, 14⁴; F. Marx, *Abh. Sächs Ges.* (1922), pp. 197–232 ('Lex Marxii'!). Where Virgil has an exception it 'corresponds to some special weight of feeling' (R. S. Conway on *Aen.* I, 26).

coincidence would have exceeded conflict in the first four feet. (This seems just as plausible as the view that the preference reflected a dislike of letting the line seem to fall into two corresponding parts:[1]

> arma virumque cano qui
> Troiae primus ab oris,

or

> et multo nebulae dea
> circumfudit amictu.

Surely the strong caesura was enough to preclude that impression. The correspondence would not have been nearly so jog-trot in effect as that precluded by the caesura in trimeters; for example,

> Beatus ille ‖ qui procul negotiis

instead of divisions analogous to

> Beatus ille qui
> procul negotiis.

And in pentameters the fixed caesura often *produces* precisely such correspondence.)

Why did Virgil allow elision freely at 4¾ but not at 5?

That is, why is the type *sider(a) adibam* fairly common, whereas the type *cerealia(que) arma* occurs only with *-que* or *-ve* except at *Aen.* III, 581, *intremer(e) omnem*?*

Because in 'síder(a) adíbam' coincidence is preserved; so also in 'cereália(que) árma', if it is true that elided *-que* or *-ve* did not displace the accent of the word to which it was attached.[2] 'Intrémer(e) ómnem' may be intended as expressive of the upheaval of Sicily by Enceladus.†

Similarly, though elision in the second half of a pentameter is rare, the type 'dícer(e) amíca pótest' is rather commoner than 'desíner(e) esse mea'.‡

* There are a few other odd cases of elision at 5, for example *Aen.* IX, 351, 'ibi ignem'; X, 508, 'haec eadem aufert'.

† Cf. Val. Fl. II, 519, 'intremere Ide', an imitation. Soubiran gives examples of rhythms of the similar type 'et tremit artus' which also seem designed to express trembling, liveliness or acceleration (*Pallas*, VIII, 1959, 43–5).

‡ The figures given for the latter type in my article in *C.R.* (1940), p. 38 n. 6 are, however, unaccountably wrong: they should be, Ovid 35, Propertius 12, Tibullus 0 (M. Platnauer, *Elegiac*,

Why do pentameters end so much more rarely with a trisyllable than a quadrisyllable?

Because the type 'suppŏsuit pĕdibus', found in Catullus, produces two conflicts and no coincidence (perhaps that is why it hardly occurs in the Augustans),[1] and the type 'rúre frŭi lĭceat' produces two conflicts to one coincidence; whereas the relatively commoner type 'vívere consĭlio' produces one conflict only to one coincidence. This process of groping towards the disyllabic ending, which produces one conflict to two coincidences, does seem significant, especially as Greek had no prejudice against trisyllables here.

Martial has plenty of trisyllabic endings; but he, like Horace in the *Satires*, was deliberately adopting a style that sacrificed poetic polish to colloquial naturalism. In fact he sometimes seems to exploit the arresting accentual conflict they produce for pointing his epigrams at the end.[2]

Why is a pentameter-ending with an accented monosyllable in the middle avoided?†

The type 'flórida vér ăgeret', quite common in Greek, does produce two coincidences to one conflict. But it involves accentuation of adjacent syllables, which causes stumbling. Since, however, there are only four examples even in Catullus, there may also be operating in this case some deterrent not connected with accent. Certainly a monosyllable here brings the line up with a jolt, and leaves an anapaestic hangover which upsets the dactylic flow of the metre.

1951, pp. 87–9). I must also withdraw what I said there (p. 39, cf. Lindsay, *Captivi*, p. 369) about enclitics being used by Ovid at the end of pentameters because they involved no clash of accent with ictus, in view of the criticisms of B. Axelson in *Ovidiana* (1958), pp. 131–4.

* If we regard trisyllables preceded by a closely linked monosyllable as quadrisyllables, the figures are as follows:

	Tibullus	Propertius	Ovid
Trisyllable	20	30	3
Quadrisyllable	18	166	31

Ovid's three trisyllables (in over 10,000 pentameters) are all from the late and less fastidious *Epistulae ex Ponto* (Platnauer, *Elegiac*, pp. 15–17).

† Catullus 4, Tibullus 1, Propertius and Ovid 0. There are plenty of lines with an *unaccented*, usually proclitic, monosyllable in the middle (G. A. Wilkinson, *C.Q.* 1948, pp. 68–9, 72–3).

There are a few cases where an accented monosyllable in the second half of a pentameter conflicts with the pulse, such as 'híc vir et ílle púer' (where no doubt the accent on *hic* weakened that on *vir*), and even such as 'dúra vir árma férat', producing equality of conflict and coincidence. (The type 'praesídium dát equis', which would produce three conflicts and no coincidence, never occurs in Latin.)

It is no refutation of the Pulse–Accent theory to point out occasional oddities.* Thus we are reminded that *exínde* was so accented, and that this spoils the coincidence at the end of *Aen.* VI, 743,

> quisque suos patimur manes; ex|índe per | ámplum....

Again, the fact that *adhuc*, like a few other words ending in -*c* for -*ce*, was accented on the last syllable makes possibly complete coincidence in the line

> sanguin(e) adhúc campíqu(e) ingéntes óssibus álbent[1]

(not quite complete, if elided -*que* does not displace the accent on *cámpi*). But these are insignificant details; and in any case Virgil felt free to break any rule, whether for expressive effect or simply for variety. A more concerted attack is made by O'Neill. He investigates all the hexameter-endings in Virgil and in Ovid's *Metamorphoses* which (generally through the presence of a monosyllable) do *not* come under the types listed above as normal, types which (including *primus ab oris* and *iactatus et alto, vocibus usa est*, etc.) amount to nearly 98 per cent in Virgil, 99 per cent in Ovid.† He finds that the majority of these 'uncanonical' endings do not produce coincidence of pulse and accent—231 out of

---

* If it were true, as Diomedes and later grammarians suggest, that -*que* drew the accent on to the preceding syllable *even if it was short*, for example *belláque*, that would create a few exceptions (only 28 in *Aen.* I–VI). But they may well have been mistaken, at least for Augustan pronunciation. Müller, *De re metrica* (1894), p. 468; P. Langen, *Philologus* (1872), p. 108; F. W. Shipley, *Cl. Ph.* (1913), pp. 31–2.

† Viz.: spectat et in me, dum gravis aut hos, subter mare qui nunc, impius ex quo, forte virum quem, cum rapidus sol, et magnis dis, ilicibus sus, et tremit artus, apibus quoque nostris, sed quis Olympo, aut Erymanthi, ducis Meliboei, depressas convalles, circumspexit, Deïopea. (*T.A.P.A.* 1940, pp. 339–41.)

347 in Virgil, 76 out of 132 in Ovid. This fact is not significant. For in some cases there is the extenuation of a Greek word, in some of intentional Ennian reminiscence, in some of obvious expressive intention. And quite apart from this, if 231 and 76 seem large numbers, they are barely appreciable in effect amid totals of 12,900 and 14,410 respectively.

And why, he asks,[1] did the Romans introduce the feature of hypermetron (extra syllable at the end of the line elided against an initial vowel at the beginning of the next)? This is liable to upset coincidence of accent with pulse in the sixth foot. We may answer that nearly all the cases involve -*que* or -*ve*, and it is not certain that the elided particle did in such cases affect accent.[2] Otherwise Virgil only has two instances (*G.* I, 295–6; *A.* VII, 160–1). In the former at least some expressive effect *may* be intended:

> aut dulcis musti Volcano decoquit umor(em)
> et foliis undam trepidi despumat aëni.

or boils down the moisture of sweet must over the fire, and skims with leaves the liquid in the bubbling vat.

SOME MODERN THEORIES OF LATIN PROSE RHYTHM

A. CLAUSULAE

To the generalization that prose rhythm should not be thought of in terms of feet I would consider one exception as at least conceivable. Terentianus Maurus (*c.* A.D. 190) wrote a poem *De Cretico*, in which he stated that the cretic (–◡–) has a favoured position (*sedes beata*) just before the end (*paene in ultimo*), followed by a dactyl, spondee or trochee. This was the 'secret' on which Zieliński built up his theory of Ciceronian clausulae.* If, with Cicero, we take the last syllable to be indifferent in quantity (*anceps*), we recognize here two of the chief Ciceronian clausulae: – ◡ – | – ◡ ⌣ and – ◡ – | – ⌣; and if we allow a ditrochee to count among the feet that follow, we can include another favourite, – ◡ – | – ◡ – ⌣.† It may be that Cicero *felt* that the cretic as such was basic to at least some of his clausulae; but it must be pointed out that his *references* to it suggest that he has in mind the ultimate, not the penultimate, position (Quintilian's examples make it clear that he too had this in mind); that immediately afterwards he treats the *dochmius*, ◡ – – ◡ –, as a unit, instead of resolving it into cretics, (–) ◡ – | – ◡ –, as he might have done in the majority of cases; and that he classes 'compărant cŏntrā nōs' as a clausula of two spondees, when he might have classed it as cretic + molossus.[1]

The human urge to reduce categories to a minimum led Zieliński to postulate a single original 'integral clausula' (– ◡ – | – ◡ – ◡ ...), based on the cretic; and others, such as Norden, to derive all forms from a few archetypes. These theories have a fundamental flaw, in that the whole history of clausulae, both in Greek and Latin, shows a process of *reducing* rather than expanding the number of varieties used. Again, their working out by some requires so many licences that rules cease

---

* First let out in a review of J. Wolff's 'De Clausulis Ciceronianis' (*Deutsche Literaturzeitung*, 1901, p. 3243). Just as the final syllable was of indifferent length, the final foot, he maintained, was not so important as the penultimate.

† Even the dispondaic ending, usually shunned by Cicero, was made palatable by a preceding cretic, as in 'consules designati' (Zieliński, *Der constructive Rhythmus*, 1914, p. 57).

to be recognizable as such: a short syllable can be replaced by a long, which in turn can be replaced by two shorts, and so forth.[1]

But it is time to say that there is a different approach to the problem, based not on syllables or feet, but on words and their 'typology', that is, their metrical form—the so-called 'French System'. Havet, working back from Symmachus, found that in Cicero too the metrical form of the final word determined that of the preceding one. His pupil Bornecque worked this out in great detail, applying a comparative method to determine the relative frequency in Latin of words of the various typologies.[2] (Novotný has carried the system still further, with variations.) A minor objection is that there are clausulae which clearly consist of more than two, or of one or less than one, words. It is also true (though this is an argument that is not decisive) that Greek prose rhythm seems indifferent to typology and that the classical Romans were *conscious* of rhythm as depending on long or short syllables expressed in terms of feet, rather than on words and their typology. The first sign of interest in typology is Quintilian's strictures on long words as clausulae and insistence on the relevance of caesura—the point where the break between the words forming a clausula comes.* The French system, though it may describe the phenomena accurately, seems an inverted way of recording them, and has no explanation to suggest.[3] We must look for an aesthetic factor determining what combinations of typologies were rare or frequent beyond what would naturally follow from the proportions of such words in the language.

Typology does indeed play some part.[4] Final monosyllables, unless

---

* Quintilian's remarks occur at IX, 4, 64–6 and 97–8. He has said (62) that the clausula must not be *durum* or *abruptum*, and must not be led up to by *via rupta*. Demosthenes' πᾶσι καὶ πάσαις and μηδὲ τοξεύῃ were approved by all (save Brutus) as *severum*, whereas Cicero's *balneatori* and *archipiratae* were criticized as *durum*. Polysyllables at the end should be avoided (64–6). It makes a considerable difference whether the last two feet are contained in a single word. *Criminis causa* forte, *archipiratae* is *molle* (*facilitates* still *mollius*). For between words there is a 'rest' (*latens tempus*) (97–8; cf. 51).

Severum must mean something like 'firm'; but it is startling to find *archipiratae* criticized as both *durum* and *molle*. *Durum* seems to denote a general disapproval ('harsh'), *molle* a flaccidity which is more marked in ∪ ∪ ∪ – – than in – ∪ – – – (cf. *praemolle* at 65). But Quintilian's treatment is confused. Once, at 105, he does speak in terms of typology, when he says that the phrase *in Africa fuisse* ends with an amphibrach (*fuisse*). But at 73 he has treated this same phrase in orthodox classical fashion as potentially the beginning of an iambic senarius; and at 101 he allows the phrase *Brute, dubitavi* to be analysed alternatively as – ∪ ∪ ∪ | – – or – ∪ ∪ | ∪ – –. Nothing here of caesura or typology.

enclitic, were always avoided, as we have seen. Iambic and pyrrhic words were apparently felt to be too slight, and the former too abrupt, for a cadence. In the clausula $- \cup - - \asymp$ Cicero shows a strong absolute, and slight relative, preference for the types *continebatur* and *omne debebat* over *arbores essent*.* In $- \cup - - \cup \asymp$ the type *possem cognoscere* is sought, *credatis postulo* rather avoided (the former word perhaps overweighs the latter). In $- \cup \cup \cup - \asymp$ the type *esse videatur* is fifteen times as common as *dicere nequivit*. In $- - - \asymp$ the figures for a sample four of Cicero's speeches are striking: the type *contenderunt* is four times as common as all types ending in *contendit* put together.[1] Cicero's preference for a long word at the end, however *molle* his critics might find it in some cases, may be largely due to the well-established principle that light and short words should come first, leading up to heavier and longer.[2] He may also have had an inclination to avoid in the cadence the slight roughness, the catch in the breath, caused by division between words.[3]

It has also been shown that, in so far as Cicero does use the 'heroic' clausula $- \cup \cup - \asymp$ (107 times in 17,092, according to Zieliński), he shows a slight preference for precisely the typology that he and his successors avoided in verse-endings—for *non superabat* or *composuisset* over *esse putabat* or *moenia Troiae*.[4] But the figures may be too small to signify.

Typology is also relevant to Broadhead's theory.† He rejects the assumption of Zieliński and many others that in prose, as in verse, rhythm depended on sequences of long and short syllables irrespective of the grouping of words in natural speech. What he calls 'rhythmical feet' were marked off by successive stress-accents (secondary accent counting for this purpose). The accent, so to speak, gives a shove off to the foot, which itself is quantitative. Clausulae begin with the penultimate (or in some cases antepenultimate) stress. Accent in Latin was dependent on typology, and Broadhead's statistics usefully distinguish the various typologies composing the groups of feet, employing a convenient notation. In order to establish true preferences and avoidances

---

* Also, however, over *mens refellebat*. Here the monosyllable may somehow have upset the rhythm. (De Groot, *La prose métrique*, 1926, pp. 6–7.)

† *Rhythm* (1922). Summary of his views in *C.Q.* (1932), pp. 40–4. I am most grateful to Professor Broadhead for his courtesy and patience in elucidating his complex theory to me. If I have misconceived it, I have no excuse.

he compares sentence-clausulae with the ends of *membra* and *articuli*,* and with the remaining, 'internal', parts of the period. He finds that in clausulae his trochees and cretics predominate both in the ultimate and the penultimate position, the more so when permitted resolutions are taken into account; that the ends of *membra* have the same tendencies, though less pronounced, whereas those of *articuli* are practically indifferent; and that in the case of some clausulae certain antepenultimates are preferred.

Broadhead's theory is ingenious, and certainly deserves serious consideration. The obvious objection, which he anticipates (pp. 36–7), is that no ancient authority mentions accent as even an accessory in classical Latin prose rhythm, let alone as the regulator of it. It is true that ancient writers were often imperfectly conscious of the motives behind their tendencies, but to be unaware of one's basis is very different from being hazy about attendant circumstances—more fundamental, for instance, than not realizing whether one's accent was primarily one of pitch or stress. Another objection is that Cicero's preferences in clausulae seem largely derived from those of the Greek Hegesias, to which accent was irrelevant. I have also already expressed my scepticism about the application of the conception of 'feet', and their resolutions, to prose rhythm.

Of course there is no suggestion that rhythm was a matter of *accentual pattern*: else why, for instance, should Cicero have greatly favoured the type 'multa cognoscunt' in clausulae and shunned its accentual equivalent 'multi cognoscunt'? If indeed, as Zieliński and Zander tried to make out, coincidence of accent with ictus was aimed at in prose, it would naturally strengthen the argument for the significance of this in dactylic verse, as acceptance of Broadhead's theory would also do; but I have already deprived myself of this prop by saying that I cannot believe there is such a thing as ictus in prose. Nor has the 'shifting accent' which Zieliński had to assume to make his theory work found favour.

---

* The term *membrum* or *colon* seems to denote the smallest group of grammatically coherent words which is followed by a pause. *Commata* or *articuli* were even smaller units.

B. BEGINNINGS AND MIDDLES

There have been elaborate analyses of whole texts from the rhythmic point of view based on a theory called *responsio*, that rhythm was pervasive and depended on repetition.[1] But in the first place some accidental repetition is inevitable; moreover the applications of the theory were forced; and in any case what Cicero insisted on was variety,[2] not recurrence (the citation of *Orator*, 38 in support of the theory rests on a misapprehension). No one seems now to believe in this theory, so we may disregard it.

Otherwise the most thorough such analysis seems to have been that carried out by Fr. Novotný, in a book too little known because written in Czech.[*] He claims to have determined against a more scientifically established norm what clausulae were *comparatively speaking* preferred. Further, he found that Cicero had, against his own advice quoted above,[3] a dislike for dactylic rhythm which is not shown by Sallust, tending to put words consisting or ending in a dactyl in synaloepha or before a pause.[4] His work has some affinity to Broadhead's.

In 1959, after a considerable dormant period, the volcano of Latin prose rhythm studies erupted again. Walter Schmid came out with an elaborate theory based on what Aristotle says at *Rhetoric*, III, 8–9.[5] He presses the metaphor of 'period' and 'colon' as taken from a hairpin-shaped race-track, and seeks to analyse rhythm through the sentence, using the ideas of *arsis* and *thesis*. Aristotle's recommendation of $- \cup \cup \cup$ for opening and $\cup \cup \cup -$ for close is expanded into a regular 'looking-glass' theory of rhythm; and the relevant passages from the *De Oratore* and *Orator* are adduced as supporting the view that rhythm runs right through prose, and as not countenancing much special attention to clausulae. The application of this theory is extremely complicated, and I cannot claim that I follow it clearly.[6] But I have already expressed my doubts about the applicability of 'feet', and so of 'arsis' and 'thesis', to prose, and great use has to be made of substitution and resolution, and even of 'rests' (Quintilian's 'inane tempus') to make it work. *A priori* one would not expect any prose writer to conform to

---

[*] *Eurythmie řecké a latinské prósy* (Prague, 1921). He summarizes its scope in his *État actuel* (1929), pp. 25–7, and gives some of his conclusions elsewhere in the same survey.

such elaborate schemes, and we must remember Aristotle's qualifications μὴ ἀκριβῶς and μέχρι του, as well as Cicero's constant reminders that prose rhythm is not an exact art.

It is not surprising, however, that most researchers have concentrated on the question, to what extent do the members also that comprise a period exhibit marked clausulae?* Here a methodological difficulty at once arises: how can we determine the correct *distinctio* or subdivision of sentences? Both the inevitability and the dangers of subjectivity here are obvious.†

The terms *cola* (*membra*) and *commata* (*incisa*) were also used, rather confusingly, of short and very short sentences, when speech was broken up into these. Cicero said that they should be used like little daggers to vary the longer thrusts of the period, and should also be rhythmical; but their very brevity allowed of more freedom. His words seem to imply that in a group of short sentences one may end, for instance, with a double spondee like *insanisti*, which would not be a good clausula for a longer period; but that the group should end with a good one.[1] In fact such a group constitutes a sort of period.

* For example Zieliński, Broadhead. Occasionally an ancient critic seems to suggest such a line of approach. Demetrius quotes a passage from Dicaearchus with the comment, 'The close of each member has something of a metrical cadence, but the fact is disguised through the linking of words in a single series; and great pleasure results' (*De Eloc.* 182, tr. Rhys Roberts).

† An unscientific and subjective approach to this problem of 'colometry' vitiated in part the Herculean labours of Zieliński and Zander. Discussion of it occupies a considerable part of Broadhead's book. The ancients themselves were confused about the meaning of these terms (see Laurand, *Études* (1907), p. 138 n.).

REFERENCES IN THE TEXT

PAGE xi

1 *De Or.* III, 24.
2 F. Maxa, *Lautmalerei und Rhythmus in Vergils Aeneis* (*Wiener Studien*, 1897), pp.78–116., K. J. Lüdke, *Ueber Lautmalerei in Ovid's Metamorphosen* (1871); *Ueber rhythmische Malerei in Ovid's Metamorphosen* (1878–9).

PAGE 3

1 For a brief account of the subsequent controversy in European countries see A. Traina, *L'alfabeto* (1957), pp. 30–2.
2 *Ueber Aussprache, Vokalismus und Betonung der lateinischen Sprache.*
3 F. Brittain, *Latin in Church*² (1955), pp. 38–9.
4 *Ibid.* pp. 65–6.
5 *Syllabus of Latin Pronunciation* (1872).

PAGE 4

1 See also *The Academy*, 15 February 1871, pp. 145–7.

PAGE 5

1 *Acta Apostolicae Sedis*, vol. IV (1912), no. 17, pp. 577–8.
2 J. Marouzeau, *Prononciation* (1943), pp. 12–20 (see also the unconvincing counterblast from Brazil by N. Romero, *L'argument historique*, 1948); F. Brittain, *Latin in Church*, pp. 39–40.

PAGE 6

1 *Epistolae* (1627), IV, no. 362, p. 700; referring to the visit of an English scholar in 1608.
2 F. Brittain, *Latin in Church*, pp. 44 ff. and *passim*; G. C. Moore-Smith, *Grammatical Miscellany O. Jespersen* (1930), pp. 170 ff.
3 *Life*, ed. Graveson (1906), p. 123.
4 W. Rhys Roberts, edn. of Dion. Hal. *On Lit. Comp.* (1910), p. 46.

PAGE 7

1 *A Defence of Poetry.* Italics mine.
2 W. P. Ker Memorial Lecture (Glasgow, 1942), pp. 17–18.

PAGE 8

1 *Rambler*, no. 94; 9 February 1751.
2 *Style* (1902). Tr. R. Aldington, *Selections*, pp. 104–5. I owe this reference to Mr G. H. W. Rylands.

PAGE 10

1 Plato, *Phaedr.* 266 E, 267 C; Arist. *Rhet.* III, 2, 13.

2 περὶ καλλοσύνης ἐπέων and περὶ εὐφώνων καὶ δυσφώνων γραμμάτων (frr. 18 and 21 Diels, Diog. Laert. IX, 48; Cic. *De Or.* II, 194, *De Div.* I, 80; Hor. *A.P.* 295–7).

3 *Euagoras*, 10. Cf. Plato, *Rep.* 601 A.

4 W. Kroll, *Rh. Mus.* (1907), pp. 93–101.

5 Strabo, p. 618, 13.

PAGE 11

1 174; 69–70; 73.

2 71; 74.

3 Chirius Fortunatianus, *Rh. Lat.* p. 124 Halm; see G. C. Fiske, *Lucilius and Horace* (1920), p. 110.

4 Quint. I, 7, 23; 35.

5 *Idem*, VIII, 3, 16.

6 *Idem*, XII, 10, 27–33. R. G. Austin *ad loc.* (with correction, p. 237), and *C.R.* (1943), pp. 9 ff.

PAGE 12

1 Varro, *L.L.* X, 70.

2 *Sat.* I, 10, 20–6.

3 *Odes*, I, 1, 32–4. (Marouzeau, *Traité* (1954), p. 176. He gives the percentages of Greek words in various Latin poets.)

4 II, 412–13; 505. Cf. C. Bailey, Proleg. VII, 9.

PAGE 13

1 *A.P.* II, 23–4.

2 *Or.* 68.

3 *Or.* 162–3; cf. 78, 149, *De Or.* III, 150. Quint. I, 5, 4; VIII, 3, 16; IX, 4, 58.

4 *Or.* 159; *Brut.* 192.

5 Ael. Arist. *ap.* Eustathius on *Il.* x, 385.

6 *Or.* 153, 163; cf. 157. It is 'barely human': Quint. XII, 10, 29.

7 IX, 4, 37.

PAGE 14

1 *Asphodel* (1949), p. 13.

2 *P.L.* II, 879–82; VII, 205–7; H. Blair, *Rhetoric*, No. 13, vol. I, p. 259 (1819).

3 *P.L.* V, 195–6; *Rambler*, No. 94.

PAGE 15

1 *Ecl.* III, 26–7.
2 *De Vulg El.* (*c.* 1305), II, 7, ultimately from Varro. (E. R. Vincent, 'Dante's Choice of Words', *It. Stud.* 1955, p. 4.)

PAGE 16

1 *De Comp.* XIV. Cf. Quint. VIII, 3, 17: 'optima...creduntur quae... maxime exclamant'.
2 H. J. C. Grierson, *Rhet. and Eng. Comp.*² (1945), p. 31 n.
3 *Biog. Lit.* (1817), cited by Grierson, *ibid.*
4 *Traité* (1954), p. 23; cf. p. 91. Cf. *Quelques aspects* (1949), p. 204 n.; Virgil, G. IV, 343; 460; I, 437.
5 N. I. Herescu, *Poésie* (1960), p. 62.

PAGE 17

1 Cat. 68, 74. Ov. F. II, 43. Virg. G. I, 502; *A.* III, 248; cf. VIII, 158, 162.
2 *Life of Pope* (1780).
3 *Properce* (1928), pp. 120–1.
4 *Rhet. and Eng. Comp.*², p. 30 n.

PAGE 18

1 *Rhet.* III, 5, 6.
2 Quint. I, 4, 16; 6, 40.
3 *Top.* 7, 30. Cf. '*e republica*', *Or.* 158.
4 T. Gomperz, *Sitz. Wien. Akad.* (1891), vol. 123, Abh. VI, p. 35; J. S. T. Hanssen, *Symb. Osl.* (1942), pp. 84–5.
5 Augustine, *Principia Dialecticae*, VI, col. 1412 (Migne). Cf. Philodemus, περὶ ποιημάτων, VI, 182; Gomperz, *ibid.* p. 44; Lucretius, II, 398–407; P. Friedländer, *A.J.P.* (1941), p. 22.

PAGE 19

1 *De Comp.* XII.
2 *N.A.* XIII, 21, 1–8. Cf. N. I. Herescu, *Poésie* (1960), pp. 95–104.

PAGE 20

1 *De Glor. Ath.* 8.
2 *De Eloc.* 68. From the μεγαλοπρεπής style of Thucydides he quotes μὴ ἤπειρος (VI, 1) and Κερκυραῖοι· οἰκιστής (I, 24): 72.
3 *Od.* XVII, 36–7; *De Comp.* XVI.

PAGE 21

1 *Or.* 152.
2 *N.A.* VI, 20. Cat. 27, 1–4.

3 Quint. IX, 4, 33; J. S. T. Hanssen, *Symb. Osl.* (1942), pp. 104–5; N. I. Herescu, *Poésie* (1960), pp. 39–59.
4 IV, 18. Cf. Quint. XI, 3, 33–4.
5 *Or.* 150.
6 *Or.* 152.

PAGE 22

1 *Or.* 77; cf. Quint. IX, 4, 36.
2 L. Laurand, *Études* (1907), pp. 114–16.
3 XXIII; tr. W. Rhys Roberts.

PAGE 23

1 Dionysius quotes as an example from prose Isocrates, *Areopagiticus*, 1–5 (*De Comp.* XXIII); cf. his *De Isoc.* XV.
2 *De Or.* III, 171–2. Cf. *Or.* 149–51; *Part. Or.* 21; Auct. ad Her. IV, 18; Quint. IX, 4, 33. Apologies: *Or.* 140, 147.
3 *De Or.* III, 171; *Or.* 149.
4 Only six exceptions in *Odes*, I–III. (Verrall, *Studies in Horace*, 1884, pp. 179 ff.)
5 Macr. *Sat.* VI, 1, 9; *Aen.* IV, 482.
6 I, 5, 42. Cf. Cic. *Or.* 157; though hardly any example of *-ere* is found in a good MS. of Cicero, according to J. S. Reid in Sandys's commentary.
7 Wordsworth, on the testimony of Leigh Hunt. (R. Graves, *Asphodel* (1949), p. 15.) Keats, in the testimony of Bailey, letter of 7 May 1848, to Lord Houghton. (W. J. Bate, *Styl. Devel. Keats*, 1945, p. 51.)
8 *Techn. Elem. Style*, Pentland edn. XV, p. 282.

PAGE 24

1 *Asphodel* (1949), p. 15.
2 *De Comp.* XIX: φυλακὴ συμπλοκῆς φωνηέντων ἡ αὐτή.
3 *N.A.* XIII, 21, 12. *Aen.* II, 554; cf. V, 384, 'quae finis standi'.
4 Vandvik, *Symb. Osl.* (1936), pp. 185 ff.

PAGE 25

1 J. D. Denniston, *Greek Prose Style* (1952), p. 127; H. Diels, *Sitz. d. Preuss. Akad.* (1914), p. 467.
2 L. R. Palmer, *The Latin Language* (1954), pp. 104–5.
3 *Ap.* Cic. *De Div.* I, 42.

PAGE 26

1 I, 199–202.
2 H. A. J. Munro, edn. Lucretius, II^4, 15–16.

PAGE 27

1 Cat. 64; Lucr. III; Virg. *E.* 1; Hor. *Odes*, II, 1; III, 2.
2 Hallam Tennyson, *Memoir*, II (1897), p. 15.
3 'Non raro assonantia fere Celtica gaudet.' Pref. to Plautus in *O.C.T.*

PAGE 28

1 IV, 12, 18. For examples from Cicero see R. Volkmann, *Rhetorik* (1885), p. 516. The epilogue to *Tusc.* 1 (119) exhibits an extreme case.
2 Sturtevant, *Pronunciation*, p. 180².
3 Ennius, Sc. Fr. 56 V.; Pacuvius, fr. 254 V.
4 *Ad Her.* IV, 18; Quint. IX, 4, 42. Norden, *Aeneis VI*, Appendix IV.
5 Isocrates, τέχνη, fr. 6 (Benseler), seems to have started this hare. Cf. Quint. IX, 4, 41; Serv. on *Aen.* II, 27; A. Biese, *Rh. Mus.* (1883), pp. 634–7, and F. M. Austin, *A.J.P.* (1903), pp. 452–5, collect and discuss examples from Latin poets, N. I. Herescu examples from French poets as well: *Poésie* (1960), pp. 42 ff.

PAGE 29

1 *Poésie*, p. 52. Further examples in J. S. T. Hanssen, *Symb. Osl.* (1942), pp. 104–5.
2 *A.P.* 347; 263.
3 Herescu, *Poésie* (1960), p. 51.
4 In a lost letter to Brutus: Quint. IX, 4, 41; *De Off.* 1, 61; *Pro Cael.* 77. Cf. *Pro Clu.* 96.
5 Juv. X, 122; Cic. *De Off.* 1, 77; Quint. XI, 1, 24.
6 *De Div.* II, 63, 4–5. See A. S. Pease's note on p. 102 of his edition.

PAGE 30

1 *De Div.* 1, 20, ll. 50–64. Cf. J. Marouzeau, *Traité* (1954), p. 63. Full analysis in Herescu, *Poésie* (1960), pp. 156–8.
2 *De Or.* III, 206.
3 *Am* III, 11 a, 18; Tib. 1, 4, 17–20.
4 *El.* 1036.
5 *De Eloc.* 69; *Aen.* III, 386.
6 Tib. II, 6, 37–8.

PAGE 31

1 Ov. *Am.* 1, 15, 33–6.
2 IV, 3 and 4.
3 III, 18; 1, 22; III, 30. Cf. Herescu, *Poésie* (1960), pp. 139–41.
4 R. Ellis on Cat. 84, 8, quoted by W. J. Evans, *Allitteratio* (1921), p. xxii.

PAGE 32

1 A similar tendency is found in the fragments of Philetas.
2 *Pal.* 37. Norden, *Aeneis VI*, pp. 395–6[3].
3 *De Agr.* 160.
4 *Varro, R.R.* I, 2, 27.
5 *Carm. Epigr.* (Buecheler), p. 242, 10.
6 *E.* VIII, 80. Cf. Theocr. II, 43–6, where anaphora creates the assonance.

PAGE 33

1 Norden, *Aeneis VI*, p. 398[3].

PAGE 34

1 *E.* VIII, 28; *G.* I, 183 (Norden, *Kunstprosa*, p. 839, n. 3).
2 *A.A.* I, 59.
3 See F. A. Wright and T. A. Sinclair, *Hist. Later Lat. Lit.* (1931), pp. 273–81.
4 Norden, *Kunstprosa*, pp. 825–42.

PAGE 35

1 *English Poetry* (1950), pp. 31–2.
2 C. D. Locock, *Shelley MSS. in the Bodleian* (1903), pp. 3–13.
3 J. Press, *Fire and Fountain* (1955), pp. 100, 118.
4 Augustine, *Conf.* V, 13. Petrarch to Penna, Basle edn. (1581), p. 946 (cf. 1044); W. H. Auden, *Making, Knowing and Judging* (1956), pp. 13–14.
5 E. A. G. Lamborn, *Rudiments* (1916), pp. 19–20.
6 *English Poetry* (1950), p. 23; cf. A. C. Bradley, *Oxf. Lect. Poetry* (1923), p. 30; R. Wellek and A. Warren, *Theory of Lit.* (1949), p. 159.
7 E. Ludwig, *Schliemann* (1931), p. 45.
8 *Father and Son* (1907), end of ch. VII.
9 *The Elder Brother*, II, 1.

PAGE 36

1 Article 7 of the 'Imagist Manifesto'.
2 *The Music of Poetry* (1942), p. 13.
3 *A.P.* 319–22.

PAGE 37

1 Rostagni *ad loc.* and Introd. pp. lxx–lxxi. Philodemus, περὶ ποιημάτων, II, fr. 48, ed. A. Hausrath (*Jahrbücher für class. Philologie*, 1889); reconsidered by T. Gomperz, *Sitz. Akad. Wien*, 123, VI (1891).
2 *Tusc.* III, 19, 45; *Or.* 68. (See p. 13.)
3 *Ecl.* V, 56–71.

PAGE 38

1 317–526.
2 See p. 12.
3 N. I. Herescu, *Poésie* (1960), p. 66. (See above, p. 16.)

PAGE 39

1 61 and 62.
2 *Harm.* I, 18.
3 *De Comp.* XI; Aristoxenus, *Harm.* I, 3 (D. B. Monro, *C.R.* IX, 1895, p. 468). K. M. Wilson, *Sound and Meaning* (1930), p. 54.
4 Aristoxenus, *Harm.* I, 9. Sturtevant, *Pronunciation*, pp. 96–8[2].

PAGE 40

1 *Or.* 57; *De Or.* III, 174. The Auctor ad Her. advised 'torquere sonum' (III, 25).
2 Cic. *Or.* 57: 'rhetorum epilogus paene canticum', cf. 27; Quint. XI, 3, 57.
3 I, 8, 2.
4 K. M. Wilson, *Sound and Meaning* (1930), pp. 207 ff.
5 See R. Wellek and A. Warren, *Theory of Lit.* (1949), pp. 159–61.

PAGE 41

1 J. Press, *Fire and Fountain* (1955), pp. 97 and 101. I have added Housman to his list.
2 Dion. Hal. *De Comp.* XXIII. Cf. Quint. IX, 4, 116. For studies and experiments see R. C. Givler, *Speech in Relation to Poetry* (1915); O. Brik, 'Zvokovie Povtory' (sound-figures), *Poetika* (1919); G. D. Birkhoff, *Aesthetic Measure* (1933).
3 *The Medium of Poetry* (1934), pp. 132–4.

PAGE 42

1 *The Music of Poetry* (1942), p. 19.
2 *Collected Essays*, II, p. 225 n. Cf. K. M. Wilson, *Sound and Meaning* (1930), pp. 252–3.
3 *Practical Criticism* (1929), p. 232.

PAGE 43

1 *The Medium of Poetry* (1934), p. 130.
2 *Od.* IX, 289–90; *De Comp.* XVI.

PAGE 44

1 Panaetius, reflected in Cicero's *De Off.* I, 97; *Or.* 70; 72; 100; cf. *De Or.*
III, 37; Philodemus, Gomperz, *Sitz. Akad. Wien*, 123, VI (1891), p. 12;
Quint. VIII, 3, 17.
2 III, 7, developing Platonic ideas suggested in *Phaedrus*, 271 D–E.
3 2, 13.
4 Tr. Rhys Roberts.

PAGE 46

1 426 C–427 C.
2 IV, ch. 47 f.

PAGE 47

1 414 C–D, 430 D–433 C, 435 A–C.
2 Augustine, Migne 32, col. 1412. Cf. Varro, *L.L.* fr. 238 G.S.
3 Gellius, *N.A.* X, 4.
4 Johnson's Dictionary.

PAGE 48

1 Migne 32, col. 1413.
2 O. Jespersen, *Language* (1922), p. 409.
3 *Human Speech* (1930), p. 174.

PAGE 49

1 *Prononciation* (1943), p. 30.
2 See, for example, Quint. I, 5, 72; VIII, 6, 31.
3 In this chapter I have drawn freely on my article 'Onomatopoeia and
the Sceptics', *C.Q.* (1942), pp. 121–33. I also profited at that date from
conversations with Mr T. F. Higham.
4 *Rambler*, no. 94.

PAGE 50

1 *Asphodel* (1949), pp. 10–13.
2 For τὸ πρέπον see W. Kroll, *Rh. Mus.* (1907), p. 99.
3 Ch. 15, tr. Rhys Roberts. ποικίλως φιλοτεχνοῦσιν.
4 On the Scholiasts see Norden, *Aeneis VI*, 419³.
5 *Quaest. Conv.* IX, 15, 2.

PAGE 51

1 See R. Philippson, *Philologus* (1930), pp. 403–8.
2 W. Kroll, *Sokrates* (1918), pp. 91 ff.
3 II, 364–73; *Rambler*, No. 92.
4 A. C. Bradley, *Oxf. Lect. Poetry* (1923), p. 19.

5 'Carte Blanche' in *Le rappel à l'ordre* (1920); *Œuvres*, IX, 74; quoted by Dame Edith Sitwell, *Notebook* (1943), p. 24.
6 *English Poetry*, p. 28.
7 *Life of Pope* (1780).

PAGE 52

1 *Les vers français* (1904), pp. 167–8. Cf. Marouzeau, *Traité* (1954), pp. 33–4; Wellek and Warren, *Theory of Lit.* (1949), pp. 159, 161.
2 As O. J. Todd has done, *C.Q.* (1942), pp. 29–39. Cf. Bateson, *English Poetry* (1950), p. 26; Lucas, *Style* (1955), p. 249.
3 V, 993.

PAGE 54

1 Soph. *O.T.* 371.
2 Racine, *Athalie*. Cf. K. M. Wilson, *Sound and Meaning* (1930), p. 241.

PAGE 55

1 *C.Q.* (1957), p. 102.
2 *English Poetry*, p. 28.
3 *Remarks on the Beauties of Poetry* (1764), p. 37; Bateson, *English Poetry* (1950), p. 32. For further examples from Shakespeare see K. M. Wilson, *Sound and Meaning* (1930), pp. 193–7.

PAGE 56

1 Virgil, *G.* IV, 460–3.
2 I, 5, 72; VIII, 3, 36; 6, 31.
3 *G.* III, 554; *A.* II, 313; cf. XI, 192.

PAGE 57

1 *Epod.* XVI, 48; *Odes*, III, 13, 14–16.
2 Hesychius; *Et. Mag.* 555, 47; Gow on Theocr. XXII, 39.

PAGE 58

1 Lyric from *The Princess*, 'Come down, O maid...'; *A.P.* 17; *Ecl.* I, 58.
2 *Geraint and Enid*; *Charge of the Light Brigade*.
3 *Il.* XXIII, 116; *Ann.* 275 V.[3]; *Aen.* VIII, 596.

PAGE 59

1 Hephaestion, 39, 1; Cat. 63, 1.
2 *A.* VII, 76; Lessing, *Werke*, ed. Lachmann–Müncker, XV, 438.
3 *A.* VI, 576. Postgate, *How to Pronounce Latin* (1909), p. 11.
4 *Six Tennyson Essays* (1954), p. 194.

PAGE 60

1 *Odes*, I, 28, 1–3. Cf. Scaliger's list of vowel-values, p. 46 above.
2 *Od.* XI, 596; τὸ μεταξὺ τῶν ὀνομάτων ψῦγμα (*De Comp.* 20; and much
   more explicitly Eustathius *ad loc.*). Cf. Demetrius, *De Eloc.* 72.

PAGE 61

1 Terpander, fr. 3B. (Keil, *Anal. Gramm.* 6, 6). Arist. Quint. *De Mus.* II,
   15 (p. 59, 28 Jahn).
2 *Il.* XXIII, 221.
3 *Odes*, IV, 2, 45–8.
4 *E.* IV, 4–10; R. G. Austin, *C.Q.* (1927), pp. 100–5.

PAGE 62

1 *Il.* IV, 125; Schol. Ven. A, cited by Norden, *Aen. VI*, 415[3].

PAGE 63

1 Hor. *Odes*, III, 30, 4–5; *Ep.* I, 14, 7; *Odes*, I, 7, 32. See J. Marouzeau,
   Traité (1954), pp. 96–103; Jespersen, *Language* (1922), pp. 403–4.
2 *Aen.* VI, 314; *Oxf. Lect. Poet.* p. 21.
3 *G.* II, 157; *Essays*, II, p. 56.
4 *Nine Essays* (1927), to which Housman wrote the introduction, p. 178.
5 IX, 4, 130–1.
6 R. Étiemble, *Rev. lit. comp.* (1939), pp. 235–61.
7 *Les vers français* (1904).

PAGE 64

1 *Theory of Lit.* p. 164, and bibliographical notes, pp. 324–5, 366–7.

PAGE 65

1 IV, 472.
2 *Epode* 13, 12.

PAGE 66

1 IX, 346. A. M. Young, *T.A.P.A.* (1933), p. li; *Cat.* I, 5, 11; *C.J.* (1932),
   p. 516 n. Cf. V. Pöschl, *Maecenasode* (1961), p. 11.
2 *P.L.* I, 742–5.
3 For instances from French poetry see Grammont, *Les vers français*
   (1904), pp. 172–6.

PAGE 67

1 But a striking instance occurs at Hesiod, *Erga*, 5–7.
2 *Il.* XXII, 126–8.

PAGE 68

1 Coleridge, *Mariner*.
2 Eur. *Bacchae*, 1065.
3 *P.L.* II, 1021–2.
4 IX, 4, 127. For the general principle, Hermogenes, περὶ ἰδεῶν B, 379 R.
5 *Ann.* 164.

PAGE 69

1 *Am.* I, 15, 5–6.
2 *F.Q.* I, 40; *Amoretti*, LXVIII ('Easter').
3 *Epode* 11, 20; *Odes*, III, 18, 15–16; I, 11, 5.

PAGE 70

1 *A.P.* 263. A break after *im-* would be regular.

PAGE 71

1 *Ep.* I, 2, 42–3 (a regular line would have a break in the middle of *omne*). *G.* I, 514 (a regular line would have a break in the middle of *audit*). *A.* V, 591 (a regular line would have a break after the *in-* of both *indeprensus* and *inremeabilis*). Norden recognizes the last two instances and gives analogous examples (*Aeneis VI*, 433³). The possibility of using caesura for such purposes was recognized by Hermogenes, περὶ ἰδεῶν B, 379 R.
2 *Odes*, II, 3, 9–11.
3 Hor. *Odes*, IV, 1, 35–6.

PAGE 72

1 XI, 22–4.
2 Fr. 478 V.³
3 Note in Eversley edn. I, 372.

PAGE 73

1 *Odes*, I, 35, 13 ff.; L. P. Wilkinson, *Horace and his Lyric Poetry* (1945), p. 142.
2 *Epod.* 15, 9; Wilkinson, p. 141.
3 *Od.* XI, 598; tr. Sandys.

PAGE 74

1 In his admirable *Essay on the Georgics* prefixed to his translation.
2 Suet. *Vita Verg.* 22.

PAGE 75

1 *De Eloc.* 255.

PAGE 77

   1   II, 3–4.
   2   *Aeneis VI*, p. 424[3].

PAGE 78

   1   *Odes*, I, 2, 18–20.

PAGE 80

   1   *Traité* (1933), pp. 408–9.

PAGE 81

   1   *S.* I, 10, 1.
   2   *Il.* XV, 678; E. Fraenkel, *Horace* (1957), p. 76 n.
   3   *P.L.* VII, 411.

PAGE 82

   1   III, 3, 31. The other instances are: 1, 5, 29; 8, 7; 17, 1; 18, 21.

PAGE 83

   1   *M.* VI, 376.

PAGE 84

   1   *Aeneis VI*, 420[3]. Cf. C. Bailey, Introd. VI, 7.
   2   64, 261–4; Norden, *Aeneis VI*, 415–16[3].

PAGE 89

   1   *Rhythm* (1925), p. 16.
   2   *De Or.* III, 186.
   3   *El.* 1384. Cf. Aesch. *Ag.* 1019.

PAGE 90

   1   By G. M. Young in a lecture.
   2   Sturtevant, *Pronunciation*, ch. IV.

PAGE 91

   1   Sturtevant, *Pronunciation*, pp. 177–8; Palmer, *The Latin Language* (1954), pp. 212–13.
   2   Cic. *Or.* 56–8; Varro, *L.L.* p. 210, 10–16; Nigidius *ap.* Gell. XIII, 26, 1–3.
   3   *Att.* XII, 6, 2.
   4   A. Schmitt, *Akzentlehre* (1924); O. Seel, *Philologus* (1959), pp. 244–5.

PAGE 92

   1   Beare, *Latin Verse* (1957), p. 164.

PAGE 93

1 *Schediasma de metris* prefixed to his edition of Terence (1726), p. xvii. See Beare, *Latin Verse* (1957), p. 61.
2 *Hermathena* (1953), p. 39.
3 *A Hope for Poetry* (1934), p. 10.

PAGE 94

1 A. Schmitt, *Akzentlehre* (1924), pp. 158–9.
2 B. O. Unbegaun, *Russian Versification* (1956), pp. 15–20, 41, 36.
3 J. B. Trend, *Rubén Darío* (1952), pp. 21, 10.
4 A. Schmitt, *Akzentlehre* (1924), p. 192.
5 F. Schoell, *De accentu linguae latinae* (1876), pp. 25, 29; A. Schmitt, *Akzentlehre* (1924), pp. 203–4.
6 Cf. A. Schmitt, *Akzentlehre* (1924), p. 35; F. W. Shipley, *T.A.P.A.* (1924), p. 158 and (1938), p. 160; F. R. Dale, *The Stateliest Measure* (1952), pp. 9–10.
7 *Poésie* (1960), pp. 197–9. Hor. *A.P.* 323; *Odes*, III, 4, 21.

PAGE 95

1 *Andr.* 126; *Ep.* I, 19, 41; *Eun.* 49; *S.* II, 3, 264.
2 *Or.* 184.

PAGE 96

1 *Ovidiana* (ed. N. I. Herescu, 1958), p. 130.
2 S. E. Winbolt, *Hexameter* (1903), p. 70.
3 H. Ebbinghaus, *ap.* de Groot, *Mnemosyne* (1935), p. 90.

PAGE 97

1 De Groot, *ibid.* pp. 92–3, 112.

PAGE 98

1 *Ann.* 213 f.
2 Balsdon to Fitzjames Stephen at Eton in 1840 (Leslie Stephen, *Life of Sir F.S.*, 1895, p. 81, quoted by M. L. Clarke, *Classical Education in Britain*, 1959, p. 56).

PAGE 99

1 *Odes*, IV, 6, 35.

PAGE 100

1 Fr. 28 Morel; Cat. 32.
2 *Acad. Post.* I, 9.
3 Fr. 230. R. Heinze, *Die lyrischen Verse des Horaz* (1959 ed.), 36–47.

4   U. von Wilamowitz, *Griechische Verskunst* (1921), p. 265 n. 1.
5   C. Cichorius, *Römische Studien* (1922), pp. 207 ff. 'Illa vetera nostra', Cicero to Varro in 45 B.C. (*Acad. Post.* I, 8.)
6   Fr. 275. Four more Galliambics in frr. 131–2.

PAGE 101

1   Also *Priapeum* 2 (21 lines) and *Catalepton* 6 (6 lines) from the *Appendix Vergiliana*.

PAGE 102

1   Inevitably in this section I shall sometimes repeat what I have said in my book *Horace and his Lyric Poetry* (1945), especially pp. 143–5, 152, 170–2.
2   *Ep.* I, 19, 23–4.

PAGE 104

1   *Sitz. Bayr. Akad. d. Wiss.* (1868), I, 1.
2   *Berl. Phil. Woch.* (1911), coll. 707 ff.
3   'Die lyrischen Verse des Horaz,' *Verh. Sächs. Ges. der Wiss.* (Leipzig, 1918), now reprinted separately by A. M. Hakkert (Amsterdam, 1959).

PAGE 105

1   Stob. III, 7, 12. For Melinno see C. M. Bowra, *J.R.S.* (1957), pp. 21–8.

PAGE 106

1   I, 10, 12; III, 27, 28; I, 2, 52; I, 18, 16.

PAGE 107

1   I, 22, 24; I, 30, 8; III, 14, 28; IV, 2, 60.
2   II, 6, 24; IV, 6, 44.
3   122 out of 165 in *Odes*, I.
4   I have discussed this in *C.R.* (1940), pp. 131–3.

PAGE 108

1   D. Norberg, *Versification latine médiévale* (1958), pp. 94 f.
2   For example, E. A. Sonnenschein, *C.R.* (1903), pp. 252–6, modifying P. Eickhoff, *Der horazische Doppelbau der sapphischen Strophe* (1895); Verrall, *C.R.* (1903), pp. 339 ff. (= *Studies in Greek and Latin Scholarship*, pp. 231 ff.); J. B. Greenough, *Harv. Stud.* (1893), pp. 105–15; E. H. Sturtevant, *T.A.P.A.* (1939), pp. 295–302.

PAGE 110

1   Stat. *Silv.* IV, 7; Seneca, e.g. *Medea*, 579–669.
2   *Die lyrischen Verse des Horaz* (1959 edn.), p. 68.

PAGE III

1 *Horace* (1945), p. 152.
2 First noted by Lachmann in C. Franke's *Fasti Horatiani* (1839), pp. 238 f.

PAGE 112

1 'Malende Absicht' (R. Heinze, *Die lyrischen Verse des Horaz*, p. 80).

PAGE 113

1 *Classical Tradition* (1927), p. 114.
2 Fr. 350, 348 L.P.
3 R. Heinze, *Die lyrischen Verse des Horaz* (1959 edn.), pp. 58–9. No caesura at tenth syllable in *Odes*, 1, 19, 16 and perhaps 2.

PAGE 117

1 *Privilege* (1955), p. 101 (Pelican ed.).

PAGE 118

1 Th. Birt, *Hist. Hex. Lat.* (1876), p. 7; E. H. Sturtevant, *Cl. Ph.* (1919), p. 379.
2 *Cic.* 2.

PAGE 119

1 *Sitz. Bayer. Akad.* (1884), pp. 1024 f.

PAGE 120

1 *The Music of Poetry* (1942), p. 12.

PAGE 121

1 The existence of secondary accent on polysyllables is disputed. The evidence for it is given by W. M. Lindsay, *The Latin Language* (1894), pp. 159–61.

PAGE 122

1 P. Langen, *Philologus* (1872), p. 105.

PAGE 123

1 For a full and satisfactory account see E. H. Sturtevant, *T.A.P.A.* (1924), pp. 73–86.
2 *Trans. Camb. Philos. Soc.* (1864), p. 388.

PAGE 124

1 *T.A.P.A.* (1938), pp. 136–7, 143–4.
2 *Papiri Greci e Latini*, pubblicazione della Società Italiana, 1, plate 21 (1912), C. H. Moore, *Cl. Ph.* (1924), pp. 322–5.

PAGE 125

1   *Aeneis VI*, 434³.
2   *Ibid.* 428–9.

PAGE 127

1   *Ibid.* p. 448. Cf. C. Bailey, *Lucretius* (1947), I, p. 109.
2   Statistical analyses in Sturtevant, *T.A.P.A.* (1923), pp. 57–63, and conclusions drawn for Virgil on p. 66.
3   *Accentual Symmetry* (1939), pp. 12–14.

PAGE 128

1   *Ibid.* pp. 28–9.
2   *Ibid.* pp. 66, 70.

PAGE 130

1   Gell. 19, 9, 14; Callim. *Ep.* 41.
2   M. L. Clarke, *Richard Porson* (1937), p. 12.

PAGE 131

1   O'Neill, *T.A.P.A.* (1940), p. 353 n.

PAGE 133

1   E. Bethe, *Ilias* (1914), pp. 37–8.
2   C. M. Bowra, *Tradition and Design* (1930), pp. 57–8; D. L. Page in *Greek Poetry and Life* (1936), p. 221.
3   Hardie, *Res Metrica* (1920), pp. 208–9. K. F. Smith, edn. of Tibullus (1913), pp. 96–7.

PAGE 134

1   For details of Ovid's practice see W. F. J. Knight, 'Ovid's Metre and Rhythm', in *Ovidiana* (ed. N. I. Herescu, 1958).
2   L. P. Wilkinson, *Ovid Recalled*, pp. 31, 424–5.
3   *Am.* I, 1, 27.
4   L. P. Wilkinson, *Ovid Recalled*, p. 34.

PAGE 135

1   L. Laurand, *Études* (1907), pp. 223–8.
2   *État actuel*, Eus supplementa, vol. v (1929).
3   Convenient summary by W. H. Shewring, *C.Q.* (1930), pp. 167–9.
4   *Prosarhythmus* (1921), pp. 13–14, 16.
5   *Handbook* (1918), pp. 96–7.

PAGE 136

1   Cic. *Or.* 175.
2   W. Schmid, *Prosarhythmus* (1959), pp. 119–20.

PAGE 137

1   *Or.* 214, 217–18, cf. 224; Quint. IX, 4, 93.
2   De Groot, *Handbook* (1918), pp. 61–2, 121–2.

PAGE 138

1   Similar confusion at *Or.* 220.
2   *Or.* 226.
3   *Or.* 170.
4   Fr. 1294 M., and Marx's note. (*G.L.* VI, p. 609, 7.)

PAGE 139

1   *Or.* 202, answering questions raised in 181–2. Cf. 204.
2   *Hermes*, Einzelschrift 12 (1959).

PAGE 140

1   M. G. Nicolau, *Cursus* (1930), pp. 37–9.
2   A. E. Douglas, *C.Q.* (1960), p. 67.

PAGE 141

1   See M. G. Nicolau, *Cursus* (1930), pp. 34–6.

PAGE 142

1   E. Norden, *Kunstprosa*[5] (1958), pp. 44–5.
2   De Groot, *Handbook* (1918), pp. 20–9.
3   Norden, *Kunstprosa*[5] (1958), pp. 41–3, 46–8.
4   *A Defence of Poetry*, ed. H. F. B. Brett-Smith (1921), p. 29.

PAGE 143

1   *De Comp.* 18.
2   IX, 4, 107. Cf. H. D. Broadhead, *Rhythm* (1922), pp. 35–6.

PAGE 144

1   IX, 4, 87.

PAGE 145

1   *Rhythm* (1922), p. 39. Cf. A. C. Clark, *C.R.* (1916), pp. 54–5; M. G. Nicolau, *Cursus* (1930), pp. 83–5.
2   Cic. *Or.* 198 and Kroll's note; Laurand, *Études* (1907), p. 195 n.
3   *De Or.* III, 182.
4   'Pulsum': IX, 4, 55.
5   A. C. Clark, *Prose Rhythm in English* (1913), p. 6.

PAGE 146

1 *Style* (1955), pp. 232–6.
2 179 ff. tr. Rhys Roberts. Many examples in Bornecque, *Clausules* (1907), pp. 50 ff.; Zander, *Eurhythmia*, II (1913), 525 ff.
3 Cic. *De Or.* III, 176; *Or.* 187, 194–6; Dion. Hal. *De Comp.* 25; *De Dem.* 50.
4 Cic. *Or.* 189; *De Or.* III, 182; Quint. IX, 4, 76.

PAGE 147

1 IX, 4, 72–8.
2 *Ibid.* 52–3.

PAGE 148

1 *Clausules* (1907), p. 595. Cf. *Or.* 194.
2 De Groot, *Handbook* (1918), pp. 126–8.
3 *Prosarhythmus* (1959), pp. 51–9.
4 Cic. *Or.* 216; cf. Quint. IX, 4, 79–80.

PAGE 149

1 Cic. *De Or.* III, 192–3; Quint. IX, 4, 62.
2 *Handbook* (1918), pp. 36–8; 148–9.
3 De Groot, *Handbook* (1918), pp. 114–17.
4 *Ibid.* p. 128. Cf. *La prose métrique* (1926), p. 34.

PAGE 150

1 Cic. *Or.* 199.
2 Dion. Hal. *De Comp.* 25; Quint. VIII, 6, 64.
3 *O Stikhe: Statyi* (1929); cited by Wellek and Warren, *Theory of Lit.* (1949), p. 166.
4 III, 191. Laurand, *Études* (1907), pp. 148–9.
5 IX, 4, 61, tr. H. E. Butler.
6 III, 191, tr. H. Rackham.

PAGE 151

1 See *Or.* 197.
2 IX, 4, 91.
3 199 f. tr. Hubbell.
4 *De Or.* III, 194.
5 *Or.* 198.

PAGE 152

1 *De Or.* III, 192.
2 *Études* (1907), pp. 166–7.

3 *Der Constructive Rhythmus* (1914); criticized by F. Novotný, *État actuel* (1929), pp. 19–20.

4 *Études* (1907), p. 228.

PAGE 153

1 Varro, *L.L.* VI, 86.

PAGE 154

1 X, 3, 17.
2 *Ad Her.* IV, 21, 29.
3 *Or.* 195.
4 *Or.* 213–14.

PAGE 155

1 *De Doctr. Christ.* IV, 56; Norden, *Kunstprosa*, p. 5[5].
2 Cic. *De Or.* II, 34.
3 *Or.* 212–13. De Groot, *La prose métrique* (1926), pp. 3–4, 12, 16, 52, 56; statistics in his *Prosarhythmus* (1921), pp. 105–13.
4 *Ibid.* pp. 96–7.
5 *Or.* 171.
6 I, 6; VII (VI), 11; XII, 9.

PAGE 156

1 A. E. Douglas, *C.R.* (1956), 134–6; (1960), 65–78.
2 De Groot's figures, conveniently set out by Shewring, *C.Q.* (1931), pp. 13 and 15.

PAGE 157

1 *Or.* 197; 209.
2 Laurand, *Études* (1907), p. 192 n. Cf. Quint. IX, 4, 19.
3 *Or.* 209–10. Laurand, *Études* (1907); p. 186.
4 *Or.* 180; cf. Quint. IX, 4, 126.
5 *Verr.* II, 1, 21; *Tull.* 8.
6 Laurand, *Études* (1907), pp. 188–9, 191; *Or.* 229–31; Quint. IX, 4, 144.
7 Tac. *Dial.* 23; Quint. X, 2, 18.
8 *Or.* 220.

PAGE 158

1 G. Wüst, *De Clausula Rhetorica* (1881), p. 96.
2 *Or.* 172.
3 *Or.* 217; Shewring, *C.Q.* (1931), pp. 18–19.
4 *Or.* 232. W. Kroll, *Glotta* (1916), p. 144 n. 3.
5 De Groot, *La prose métrique* (1926), pp. 12, 52–5.
6 *Ibid.*

PAGE 159

1 De Groot's tables, *Prosarhythmus* (1921), pp. 106–9.
2 Sen. *Contr.* VII, 4, 6. Cat. 53.
3 *Dial.* 18, cf. 25. Quint. XII, 10, 12; see also IX, 4, 1; 64; XII, 1, 22.
4 *Or.* 28, 32, 171. Cf. Sen. *Ep.* 100, 6.
5 *Or.* 234. Cf. 235–6.
6 De Groot, *La prose métrique* (1926), p. 55.

PAGE 160

1 De Groot, *Prosarhythmus* (1921), p. 100.
2 *Ep.* 100, 6; Quint. X, 1, 113.
3 *Dial.* 25, 4.
4 *De Leg.* I, 5.
5 X, 1, 31.
6 IV, 18.
7 *Or.* 229–30.

PAGE 161

1 Ar. *Rhet.* III, 9.

PAGE 162

1 Sen. *Ep.* 114, 17.
2 Sen. *Suas.* VI, 17 and 22; Quint. II, 5, 20; X, 1, 39. Sen. *Contr.* IX, 1, 13 and II, 26; Quint. VIII, 2, 18.
3 R. Syme, *Tacitus* (1958), p. 347.

PAGE 163

1 A. C. Clark, *The Cursus* (1910), pp. 9–10.
2 M. G. Nicolau, *Cursus* (1930).
3 *Kunstprosa*, II, p. 951.
4 *Or.* 168.

PAGE 164

1 IX, 4, 59; 119.
2 See F. L. Lucas, *Style* (1955), pp. 254–9.
3 *Eng. Prose Rhythm* (1912), p. 450.
4 *Theory of Lit.* (1949), p. 166.

PAGE 167

1 Suda; Cic. *Or.* 175–8.
2 J. D. Denniston, *Greek Prose Style* (1952), pp. 66–7.

3 Cic. *Or.* 207–9.
4 For full discussion see J. Zehetmeier, *Philologus* (1930); W. Schmid, *Prosarhythmus* (1959), pp. 112–30.

PAGE 168

1 J. Zehetmeier, *Philologus* (1930), pp. 273–4.

PAGE 169

1 *Prosarhythmus* (1959), pp. 117–22.
2 III, 8, 2, 1408 b 27.

PAGE 170

1 *Philologus* (1930), p. 264.
2 περὶ εὑρέσεως Δ, 154 Rabe. Cf. Quint. IX, 4, 29–30. Examples in J. D. Denniston, *Greek Prose Style* (1952), p. 67.
3 *Or.* 225. Cf. Quint. IX, 4, 125.

PAGE 172

1 40, tr. Rhys Roberts.
2 *Or.* 37–8, tr. Hubbell.

PAGE 173

1 *Or.* 62–5, 207–9.
2 For the small differences of opinion see J. Cousin, *Études sur Quintilien*, I (1936), 518 ff.
3 See especially Cic. *Or.* 204 and Sandys's note.
4 IV, 27.
5 Cic. *Or.* 204, 208; Quint. IX, 4, 22.
6 *Ad Her.* IV, 18; Cic. *De Or.* I, 261; III, 171; *Or.* 222; *De Or.* III, 182, 190.
7 *De Or.* III, 186.
8 *Or.* 178.
9 *De Or.* III, 186.

PAGE 174

1 II, 34.
2 *Or.* 199–200.
3 *De Or.* III, 176.
4 *Or.* 229–30.
5 *Or.* 164, 168, 174; *Part. Or.* 18; 72. Cf. Ar. *Rhet.* III, 9, 5–6, 1409 b 17; *De Or.* III, 191.
6 *Or.* 230. Cf. Dion. Hal. *De Comp.* 22; *De Isoc.* 3; Sen. *Contr.* IX, 2, 27.

PAGE 175

1　*De Or.* III, 190; *Or.* 224–6.　Dem. *De Eloc.* 15.
2　*De Eloc.* 18.
3　*De Or.* III, 186.

PAGE 176

1　C. N. Smiley, *C.J.* (1917), pp. 125–8; G. Highet, *The Classical Tradition* (1949), p. 334.
2　*Greek Prose Style* (1952), p. 68.
3　Hermogenes, περὶ εὑρ. Δ, 153 Rabe.

PAGE 177

1　*Ap.* Quint. IX, 3, 94.
2　*Pro Arch.* 19; Quint. IX, 4, 44.
3　*Cat.* II, 1.
4　Cic. *Verr.* IV, 101.
5　*Or.* 223, from *Pro Scauro.*

PAGE 178

1　IV, 26.
2　*Contr.* II, 4, 11 ff.

PAGE 179

1　Gell. VI, 3, 15.　*Or. Rom. Frr.* ed. Malcovati, I, 191–4.

PAGE 180

1　*De Or.* III, 198; *Brut.* 33; *Or.* 177.
2　*Brut.* 96.

PAGE 181

1　Quint. XI, 1, 19; 3, 97.

PAGE 184

1　*Brut.* 262.
2　Sir F. E. Adcock, *Caesar as Man of Letters* (1956), pp. 65–7.
3　Cic. *Or.* 30–2.
4　Vell. Pat. II, 36, 2.
5　For example, *Cat.* 17, 1; 21, 1; 24, 4; *Jug.* 31, 9; 19.
6　*Cat.* 25, 4.
7　*Jug.* 4, 6; 14, 15; 74, 1.　*Cat.* 48, 1; 15, 5.

PAGE 185

1　*Ep.* 114, 17.
2　K. Latte, *Sallust* (1935), p. 2.

3   *Jug.* 8, 1–2; cf. 10, 4; 18, 4–5; 21, 4; 36, 2; 38, 2; 54, 1. *Cat.* 27, 4; 29, 3; 32, 3.
4   *Jug.* 27, 2; 40, 3; 56, 5.

PAGE 186

1   *Jug.* 44, 1.
2   *Jug.* 20, 4.
3   *Jug.* 51, 1; 5.
4   *De Leg.* I, 5; *De Or.* II, 53–4; *Or.* 207.
5   II, 62–4.
6   *J.P.* (1886), p. 50.

PAGE 187

1   XXII, 39.

PAGE 188

1   W. Kroll, *Stud. zur Verständnis der röm. Lit.* (1924), p. 366.
2   XXII, 6, 6–7.

PAGE 189

1   J. B. Hofmann in Stolz–Schmalz[5], pp. 810–11.

PAGE 190

1   Cf. Prop. II, 34, 89–90.
2   F. Skutsch, *Aus Vergils Frühzeit,* I (1901), 65–8; W. Kroll, *Neue Jahrbücher* (1903), pp. 22–4; E. Fraenkel, *Vergil and Cicero,* Atti Mantova (1926), p. 225; E. Norden, *Aeneis* (1927[3]), Appendix II, 'Periodik'; J. W. Mackail, *Aeneid* (1930), pp. lxxv ff.
3   Cf. Dem. *De Eloc.* 252.

PAGE 191

1   *Roman Literature* (1954), p. 202.

PAGE 193

1   Suet. *Verg.* 22.

PAGE 194

1   *De Div.* I, 11, 17; fr. 11 Morel.
2   Wilamowitz, tr. Bion's *Adonis* (1900), pp. 38 f., *Die Textgeschichte der griechischen Bukoliker* (1906), 139.

PAGE 195

1   Theocr. *Id.* I, 66–75; Virg. *E.* X, 9–20.

PAGE 197

1 W. Kroll, *Neue Jahrbücher* (1908), pp. 526–7.

PAGE 198

1 See J. Henry, *Aeneidea* (1873–89), index under 'Theme and Variation'.
2 Suet. *Verg.* 34. Cf. Servius *ad loc.*

PAGE 199

1 *The Aeneid of Virgil* (1930), pp. lii–liv.

PAGE 200

1 *E.* i, 62. Cf. J. W. Mackail, *Aeneid* (1930), pp. liv, lxxvii.
2 i, i, 14–19.
3 For example, ii, 2, ll. 7, 40, 41, 50, 87, 96, 101, 107, 108. J. Marouzeau, *Emerita* (1936), p. 3.

PAGE 203

1 J. S. Phillimore, Riccardi edn., and O. L. Richmond, *Propertius* (1926), pp. 6–7, 27 ff.

PAGE 205

1 'Lex Meinekiana' (*Ber. Sächs. Akad. Leipzic*, Phil.-hist. Kl., 1939, Heft 2).

PAGE 206

1 *Ibid.* pp. 8–15, 22–7.
2 ii, vii, 25–38; Ov. *Met.* iii, 568–71.

PAGE 211

1 *Metrik* (1879²), p. 654.

PAGE 212

1 P. J. Enk, 'De Symmetria Horatiana', *Mnemosyne* (1936), p. 168.

PAGE 213

1 iv, 44. Cf. Cic. *Or.* 229; Quint. ix, 4, 26–7, 144.
2 E. Norden, *Kunstprosa*, i, 179–80, 203 n., 214.
3 *Aen.* i, 109; Quint. viii, 2, 14.
4 *Tr.* iv, 10, 65–6.

PAGE 214

1 *Tr.* i, i, 18.
2 *A. and C.* iii, ii, 16–18; *P.L.* vii, 502. A. Alonso, 'Presidential Address to the Modern Humanities Research Association' (1960), pp. 27–34.

3 *Pal.* 37.
4 F. Caspari, 'De ratione quae inter Vergilium et Lucanum intercedat', *Diss. Leipzic* (1908), pp. 88 ff.

PAGE 215

1 *Phil.* 2, 66; *Tusc.* IV, 7. Norden, *Aeneis VI*, 396[3].
2 E. Fraenkel, *Iktus und Akzent* (1928), p. 334 n.

PAGE 216

1 A. M. Young, 'Schematized Word-order in Virgil', *C.J.* (1932), p. 517.
2 I, 463–8, 493–7 (cf. I, 190; II, 522); *E.* VI, 40.

PAGE 217

1 A. M. Young, *C.J.* (1932), p. 517.
2 Ov. *Am.* I, 10, 4; 13, 10; II, 16, 36.
3 Norden, *Aeneis VI*, 391[3].
4 *Aen.* VI, 51–2; XII, 192–3.

PAGE 218

1 *Ai.* 550–1; Acc. Trag. frr. 156R. J. H. Schmalz in Stolz–Schmalz[3], pp. 794–5.
2 *Ad Brut.* x Watt. R. B. Steele, *Studies B. L .Gildersleeve* (1902), pp. 339–40.
3 *S.* II, 6, 80–1; *Ep.* I, 8, 12; *A.P.* 268–9.
4 *Am.* III, 9, 1; 4, 40. *Tr.* III, 8, 6.

PAGE 219

1 H. Darnley Naylor, *Horace* (1922), pp. xiv–xv.

PAGE 220

1 I, 9, 21–2.
2 W. Wili, *Horaz* (1950), p. 248 n. (371: 239; 472: 328).

PAGE 221

1 *De re metrica* (1894), pp. 202 ff. Criticisms of the Pulse–Accent theory on pp. 333–7.

PAGE 222

1 *Sitz. Bayer. Akad. München* (1884), p. 1030. Meyer modified his views in the same journal, II (1889), 234–5.
2 *Sitz. Bayer. Akad. München*, II (1889), 237–8.

PAGE 223

1 L. Havet, *Métrique* (1896), sections 102–5.
2 *Römische Metrik* (1929), pp. 45–6.

PAGE 224

1 E. G. O'Neill, *T.A.P.A.* (1940), p. 338.
2 Crusius–Rubenbauer, *Römische Metrik*, section 37 *d*. For prose see H. Bornecque, *La prose métrique* (1898), p. 20.
3 See R. S. Radford, *A.J.P.* (1904), pp. 147–62.

PAGE 225

1 *Accentuation latine* (1855), p. 75.
2 'Est enim quoddam ipsa divisione verborum latens tempus' (ix, 4, 98).
3 *Sitz. Bayer. Akad. München* (1884), pp. 992–7, 1041. (For a point against him made by Norden: *Aeneis VI*^{3}, p. 437 n. 2.)

PAGE 226

1 *Traité de métrique* (1948), sections 119–21.
2 S. E. Winbolt, *Hexameter* (1903), section 94.
3 *Sitz. Bayer. Akad. München* (1884), p. 1040.
4 Quint. ix, 4, 64; 97. W. Meyer, *Abh. Bayer. Akad.* (1886), p. 9. F. Leo, *De Stati Silvis*, pp. 7–8.
5 *Aeneis VI*, p. 437^3.
6 H. D. Broadhead, *Rhythm* (1922), pp. 51–3.

PAGE 227

1 *T.A.P.A.* (1940), p. 357.
2 *T.A.P.A.* (1939), summary, p. 294.
3 W. R. Hardie, *Res Metrica* (1920), p. 50.

PAGE 228

1 L. Müller, *De re metrica* (1894), p. 247; W. Meyer, *Sitz. Bayer. Akad. München* (1884), p. 1043; J. P. Postgate, *Prosodia Latina* (1923), p. 86.
2 E. H. Sturtevant, *T.A.P.A.* (1924), pp. 75–8.
3 'Mechanismus', in *Ovidiana*, ed. N. I. Herescu (1958), p. 131.
4 See P. Maas, *Greek Metre*, tr. H. Lloyd-Jones (1962), sections 47–9 and Appendix.

PAGE 229

1 *Griechische Verskunst* (1921), p. 52.
2 Cf. v, 16; 110. Crinagoras: vii, 636; ix, 283.
3 P. Maas, *Greek Metre*, tr. H. Lloyd-Jones (1962), section 21.

PAGE 230

1 Edn. Tibullus (1913), p. 99. Zieliński in *Philologus*, Supplementband (1904), pp. 827 ff.
2 In Gercke–Norden, *Einleitung in die Altertumswissenschaft* (1923), I, 8, 6 (p. 14); G. A. Wilkinson, *C.Q.* (1948), pp. 68–75.
3 'Mechanismus', in *Ovidiana*, ed. N. I. Herescu (1958), p. 131.
4 *Metrik*, p. 209.
5 W. M. Lindsay, *The Latin Language* (1894), pp. 159–61.
6 H. D. Broadhead, *Rhythm* (1922), pp. 51–3.

PAGE 231

1 *Pallas* (1959), pp. 54–5.
2 *Pallas* (1959), pp. 31–40; S. E. Winbolt, *Hexameter* (1903), pp. 137–9.
3 A. G. Harkness, *Cl. Ph.* (1908), pp. 41–58; R. S. Radford, *A.J.P.* (1904), pp. 157, 160, 420.

PAGE 232

1 M. L. Clarke, *C.R.* (1947), pp. 86–8.
2 Norden, *Aeneis VI*, 438–46, cf. 445³; Havet, *Métrique* (1896), section 110.
3 Quint. XII, 10, 33; Lindsay, *The Latin Language* (1894), pp. 155, 162.

PAGE 233

1 Crusius–Rubenbauer, *Römische Metrik* (1955), section 55; cf. 89.
2 Lindsay, *A.J.P.* (1893), p. 313.

PAGE 234

1 Platnauer, *Elegiac* (1951), p. 16; G. A. Wilkinson, *C.Q.* (1948), p. 72.
2 For example, I, 70, 18; III, 49, 2; IV, 69, 4. G. A. Wilkinson, *C.Q.* (1948), p. 69; J. P. Postgate, *Prosodia Latina* (1923), p. 85. On Horace see Munro, *Trans. Camb. Philos. Soc.* (1864), p. 394.

PAGE 235

1 Munro, *Trans. Camb. Philos. Soc.* (1864), pp. 391–2.

PAGE 236

1 *T.A.P.A.* (1940), p. 343 n.
2 *A.J.P.* (1893), p. 313. See pp. 233, 235 n. J. Soubiran, *Pallas* (1959), p. 50 n.

PAGE 237

1 *Or.* 215, 218, 223; Quint. IX, 4, 107.

PAGE 238

1 Laurand, *Études* (1907), pp. 156–7, 195–6; Novotný, *État actuel* (1929), pp. 56–7.
2 *Clausules* (1907).
3 Novotný, *État actuel* (1929), pp. 8–12; Laurand, *Études* (1907), pp. 201–9; de Groot, *La prose métrique* (1926), pp. 15, 21–2.
4 A. W. de Groot, *La prose métrique* (1926), p. 7.

PAGE 239

1 H. D. Broadhead, *C.Q.* (1932), pp. 38–9.
2 E. Lindholm, *Stilistische Studien* (1931).
3 H. D. Broadhead, *Rhythm* (1922), pp. 76–7.
4 F. W. Shipley, *Cl. Ph.* (1911), pp. 410–12.

PAGE 241

1 F. Blass, C. Zander, E. Müller, J. May.
2 *De Or.* III, 191; *Or.* 213, 215, 231.
3 *De Or.* III, 191.
4 *État actuel* (1929), p. 37; cf. F. W. Shipley, *T.A.P.A.* (1910), 139–56.
5 *Prosarhythmus*, 1959.
6 Sceptical review by H. Drexler, *Gnomon* (1960), pp. 237–47, and by A. E. Douglas, *C.R.* (1960), pp. 131–2.

PAGE 242

1 *De Or.* III, 190; *Or.* 222–5; 216. Cf. Quint. IX, 4, 70–1; Laurand, *Études* (1907), pp. 213–14.

INDEX OF MODERN WORKS CITED

References are to pages of this book. Superior figures indicate references on those pages to the endnotes ('References in the text', p. 243); 'n.' denotes a footnote.

Acta Apostolicae Sedis, vol. IV (1912), no. 17 (pp. 577–8), 5[1]

ADCOCK, Sir F. E., *Caesar as Man of Letters* (1956), 184[2]

ALONSO, A., Presidential Address to the Modern Humanities Research Association (1960), 214[2]

AUDEN, W. H., *Making, Knowing and Judging* (1956), 35[4]

AUSTIN, F. M., 'Cacophony in Juvenal, Horace and Persius' (*American Journal of Philology*, 1903, pp. 452–5), 28[5]

AUSTIN, R. G.,
'Virgil and the Sibyl' (*Classical Quarterly*, 1927, pp. 100–5), 32 n., 61[4]
'Quintilian XII, 10, 27–8' (*Classical Review*, 1943, pp. 9–12), 11[6]

AXELSON, B., 'Mechanismus des Ovidischen Pentameterschluss', in *Ovidiana* (ed. N. I. Herescu, 1958), 96[1], 228[3], 230[3]

BAILEY, C., *T. Lucreti Cari De Rerum Natura* (edn., 1947), 12[4], 84[1], 127[1]

BAILEY, D. R. SHACKLETON, *Propertiana* (1955), 33 n.

BARKAS, P., *A Critique of Modern English Prosody* (1934), 96 n.

BATE, W. J., *The Stylistic Development of Keats* (1945), 23[7], 31 n., 41 n.

BATESON, F. W., *English Poetry: a Critical Introduction* (1950), 7, 35[1,6], 47 n., 51[6], 52[2], 54 n., 55[2, 3]

BEARE, W.
The Roman Stage (1950), 95 n.
'The Meaning of Ictus as Applied to Latin Verse' (*Hermathena*, 1953, pp. 29–40), 93[2], 96 n.
Latin Verse and European Song (1957), 90 n., 92 n., 92[1], 93[1], 230 n.

BEHAGHEL, O., 'Beziehungen zwischen Umfang und Reihenfolge von Satzgliedern' (*Indogermanische Forschungen*, XXV, 1909, pp. 110–42), 175 n.

BENDA, J., *Properce* (1928), 17[3]

BETHE, E., *Die Ilias* (1914), 133[1]

BIESE, A., 'De iteratis syllabis observatiuncula' (*Rheinisches Museum*, 1883, pp. 634–7), 28[5]

BIRKHOFF, G. D., *Aesthetic Measure* (1933), 41[2]

BIRT, Th., *Ad Historiam Hexametri Latini Symbola* (1876), 118[1].

BLAIR, H., *Lectures on Rhetoric and Belles Lettres* (1783), xii, 14[2], 18 n., 144 n., 59 n.

BOILEAU, N., *L'art poétique* (1674), 21 n.

BONAVIA-HUNT, N. A., *Horace the Minstrel* (1954), 104 n.

BORNECQUE, H.
La prose métrique dans la correspondance de Cicéron (1898), 148 n., 224[2]
Les clausules métriques latines (1907), 141 n., 146[2], 147 n., 148[1], 238[2]

BOWRA, C. M.
'Melinno's Hymn to Rome' (*Journal of Roman Studies*, 1957, pp. 21–8), 105[1]
Tradition and Design in the Iliad (1930), 133[2]

BRADLEY, A. C., 'Poetry for Poetry's Sake' (1901), in *Oxford Lectures on Poetry* (1923), 35[6], 51[4], 63[2]

BRANDIN, L. M. and HARTOG, W. G., *A Book of French Prosody* (1904), 66 n.

BRIDGES, R.
Milton's Prosody (1901), 54 n.
Collected Essays II (1927–36), 42[2], 63[3]

BRIK, O., 'Zvokovie Povtory', in *Poetika* (1919), 41[2]

BRITTAIN, F., *Latin in Church* (1955), 3[3,4], 5[2], 6[2]

BROADBENT, J. B., *Some Graver Subject* (1960), 66 n.

BROADHEAD, H. D.
Latin Prose Rhythm (1922), 90 n., 143[2], 145[1], 152 n., 226[6], 230[6], 239[3], 239 n., 242 n.
'Prose-Rhythm and Prose-Metre' (*Classical Quarterly*, 1932, pp. 35–44), 239 n., 239[1]

BÜCHNER, K., 'Zur Form und Entwicklung der horazischen Ode und zur Lex Meinekiana' (*Berichte über die Verhandlungen der Sächsischen Gesellschaft der Wissenschaften zu Leipzic*, Phil.-Hist. Kl. 1939, Heft 2) = *Horaz*, 1962, pp. 52–101), 205[1]

BURKE, E., *The Sublime and the Beautiful* (1767), 47

MEYER, W. (cont.)
der Bayerischen Akademie der Wissenschaften, München, 1884, pp. 979–1089),
119[1], 222[1], 225[3], 226[3], 228[1]
'Ueber die Beobachtung des Wortaccentes
in der altlateinischen Poesie' (Abhand-
lungen der Bayerischen Akademie der Wissenschaften, München, 1886, pp. 1–120),
226[4]
'Ueber die weibliche Caesur des klassischen
lateinischen Hexameters' (Sitzungs-
berichte der Bayerischen Akademie der
Wissenschaften, München, 1889, pp. 228–
45), 222[1, 2]
MONRO, D. B., Review of H. Weil and Th.
Reinach, Un nouvel hymne à Apollon
(Classical Review, 1895, pp. 467–70), 39[3]
MOORE, C. H., 'Latin Exercises from a Greek
Schoolroom' (Classical Philology, 1924,
pp. 317–28), 124[2]
MOORE-SMITH, G. C., 'The English and the
Restored Pronunciation of Latin' (in
Grammatical Miscellany Presented to O.
Jespersen, ed. N. Bogholm, 1930), 6[2]
MÜLLER, L., De re metrica poetarum Latinorum
(1894), 221[1], 225 n., 228[1], 235 n.
MUELLER, M., Letter in The Academy (15 Feb-
ruary 1871, pp. 145–7), 4[1]
MUNRO, H. A. J.
Syllabus of Latin Pronunciation (1872), 3[5]
Lucretius (edn., 1864, 4th edn. vol. II, repr.
1928), 26[2], 232 n.
'On a Metrical Latin Inscription at Cirta'
(Transactions of the Cambridge Philo-
sophical Society, 1864, pp. 374–408), 123[2],
234[2], 235[1]
MURRAY, G.
The Classical Tradition in Poetry (1927), 113[1],
121 n.
Greek Poetry and Life (presented to G.M.,
1936), 133[2]

NAYLOR, H. DARNLEY, Horace, Odes and
Epodes: A Study in Poetic Word-order
(1922), 219[1], 219 n.
NETTLESHIP, H., 'The Historical Develop-
ment of Classical Latin Prose' (Journal of
Philology, 1886, pp. 35–56), 180 n., 186[6]
NICOLAU, M. G., L'origine du cursus rythmique
(1930), 140[1], 141[1], 145[1], 163[2]
NORBERG, D.
Introduction à l'étude de la versification latine
médiévale (1958), 108[1], 124 n.
'Remarques sur l'histoire de la prononcia-
tion du latin' (in Acta Conventus Romani,
1959), 124 n.

NORDEN, E.
Die Antike Kunstprosa (1898, 5th edn., re-
print, 1958), xi, 32 n., 34[1, 4], 142[1, 3],
142 n., 149 n., 155[1], 163[5], 213[2], 237
Aeneis VI (1903; 3rd edn. 1927), xi, 28[4],
32[2], 33[1], 46 n., 50[4], 51 n., 58 n., 62[1],
68 n., 69 n., 70 n., 71[1], 77[2], 84[1, 2], 84 n.,
190[2], 197 n., 214 n., 215 n., 217[3], 225[3],
226[5], 231 n., 232[2]
NOUGARET, L.
'Les fins d'hexamètre et l'accent' (Revue des
Études Latines, 1946, pp. 261–71), 223 n.
Traité de métrique latine classique (1948),
119 n., 223 n., 226[1]
NOVOTNÝ, F.
Eurythmie řecké a latinské prósy (1921), 148 n.,
241
'Le problème des clausules dans la prose
latine' (Revue des Études Latines, 1926,
pp. 221–9), 143 n.
'État actuel des recherches sur le rythme de
la prose latine' (Eus supplementa, vol. 5,
1929), 135[2], 152[3], 153 n., 238[1, 3], 240[4]

O'NEILL, E. G.
'Final Syllables in Greek Verse' (Transactions of the American Philological Association, 1939, pp. 256–94), 227[2]
'Word-Accents and Final Syllables in Latin
Verse' (Transactions of the American Philological Association, 1940, pp. 335–59), 131[1],
223 n., 224[1], 227[1], 235 and n., 236[1]

PAGE, D. L.
'The Elegiacs in Euripides' Andromache'
(in Greek Poetry and Life, presented to
G. Murray, 1936), 133[2]
Sappho and Alcaeus (1955), 112 n.
PAGET, Sir R., Human Speech (1930), 48[3]
PALMER, A., Unpublished Edition of Horace's
Odes; report by L. J. D. Richardson
(Hermathena, 1942, pp. 87–111), 116 n.
PALMER, L. R., The Latin Language (1954),
25[2], 91[1], 136 n., 180 n.
PEASE, A. S., 'Quadripedante putrem'
(Classical Journal, 1925–6, pp. 625–8),
58 n.
PERRET, J., Horace (1959), 104 n.
PETRARCH, F., Letter to Penna (Basle edn., 1581,
p. 946), 35[4]
PHILIPPSON, R., 'Die Sittlichschöne bei
Panaitios' (Philologus, 1929–30, pp. 357–
413), 51[1]
PLATNAUER, M., Latin Elegiac Verse (1951),
33 n. 233 n., 234[1], 234 n.
PLATT, J. A., Nine Essays (1927), 63[4], 65, 72 n.

INDEX OF PASSAGES CITED

(INCLUDING MODERN POETS)

References are to pages of this book. Superior figures indicate references on those pages to the endnotes
('References in the text', p. 243); 'n.' denotes a footnote.

INDEX OF PASSAGES CITED